Where Law Meets Reality

Forging African Transitional Justice

Through the voices of the peoples of Africa and the global South, Pambazuka Press and Pambazuka News disseminate analysis and debate on the struggle for freedom and justice.

Pambazuka Press – www.pambazukapress.org

A Pan-African publisher of progressive books and DVDs on Africa and the global South that aim to stimulate discussion, analysis and engagement. Our publications address issues of human rights, social justice, advocacy, the politics of aid, development and international finance, women's rights, emerging powers and activism. They are primarily written by well-known African academics and activists. Most books are also available as ebooks.

Pambazuka News – www.pambazuka.org

The award-winning and influential electronic weekly newsletter providing a platform for progressive Pan-African perspectives on politics, development and global affairs. With more than 2,800 contributors across the continent and a readership of more than 660,000, Pambazuka News has become the indispensable source of authentic voices of Africa's social analysts and activists.

Pambazuka Press and Pambazuka News are published by Fahamu (www.fahamu.org)

Where Law Meets Reality

Forging African Transitional Justice

Edited by
Moses Chrispus Okello
Chris Dolan
Undine Whande
Nokukhanya Mncwabe
Levis Onegi
and
Stephen Oola

Pambazuka Press
An imprint of Fahamu

Published 2012 by Pambazuka Press, an imprint of Fahamu
Cape Town, Dakar, Nairobi and Oxford
www.pambazukapress.org www.fahamu.org www.pambazuka.org

Fahamu Kenya, PO Box 47158, 00100 GPO, Nairobi, Kenya
Fahamu Senegal, 9 Cité Sonatel 2, BP 13083 Dakar Grand-Yoff,
Dakar, Senegal
Fahamu South Africa, c/o 19 Nerina Crescent, Fish Hoek, 7975 Cape Town,
South Africa
Fahamu UK, 2nd floor, 51 Cornmarket Street, Oxford OX1 3HA, UK

British Library Cataloguing in Publication Data
A catalogue record for this book is available from the British Library

ISBN: 978-0-85749-093-3 paperback
ISBN: 978-0-85749-094-0 ebook – pdf
ISBN: 978-0-85749-095-7 ebook – epub
ISBN: 978-0-85749-096-4 ebook – Kindle

Manufactured in the UK by Printondemand-worldwide.com

Contents

Acknowledgments

This book is based on papers presented at the inaugural event of the Institute for African Transitional Justice (IATJ), which was jointly organised by the Refugee Law Project (RLP), Faculty of Law, Makerere University, and the African Transitional Justice Research Network (ATJRN), in Kampala, Uganda, in November 2010. The RLP and the ATJRN are grateful to the authors who contributed to this publication and to the donors who made the IATJ and this publication possible, namely the Department for International Development (UK), Open Society Foundations-Africa Regional Programme, the International Development Research Centre (Canada), the Swedish International Development Cooperation Agency (SIDA), and the Norwegian Agency for Development Cooperation (Norad). The views expressed in this publication do not necessarily represent those of the donors.

Finally, the ATJRN would like to thank its partners – the Centre for the Study of Violence and Reconciliation (CSVR), South Africa; the Centre for Good Governance, Sierra Leone; the Centre for Democratic Development, Ghana; and the Refugee Law Project, Uganda – all of whom developed the proposal to establish an IATJ aimed at addressing transitional justice issues in the context of Africa's challenges. A special note of thanks must be extended to Levis Onegi, Great Lakes coordinator of the ATJRN and lead coordinator of the IATJ, and Nokukhanya Mncwabe, Southern Africa coordinator for the ATJRN, for ably preparing the manuscript for this book with the valuable input of their colleagues at RLP and CSVR.

About the African Transitional Justice Research Network

www.transitionaljustice.org

The African Transitional Justice Research Network (ATJRN) seeks to promote and encourage transitional justice research in Africa through the development of research capacity, the building of transitional justice content knowledge, and the creation of spaces for practitioners and researchers in Africa to share experiences, expertise, and lessons learned. The goal is to ensure that the transitional justice agenda in Africa is locally informed and owned. It is managed by representatives from four steering committee member organisations: the Centre for the Study of Violence and Reconciliation (CSVR), South Africa; the Refugee Law Project (RLP), Uganda; the Campaign for Good Governance (CGG), Sierra Leone; and the Centre for Democratic Development (CDD), Ghana. The regional representation and continental reach of the network positions it well to drive the African debate on transitional justice. Further, the network is able to attract critical facilitators and participants, who are committed to addressing Africa's challenges.

About the authors and editors

Christine Alai is a human rights lawyer with a keen interest and experience in human rights and transitional justice. She is currently the interim head of office and programme associate of the International Centre for Transitional Justice (ICTJ), Kenya Programme where she is responsible for legal and policy-oriented research, technical assistance and policy advice on ongoing transitional justice measures in Kenya. Christine has previously worked with the non-governmental Kenya Human Rights Commission and the state-established Kenya National Commission on Human Rights, among other organisations. She has also published several chapters in various publications including: with, Njonjo Mue (2011) 'Complementarity and the impact of the Rome Statute and the International Criminal Court in Kenya', in Carsten Stahn and Mohamed M. El Zeidy (eds) *The International Criminal Court and Complementarity: From Theory to Practice*, Cambridge University Press; and 'The promise of truth, justice and reconciliation: will the Truth, Justice and Reconciliation Commission deliver?' in the International Commission of Jurists – Kenya, Rule of Law Report 2011–2012. Christine is also the chair of the board of directors of the East African Centre for Human Rights.

Chris Dolan is best known for his work on gender dynamics, sexual violence and masculinities in conflict and post-conflict settings. He first worked with Mozambican refugees in South Africa as it was transitioning out of apartheid in the early 1990s. This led to work with former Renamo and Frelimo combatants in Mozambique in the mid-1990s and conflict analysis with internally displaced persons in northern Uganda in the late 1990s. The latter research resulted in the publication of *Social Torture: The Case of Northern Uganda, 1986–2006* by Berghahn Books in 2009. After completing his doctorate at the London School of Economics in 2005, he spent a year with UNHCR in Democratic Republic of Congo as a reintegration officer, before taking up his current position as director of the Refugee Law Project, a community outreach project of the School of Law at Makerere University in Kampala, in 2006 (www.refugeelawproject.org). In that position he has also served as project advisor to the Beyond Juba Project, which in turn gave rise to the Institute for African Transitional Justice and the Kitgum Peace Documentation Centre.

Robert Senath Esuruku is a senior academic and researcher in development policy and administration. He is the author of *Horizons of Peace and Development in Northern Uganda* (2011); *Engendering Social Capital: Perspectives from Rural Development Networks in Uganda* (2010); *The Political and Social Economy of Gender and Rural Livelihoods in Uganda* (2010); *Gender, Land Rights and Development in Uganda* (2008); *Fiscal Decentralisation and Poverty Reduction in Uganda: Veracity or Tokenism* (2006) and several other publications. He is currently International Alert's deputy representative for the Africa region in Kampala, Uganda. He holds a BA (philosophy) from Urbania University, Rome and an MA and a PhD in development policy and administration from Dar es Salaam University, Tanzania. In 2010, he was a visiting fellow at the Helen Kellogg Institute for International Studies, University of Notre Dame, USA. He was a senior lecturer at the Uganda Martyrs University, as well as a part-time lecturer at the Faculty of Arts, Makerere University, in Kampala. His current project is, 'Gender, local governance, and participatory development in Uganda'. He is investigating how gender is constructed and institutionalised in local politics and development programmes. He is also working closely with the institute's Ford Programme to advance community engagement in Uganda.

Lucy Hovil is currently the senior researcher for the International Refugee Rights Initiative where she has initiated a region-wide policy-based research programme focusing on issues of citizenship and displacement in Africa's Great Lakes region. She is also the managing editor for the *International Journal of Transitional Justice*, Oxford University Press. Previously she founded the Refugee Law Project's research and advocacy department including pioneering the RLP's working paper series, which enjoys extensive national and international readership. She has written extensively on issues of displacement and conflict, and received a doctorate from the School of Oriental and African Studies, London University, in which she investigated the relationship between violence and identity in the pre-1994 election violence in KwaZulu-Natal, South Africa.

Brian Kagoro is a human rights activist and constitutional and international economic relations lawyer. He is a founding member of the National Constitutional Assembly and the Crisis in Zimbabwe Coalition, of which he was the spokesperson and national coordinator respectively. He served as a board member for Amani Trust and is also legal advisor to the Zimbabwe Congress of Trade Unions. Brian is a frequent writer on human rights, constitutional reform and political affairs. He holds a master's degree in law from Warwick University in the United Kingdom. He has worked for Action Aid International, in their Africa regional office as the pan-African policy manager. Brian is currently the chairperson of the Development Foundation for Zimbabwe.

David Kaulemu holds a PhD from the University of Zimbabwe. His doctoral thesis focused on 'Morality and the construction of social orders in African modernity'. He also holds an MS in philosophy, University of Oxford; an MA in philosophy, University of Zimbabwe; a BA in philosophy, University of Zimbabwe; and a BA general, English and philosophy, University of Zimbabwe. David is currently the regional coordinator of the African Forum for Catholic Social Teaching (AFCAST) for eastern and southern Africa. Previously, David was the chairperson of the Department of Religious Studies, Classics and Philosophy at the University of Zimbabwe. He has been awarded numerous prizes for outstanding performance and is published widely.

Lyandro Komakech is a senior research and advocacy officer at the Refugee Law Project, School of Law, Makerere University. He has a master's degree in development studies from Uganda Martyrs University Nkozi, a master's in international relations and diplomatic studies from Makerere University Kampala, a bachelor's degree in social science with a major in international relations from Makerere University, and an associate bachelor's degree in development studies from Uganda Martyrs University Nkozi. He is currently the lead researcher on traditional justice mechanisms in Uganda. His publications include a working paper titled 'Tradition in transition: drawing on the old to develop a new jurisprudence for dealing with Uganda's legacy of violence' and a book chapter titled 'Exploring the place of traditional justice in Uganda'. Lyandro's research interests include peace and conflict analysis, transitional justice, forced migration and international human rights law.

Davis M. Malombe is the deputy-executive director of the Kenya Human Rights Commission where he was previously responsible for research, programming and advocacy in the Transitional Justice Programme. Davis is studying for an MA in political science and public administration from the University of Nairobi, and a BA in political science from Moi University, Kenya. His other areas of interest include human rights monitoring and research methodologies as well as policy advocacy. Davis has written extensively on conflict and transitional justice, including a position paper titled 'On government responses to IDP issues in Kenya' and a publication on 'Transitional justice in Kenya: a toolkit for training and engagement'. He has contributed to a documentary on the historical injustices in Kenya entitled *The Unturned Stories on Impunity and Massacre*.

Nokukhanya Mncwabe is the African Transitional Justice Research Network regional coordinator for Southern Africa. She has a BSocSci (philosophy and politics) from the University of Cape Town. Her publications include a book chapter entitled 'Negotiating with terrorists' (Routledge 2011) and an article in the *International Journal on Transitional Justice* entitled 'African Transitional Justice Research Network: critical reflections on a peer learning process'. She teaches a course on transitional justice developed by the Centre for the Study of Violence and Reconciliation for the University of Stellenbosch, Cape Town.

Tim Murithi is head of the Transitional Justice in Africa Programme at the Institute for Justice and Reconciliation in Cape Town, and research fellow in the Department of Political Sciences, University of Pretoria. He has also held posts at the Institute for Security Studies; the Department of Peace Studies, University of Bradford, in the United Kingdom; the Centre for Conflict Resolution, University of Cape Town; and the United Nations Institute for Training and Research (UNITAR) in Geneva. From 1995 to 1998 he taught at the Department for International Relations, Keele University, England, where he also obtained his

PhD in international relations. He is on the international advisory boards of the *Journal of Peacebuilding and Development* and the *African Peace and Conflict Journal* and has authored numerous journal articles, book chapters and policy papers. He is the author of *The Ethics of Peacebuilding*, published by Edinburgh University Press, in 2009; and *The African Union: Pan-Africanism, Peacebuilding and Development*, published by Ashgate, in 2005. His most recent co-edited book is entitled *Zimbabwe in Transition: A View from Within*, published by Jacana, in 2011. He is currently co-authoring a book on justice and reconciliation.

Pius Ojara is currently the national conflict advisor at the UK's Department for International Development in Uganda, and a former head of research and advocacy, and project coordinator for the Advisory Consortium on Conflict Sensitivity (ACCS) at the Refugee Law Project, School of Law, Makerere University. He holds a BA (philosophy) from Urbania University, Rome. He completed his MA and PhD from the University of Zimbabwe, and master of divinity from the School of Theology, Berkeley, California. He taught at Arrupe College, an associate college of the University of Zimbabwe for five years, and was visiting professor at Marquette University, Milwaukee. He is author of *Marce, Girard, Bakhtin: Return of Conversion* (2004), *Toward a Fuller Human Identity: A Phenomenology of Family Life, Social Harmony, and the Recovery of the Black Self* (2006), *Tragic Humanity and Hope: Understanding our Struggle to be Scientific, Sapiential and Moral* (2007), and *Faith, Culture, and Church as Family* (2009).

Moses Chrispus Okello is a senior research advisor at the Refugee Law Project, Faculty of Law, Makerere University. He holds a BA in political science and public administration from Makerere University, a postgraduate diploma in refugees and forced migrations studies, and a master's in international human rights law from the American University in Cairo. Moses has conducted research across many regions of Uganda and has contributed to a number of RLP publications. In addition, Moses has contributed to chapters as well as published in internationally acclaimed peer-reviewed journals. Moses is a member of the editorial board of the *International Journal of Transitional Justice*.

Levis Onegi is the African Transitional Justice Research Network regional coordinator for the Great Lakes and the coordinator of the Institute for African Transitional Justice, based at Makerere University's Refugee Law Project. Levis holds a BA (Honours) in political science and public administration from Makerere University, and a master's in public administration. He is currently a pre-doctoral candidate at the African Centre for Migration and Society (ACMS), University of the Witwatersrand, South Africa. He previously worked for the United Nations High Commissioner for Refugees in Uganda, Sudan, Eritrea and Ethiopia. He has also worked with the Jesuit Refugee Services in Uganda and Southern Sudan. His research interest broadly focuses on migration, community, identity and conflict analysis.

Stephen Oola a transitional justice and governance analyst and the head of research and advocacy at the Refugee Law Project, School of Law Makerere University. Oola holds an LLB degree from Makerere University and an MA in international peace studies from the University of Notre Dame, USA. Oola coordinates the Advisory Consortium on Conflict Sensitivity (ACCS). Oola is also an advocate of the High Court of Uganda and previously worked as a lawyer for the Beyond Juba Transitional Justice Project. He also has a post-graduate diploma in legal practice and a post-graduate diploma in conflict management and peace studies from Gulu University. Oola has presented several papers internationally and published with the Oxford Transitional Justice Research Network.

Undine Whande is a social anthropologist who has worked as a practitioner in conflict transformation and social change for the past 15 years. Born in Germany she has lived and worked in southern Africa since 1996. She currently resides in Cape Town, South Africa where she works as a specialist in organisational learning and conflict transformation for the Centre for the Study of Violence and Reconciliation (CSVR). Undine Whande holds a PhD in social anthropology from the University of Cape Town and has published widely. In the often-challenging context of political and social transition in post-1994 South Africa, she developed her expertise as a conflict mediator, coach and facilitator in social change processes. Working with Goethean phenomenology and systems theory, her approach in accompanying people in their professional and personal development and growth through change, is strongly rooted in principles of respect, recognition and valuing each individual biography and life journey.

Preface

The inaugural meeting of the Institute for African Transitional Justice (IATJ), held in Kampala in 2010, was an extraordinary continental move forward. It was an effort by African-born and Africa-based actors who have worked over many years in contexts of violent conflict and in the so-called transitions therefrom to a more democratic and peaceable future. Participants in IATJ 2010 had worked in situations that had often been characterised by stark continuities of violence since at least colonial times. The idea of the IATJ made manifest was a gathering of 35 African scholars, practitioners, field workers, researchers, and former participants in transitional justice processes, most of them interested in both inquiry and intervention. The participants varied from seasoned civil society human rights stalwarts who had worked all their lives to make real what is now the celebrated (and already embattled) new constitution of Kenya, to activists who continue to seek peace and justice in Zimbabwe, from scholars who live the realities of life in Democratic Republic of Congo, Rwanda and Burundi, pondering what to teach and how to research in ways that prove transformative to the situations in their countries, to civil society organisation leaders from Sierra Leone and Liberia who hold the threads of the slow and laborious building of infrastructures from which positive peace can become a reality for the people living in these West African countries. So many stories were gathered in the room, so much experience, so much substance; there was a palpable sense of being in touch with situations-in-context, sharing observations and engaging each other as peers, inhabiting a sphere of shared understanding that needed little explanation, as when discussing the engagement with external actors in northern Uganda and the structural exclusion consciously or unconsciously perpetuated by the international aid industry.

Some of the most vibrant and lively debates of the 2010 IATJ were precisely those that revealed the key fault lines in the conversations among Africans: how should we engage with the human rights violations of autocratic governments while being labelled stooges of Western governments? How do we deal with the claims of entitled (liberation) elites to stay in power forever? How to pierce the spectres of global geopolitics, which pit the West against the rest and foster continuous extractive economic practices in the name of benevolent aid dispensation? How do eminent and budding activists, scholars, practitioners and others engage with the call that resounded throughout the institute, a call to a conscious, introspective, rigorous and critical intra-African conversation about transitional justice, which in a short space of time has become a much-funded and perhaps overrated and under-performing promise for engineering stability and prosperity? The audience were, above all, people with a deep sense of caring and belonging to this continent, with a sturdy determination to see Africa succeed and thrive in this generation.

In all the valid critique of geopolitical injustices, neocolonial perpetuations and exclusions, the debate did not get stuck in either Afro-radicalism or Afro-romanticism. In fact, both were put on the table as questionable routes to pursue, as pitfalls to a robust self-reflexivity and a future-oriented exploration of the potentials of an African transitional justice rather than just transitional justice in Africa. As key questions were launched about the meaning of the word 'African' in the name Institute for African Transitional Justice, questions of colonial history, the legacies of racial oppression and indignification, struggles over identity, subjectivity and legitimacy surfaced in the debates. Reflections were offered on the conditions under which external actors from the 'international community' currently intervene. Assumptions about justice and the need for both universal imaginaries and culturally embedded sets of practices were flagged.

A self-reflexive critique was also offered of elite internals who facilitate transitional justice policymaking and strongly influence the implementation of processes. Which agendas drive the politics of transitional justice on the continent? There is no easy claim to a continental 'we' across the fault lines of race, class, gender – that much became clear. Participants asked: what are the conditions of belonging for the beneficiaries of previous violent dispensations? What are the questions for the beneficiaries of colonial privilege enjoying the vibrancy of life on the continent? What are the questions for the black political, civil society organisation and academic elites that were the majority in the room? There was a moment when presenter Brian Kagoro challenged the audience as being 'donor proxies', without a critical backbone and stance of their own. This generated heated debate. What is the responsibility of those privileged to access aid funding? How intellectually rigorous is the (pan-)African stance in the transitional justice field? How strong is the claim to connectivity to other classes, to the victims of human rights violations and in particular to those affected by structural violence, such as rural peoples that form the base and core of the majority of the societies participants came from?

Another potent debate surfaced around the notion of traditional forms of justice. There was a yearning for, and also excitement at, the promise of empowerment through reinventing African traditions to serve justice and reconciliation processes at local level. Yet women expressed frequent doubt about the unquestioning celebration of the mostly patriarchal and, in some cases, exclusive power domains in the traditional practices described. The limits of traditional approaches were outlined, yet their merit was appreciated and the discussion reached considerable depth on the role and use of language and culture in transitional justice processes.

Finally, the IATJ 2010 did not shy away from the core debate about the value and validity of human rights in the African context. While recognising that an easy complementarity of international, national and local transitional justice-related processes was impossible, people were willing to see the potential for concurring interventions, the interplay between the external and internal, the outsider's and the insider's contributions in terms of their knowledge, capacities and avenues of access to power. As most participants were themselves affected by the violence in their country, the meeting remained grounded in these local realities of pain and suffering, of resilience and hope, of local remedy and everyday repair. A need for the long term was stated and for awareness of the process and nature of any effort at dealing with any past. Rather than the (donor) hope that transitional justice could be a positivist set of mechanisms that engineers outcomes and then somehow transfixes them, the ongoing labour that transitional justice generates for societies extends far beyond the so-called transition, unfolding slowly over time and space, needing the healing and repair work of several generations.

Introduction

Levis Onegi

The early democratic gains made by African states since attaining independence from colonial powers have largely unravelled, with most countries marred by increasingly repressive and authoritarian regimes. A feature of this period has been stark violations of human rights, mass displacement of populations, state-sponsored killings and disappearances, sexual and gender-based violence, the extermination of ethnic and racial communities, the recruitment of minors as combatants and the use of rape as an instrument of warfare.

Citizens of South Africa, Rwanda, Burundi, the Central African Republic, Liberia, Sierra Leone, Morocco and elsewhere on the African continent have confronted a host of social, political and economic violations as a result of conflict or repressive regimes. Efforts to move out of this dark era have faced numerous challenges, including the question of how to heal the wounds of the past and provide a remedy for past injustices without threatening future peace and security. Many of the states in Africa which have sought to respond to such challenges have turned to transitional justice. However, as the discussions in this book illustrate, the transitional justice approaches adopted by many African states have sometimes been ill suited to the needs and contexts for which they are intended.

The contemporary guise of transitional justice is most often traced to the post-conflict accountability processes of the Second World War, most notably the Nuremberg trials. However, the overthrow of Latin America's military dictatorships, the end of the cold war, the Balkan conflicts and large-scale atrocities in Africa and Asia have further expanded transitional justice objectives to include the elimination of authoritarianism and the entrenchment of the rule of law, cultivation of social cohesion and nation building, the adoption of victim-centred and more holistic justice processes and, ultimately, the promotion of democratic practices. While this genealogy of transitional justice continues to coalesce into an academic field, the scope and boundaries of the 'field' of transitional justice remain unclear. Moreover, there is still significant disagreement over the most effective mechanisms for achieving transitional justice goals.

Further, despite the proliferation of international instruments that recognise and define transitional justice as including both judicial and non-judicial mechanisms (individual prosecutions, reparations, truth seeking, institutional reform, vetting and dismissals, or a combination thereof[1]), the breadth of endogenous processes and mechanisms used by societies recovering from the legacies of conflict is often disregarded by international actors.

This book carefully reflects on the complexities of current transitional justice policies and practices and their shortcomings in addressing the concerns of post-conflict societies in Africa. The book advances the view that contemporary transitional justice narratives dehistoricise Africa's relationship with the rest of the world; fail to adequately acknowledge the contribution of external actors to Africa's underdevelopment and the enduring effects of colonial crimes; do not reflect on the impact of geopolitics from the time of Africa's independence to the era of the cold war, then to that of globalisation and the emergence of new economic powers; and do not challenge the uncritical adoption of justice models that may not be fully responsive to Africa's needs. The book explores transitional justice mechanisms as they uniquely manifest themselves in Africa, taking keen note of the complexities of both concept and context, and so deepens comprehension of the ever-changing boundaries of transitional justice.

This book should hold wide appeal not only for an academic audience, but also to transitional justice practitioners, policymakers, researchers, the media, social commentators and humanitarian and development practitioners who want to familiarise themselves with the transitional justice debates that animate Africa. The issues presented speak to the challenges faced by countries coming to terms with a legacy of conflict and repressive authoritarian regimes. The fundamental question posed by the book is whether there is, or should be, a transitional justice model which seeks to respond to Africa's unique challenges.

There is currently limited literature on how to achieve the broad goals of transitional justice – peace, justice, healing and national reconciliation – from the perspective of African conceptions and paradigms. Much of the literature accepts the principles of Western criminal justice systems as the building blocks of any transitional justice process. This book sets out to challenge this assumption.

The emerging field of transitional justice has offered a diverse array of approaches which affected societies can use to address large-scale atrocities and past human rights abuses. The literature draws on the actual experiences of a variety of actors in communities implementing mechanisms and processes to counter the past. Although there are few empirical studies on the impact of the approaches adopted, scholars, policymakers and practitioners contribute to the design of these institutions, and therefore have first-hand experiences of the transitional justice processes they are analysing. The sheer number and variety of institutional mechanisms for promoting accountability and reconciliation suggest that questions of how people address gross human rights atrocities and move forward into the future will continue to be a source of interest to all scholars, practitioners and policymakers globally.

Note

1   United Nations Security Council (UNSC) (2003) *The Rule of Law and TJ in Conflict and Post-conflict Societies: Report of the Secretary-General*, New York, UNSC.

1

The paradox of alien knowledge, narrative and praxis: transitional justice and the politics of agenda setting in Africa

Brian Kagoro

> We cannot have democracy without peace; neither can we enjoy peace without democracy. But we will enjoy neither democracy nor peace without respect for human rights.
>
> Kofi Annan, 2005

Introduction

Economic, social and political fragility in Africa is inextricably tied in with failures to address the painful multiple legacies of the past, socio-economic exclusion and the culture of violence. It is a fragility that gives rise to and is reinforced by often precarious social cohesion, poor policy coherence and weak integration within nation states. Africa has for the past 50 years been torn apart by inter-state, intra-state, ethnic, racial, religious, and resource-based conflicts. More than 26 armed conflicts erupted in Africa between 1963 and 1968, affecting the lives of 474 million people, representing 61 per cent of the population of the continent, and claiming over 7 million lives. These conflicts spread across all the geographic regions of the continent: the Horn of Africa (Ethiopia, the Sudan, Eritrea and Somalia), Southern Africa (12 conflicts) and West Africa (some 10 wars). Until the recent uprisings in 2011–12, only North Africa, with the exception of Algeria, remained relatively conflict free. The conflicts – in Chad, Democratic Republic of Congo (DRC), Sudan, Angola,

Mozambique and Somalia – lasted for quite long periods: the war in Chad for 40 years; in South Sudan, 37 years; in Eritrea, 30 years; and in Angola, 27 years. One of the consequences of armed conflict is large-scale internal and external displacement, with refugees alone currently estimated at five million and displaced persons at not less than 20 million.

In some African countries the political situation since independence has been at best precarious and at worst chaotic. Governance in the post-colony has seen a recourse to force and coups d'état as a means of gaining power or undermining democratically elected governments. Despite pertinent treaties and declarations, Africa experienced 189 coups d'état between 1956 and 2011, half of which occurred in the 1980s and 1990s, all coinciding with the period of economic decline, externally imposed structural adjustment programmes, political liberalisation and the end of the cold war. The cold war era was marked by deep intra- and inter-state polarisation based on ideological differences and external alliances. These differences were in turn characterised by illiberal ways of doing politics based on a skewed logic of state security characterised by excessive supervision and surveillance. State security was used as an excuse for police brutality and other forms of intrusive state behaviour, which severely limited democratic space. Proxy ideological wars characterised the international projects to sabotage transitions to African rule in Ghana, DRC and Kenya, to mention but a few examples.

Three factors determined the length of African conflicts: the presence of a strong external influence or strategic interest in the affected countries; an endowment of natural and mineral resources; and the presence of two politically opposed major ethnic or religious groups. The social, economic and psychological impacts of both long and short conflicts were devastating. Historical conflicts have been superseded by newer conflicts fought over unresolved historical issues. In some instances those who were victims of previous conflicts became perpetrators in new conflicts, blurring the lines between victims and perpetrators.

Post-conflict reconstruction and development is, therefore, much more than a quick fix. The range of actors changes over time as do the issues for consideration. National aspirations for prosperity and development are not deferred by the more immediate desire for peace and stability. There is often a dilemma over whether to give priority to bringing perpetrators of past human rights violations to justice, as a means of curtailing the culture of impunity, or to focus attention more on putting in place measures to secure peace and stability as prerequisites of longer-term national recovery, reconstruction and development. This, in turn, reflects a larger problem of acquisition, exercise, transfer, retention and democratisation of political power.

Conflict destroys institutions and institutional memory, state capacity and the economy. As a conflict unfolds and until it is transformed, various layers of violations occur against individuals, communities and the basic essence of humanity. The conflicts referred to above witnessed bizarre and depraved acts of inhumanity, and the mindless destruction of physical infrastructure and personal assets as well as any sense of being, belonging and becoming a nation. Transitional societies are often faced with hard choices regarding how to handle displaced people (internal and external) on matters such as the right to vote, the right to return and the conferment of nationality upon their descendants and spouses as well as entitlement to reparations and the redemption of land and other property that they previously owned or occupied. Invariably, most displaced people and refugees live in inhumane conditions without adequate protection and assistance from national governments or the international community. Very few have adequate identification papers or certification to enable them to get decent employment in the receiving countries. With time, they may become deskilled and may be forced to turn to either socially risky behaviour or crime for survival. Displacement therefore has devastating consequences for post-conflict reconstruction, national stability and national healing efforts.

One of the frameworks that is often deployed in dealing with post-conflict societies and reconstruction is transitional justice. It is considered to be essential if Africa is to achieve an end to impunity, gross human rights violations and the reckless plunder of its precious natural resources. There is a correlation between unchecked impunity, weak institutions, unaccountable governance and the abject impoverishment of Africa and its peoples. Addressing impunity, economic fragility and poor governance will be a critical step in tackling poverty and underdevelopment in Africa. The dynamics of modern conflict require a great degree of intellectual rigour to unravel the complex layers that form the conflict jig-saw puzzle. Transforming conflict situations does not presume easy, one-size-fits-all imported 'solutions'. Ultimately, the more sustainable solutions to conflict lie in the affected countries and communities addressing concurrently or coherently their social, economic, political and environmental challenges informed by the lessons of the past, the realities of the present and the possibilities of the future.

In this regard, a critical and often under-utilised resource is traditional conflict management mechanisms (often inappropriately referred to as traditional justice). Traditional mechanisms were given prominence by the Rwandan experiment with *gacaca*, a 'modernised' approach to a traditional form of dispute settlement that was developed and implemented in the aftermath of the 1994 genocide. More recently, traditional conflict resolution mechanisms of the Acholi have been applied to the northern Ugandan conflict in efforts to achieve a peaceful settlement. Mozambique, Sierra Leone and Burundi have also – to varying degrees – utilised traditional conflict resolution mechanisms for purposes of national reconciliation and healing.

As jurists and academics we are predisposed to assume – sometimes without much interrogation – that juridical forms and processes are the *sine qua non* of the struggle to end impunity: better laws, better jurists, better courts, more vigilant prosecutions, the separation of powers, the rule of law. However, these are mere tools and approaches to legal social engineering that must recognise the messiness of reality, bounded by politics, social prejudice, economic inequity and sometimes an underlying desire for vengeance. We rationalise such forms of legal social engineering based on our idealism and need to justify our existence and central role in socio-economic and political transformation. We are, after all, embedded in both the status quo as well as the emerging alternatives. Notwithstanding a myriad of contradictions, transitional justice-speak represents and also dramatises this embeddedness. In Africa when transitional justice meets the messy reality of centuries of colonial domination and exploitation, decades of plutocratic and kleptocratic rule, deeply held social pathologies that are anti-national, notorious ethnic chauvinism and gender and class apartheid, we must ask the following irreverent questions: transition from what state (economic, social and political)? Whose transition? What justice? Whose justice? Can the justice needs of a community that has survived genocide and near annihilation ever be transitional?

The 2007–12 social and political upheavals in Kenya, Zimbabwe, South Africa, Mozambique, Madagascar, Tunisia, Egypt, Ivory Coast, Libya, Mali and Guinea Bissau dictate that any discussion of transitional justice be situated within a broader discussion of international democracy, justice, rule of law, sustainable development, inclusive economic growth and governance. These distinct political situations and those mentioned earlier were essentially internationalised internal conflicts or political crises. The process and nature of the internationalisation of these varied from case to case. The role played by both domestic and international actors in African conflicts and political upheavals since the 1950s is worth taking due note of. It informs the broader context and scope of international criminal justice. Arguably, the current debate on the International Criminal Court (ICC) is largely a proxy debate about undemocratic global governance, lopsided and faltering multilateralism. Further, the general failure to bring multinational corporations, international organisations and foreign governments to account for complicities in human rights violations since the cold war era remains the Achilles heel of international criminal justice.

Debates about transition and justice cannot – and should not – be resolved by focusing on purely juridical mechanisms and processes without factoring in the significant relevance and role of socio-economic and political contexts that might better explain the origins and other factors in the conflict continuum. It is fair to surmise that African victims of crimes against humanity, gross human rights violations, war crimes and genocide are trapped between inadequate local remedies and expensive, highly politicised, ineffective, remote and relatively low-impact international criminal justice options. In the face of indigenous tyranny, severely constrained democratic space, a lack of resources and often unsympathetic or sluggish regional actors, local activists vest their hopes in an international system whose ethos has historically been imbued with self-interest and bigotry, heavy handedness and short-term objectives. These are objectives whose logic tends towards projectisation of centuries-old structural and deeply embedded social problems.

To view the justice needs of women, girls and boys who have been raped or sexually violated during a conflict as a short-term transitional project is a travesty. National or local transition and justice can only be achieved by concurrently addressing the structural, global, politico-legal and socio-economic factors that fuel or sustain injustices. We must fashion a concept of transitional justice in Africa that has both an external and an internal dimension, one that looks at personal justice, socio-economic justice, political justice, electoral justice, ecological justice and broader collective justice claims. These dimensions of justice are mutually reinforcing and indivisible for the most part.

This chapter is not an argument against transitional justice; rather it is an argument for a self-sustaining Afro-centric transitional justice that takes on board the historiography of African conflicts as well as the broader geopolitical and geo-economic contexts of such conflicts. I intend to demonstrate that justice is – by its very nature – not transitional and that there are no differences in the standard and content of justice required in post-conflict and non-conflict situations. Further, that indigenous conflict resolution mechanisms are likely to be more successful in mono-ethnic or bi-ethnic settings (e.g. Rwanda, Burundi and northern Uganda) than in settings where the conflict involves several hundred ethnic, religious or cultural groups. The chapter also notes that most traditional mechanisms were designed to deal with personalised individual conflicts and are hardly suited to address large-scale human rights violations that include crimes which were either taboo or had complex redress mechanisms such as heterosexual rape, sodomy rape, and incineration and mass murder of the unborn while in the womb. It is not easy to find appropriate traditional mechanisms to address these issues while guaranteeing that gender, generational and other exclusions are mitigated. In order to be truly restorative and relevant within settings of multi-ethnic, multi-religious or multinational conflicts, traditional mechanisms must of necessity be significantly expanded and modernised. They must ensure that they are not, in the long term, viewed simply as the imposition of the culture of the victors upon the vanquished.

Human rights entrepreneurs do a lot to ensure that great abuses are exposed, averted or mitigated. The motivations of most human rights activists are noble and well intentioned. It would be remiss to judge the transitional justice industry purely on the intentions of its practitioners. However, this chapter seeks to analyse the objective implications of certain juridical narratives, actions and processes, their presumed saintly intentions notwithstanding. It is not intended to excuse the profligate violation of individual rights and freedoms by political elites, unscrupulous political merchants or tyrants, and my criticisms of transitional justice should be understood in this light. Abhorrence of tyranny should not necessarily make us uncritical of flawed solutions to African developmental and justice needs.

Criticism of transitional justice is by no means a denial of its relevance and potential role in post-conflict societies. This is not intended to be an academic paper and all views expressed below are mine and are not attributable to any institution that I might be associated with.

Transitional justice assumptions

The rise of the transitional justice industry and its privileging occurred as part of the post-cold war ascendancy of particular, culturally laden narratives about history, society, governmentality and justice. Transitional justice is premised on several fundamental assumptions and objectives, which include – but are not limited to – the following:

- Realising an ideal of justice for those who are vulnerable and powerless in society, transitional justice seeks to contribute to social coexistence and democratic stability.
- Breaking the cycle of impunity is necessary to prevent the recurrence of similar widespread and systematic violations.
- Dismantling or overhauling the structures that caused gross violations in the first place is regarded as a prerequisite for judicial, security sector, civil service and constitutional reforms.
- Investigating, prosecuting and punishing perpetrators of mass atrocities is a means of deterring similar minded individuals and groups.

- Engaging in honest introspection about the past, commonly referred to as truth seeking, is cathartic. In other words, when a perpetrator confesses to their wrongs, it is assumed that those who have incurred the loss or been violated will be healed by knowing who did what, when, how and why. This, it is believed, offers better prospects for the stability of a post-conflict society than indifference and denial. It is assumed that societies that confront their past are better off than those that do not.
- Ensuring the quality of democracy, characterised by well-functioning institutions, an absence of executive diktat, a responsiveness to the interests of the general populace and the inclusion of the least powerful sections of society requires truth, justice, reparations and institutional reform as well as the rule of law.

Reconciliation, an often-stated objective of transitional justice, is a contested notion that is variously understood, although at its core it is thought to constitute the establishment of civic trust, based on shared norms among citizens and between citizens and governing institutions. Transitional justice in Africa has been transacted through various mechanisms, including truth commissions, as in South Africa; mixed courts, as in Sierra Leone; and international criminal tribunals, as used in Rwanda. While some countries – DRC, Uganda, Sudan and Kenya – experienced the ICC's interventions with varying degrees of satisfaction, alternative and traditional forums, such as the *gacaca* courts and ordinary court prosecutions, have also proved successful.

Since 1994, almost every imaginable transitional justice mechanism has been tried in and on Africa. The continent has continued to witness deadly civil wars and political conflicts in which murderous armed groups target civilians (Chad, Darfur, DRC, Libya, Tunisia, Egypt, Ivory Coast, northern Uganda and Sudan). We have also witnessed an unprecedented number of peacekeeping missions and humanitarian interventions (Rwanda, Sierra Leone, Liberia, Burundi, DRC, Darfur, Somalia).

Since transitional justice may mean different things in different contexts, we need to carefully define its scope rather than just describe existing approaches. It cannot be taken as a given that transitional justice is accepted by and acceptable to all communities and peoples. The subject and concepts underlying it have not been sufficiently problematised. Most transitional justice practitioners adopt an over-simplified assumption that all forms of amnesty are tantamount to impunity. For those communities whose ethical and moral reference point is religion, forgiveness is neither impunity nor a sign of weakness. Elsewhere, for example in DRC, Sierra Leone, Sudan and Liberia, the amnesty statutes or agreements specifically excluded crimes against humanity, torture, genocide and serious human rights violations. Different conflict situations present different challenges and possibilities for their resolution. Thus to condemn all amnesty instruments, making no distinction between war situations and civil unrest, might be disingenuous.

African transitional justice practitioners also need to extensively discuss the limitations of international law and diplomacy (under the UN Charter, articles VI and VII, as well as the AU Constitutive Act). The question of intervention in the internal affairs of another sovereign state is fairly complicated, bounded by many conceptual landmines, more so in the context of the recent NATO bombardment of Libya, the Ivory Coast crisis, the war on terror and regime-change projects seen across the globe. The African transitional justice industry is surprisingly silent on these geopolitical realities.

The African state as the primary transitional justice actor?

Transitional justice is a largely statist or state-centric process. Its success in Africa will depend on the role played by the African state as well as the inter-governmental bodies such as the African Union (AU) and the regional economic communities. We need to understand the nature of the state and society, particularly state–society relations. Transitional justice nomenclature has entered African politics via the activities of international aid agencies, Western think-tanks, knowledge institutions and government funding regimes. African transitional justice practitioners often do not critically examine this knowledge imperialism, let alone Western interests beyond the positive role played in pressuring weak African governments and the comprador political elites that preside over them. Little distinction is made between the rhetorical deployment of ideas and ideals such as democracy as advanced by Western governments and their strategic interests in each context.

The dialogue about the African state is important for many reasons. It addresses the related issues of self-determination, sovereignty, national ownership and sustainability beyond donor pressure to prioritise a particular justice, truth or peace process. It speaks to the broader question of citizenship and the sovereignty of the people as opposed to the sovereignty of an abstraction called the state.

National reconstruction and reconciliation cannot be transacted without taking into account the history of the conflict that necessitated them. This struggle over history and meaning is also a struggle over the form of futures, of nationhood and citizenship. Central to this dialogue is how to collectively fashion an inclusive and egalitarian post-conflict state and society.

The role of external actors in financing insurgency and conflict and facilitating the plunder of natural resources makes them complicit in human rights violations. As a result, the resolution of situations of conflict or repression remains incomplete unless the agency of external actors such as multinational corporations, gun traders, rogue intelligence officers, mercenaries and indifferent donors is addressed. Although it is hardly ever admitted, Africa has experienced more pernicious conflicts in the age of democracy than it did under the recalcitrant dictatorships (e.g. DRC, Rwanda, Kenya, Zimbabwe, Ivory Coast, Madagascar, Sudan, Nigeria). To what extent are these new manifestations of conflict – in essence, anarchies – born out of the new democratic dispensation? This highlights the limitations of liberal democracy and the new governance models in addressing social inequity, inequality, poverty, disintegration, ethnicity and conflict in Africa.

Africa's developmental and economic challenges are tied to the ability and capability of the African state to raise independent resources to address the socio-economic and politico-legal inequities that threaten to deepen the cleavages within the nation state. In sum, the question of state architecture is important, not just for the institutional reform agenda, but also the larger nation-building and state reconstruction that is a prerequisite for a truly reconciled and sovereign nation. As seen in Liberia, Sierra Leone, South Africa, Kenya and Burundi, it is one thing to demobilise militarised and militant youth and quite another to keep them gainfully engaged after the conflict. Peace and justice will remain elusive as long as transitional justice remains disconnected from developmental questions (the creation of inclusive wealth and the eradication of poverty and inequality).

The paradox that many post-conflict countries in Africa face is whether to expend billions of dollars pursuing a few criminals, or invest more in reconstruction. The trade-off is not just between peace and justice, but also between development and vindication. Therefore we must ask: what does national healing mean to a people that remain severely impoverished, and with very little access to basic social services and life opportunities? What might the prosecution of egregious violations of human rights signify to communities that continue to live in abject poverty?

Ultimately, most transitional justice processes presume the existence of a state to implement and defend reform gains in the long term. Further, the arena of public policy, building national consent and consensus is tied to the nature and role of the state. In other words, the state leadership is central to any justice project and it cannot be replaced by civil society and international benefactors. Transitional justice presumes a law-governed state that responds to the legitimate interests, rights and aspirations of citizens. Since justice cannot be transacted in a vacuum, it is presumed that a capable, democratic and developmental state is the best guarantor for transitional justice in Africa.

Framing the dialogue

Post-conflict reconstruction – and by parity of reasoning, transitional justice – requires that one of its core objectives be the establishment of a capable democratic developmental state and an active and informed citizenry. African transitional justice should adopt an expansive view of justice, democracy and development. It should not be an end in itself, but a means of building the capacity of the state to provide basic goods to its citizens, provide social security, universal social protection and facilitate inclusive wealth creation. Africa requires transitional justice processes that are both developmental and inclusive. A capable, democratic developmental state is necessary in order to address the economic, social and institutional deficits faced by many post-conflict countries. The objective of creating a competent administrative apparatus within the state depends on the willingness of political leaders to ensure that necessary resources are deployed and appropriate policy programmes are developed and implemented. Implied in this is the political will to forge programmatic and reciprocal relationships with voluntary associations of citizens such as trade unions, businesses, faith-based institutions, civil society and so on. These efforts should be predicated on a functional, constitutional, democratic and accountable governance architecture.

The state should simultaneously promote inclusive economic growth while addressing social questions of inequality, poverty, unemployment and environmental degradation. This raises fundamental questions about the objectives of transitional justice in Africa. Transitional justice should not have a single role, but should have multiple objectives. It should simultaneously ensure policy reforms and targeted institutional redesign. It should establish developmental and transformative institutions to overcome under-capacity or limited capacity. The weak capacity of the state during the moment of transition should not be an excuse but an incentive for constructing a developmental state.

Sustainable transitional justice requires a state that has the capacity to give leadership in the definition of a common national agenda and in mobilising all sectors of society to participate in implementing that agenda. This includes the capacity to prioritise in a strategic manner, to identify which goals and initiatives have the potential to forge national consent, consensus and unity in an effort that kick-starts the rest of the national reconstruction agenda. This leadership role and capacity presumes a popular mandate and effective systems and processes of broad-based engagement with citizens and other stakeholders. Justice in these settings is the process of re-humanisation and empowerment to live a life of dignity.

As intimated earlier, transitional justice is not a politically neutral, non-ideological and well-intentioned discipline of universal application. It has to be decoupled from its neoliberal and neo-imperial hue in order to guarantee its success in Africa. Current transitional justice narratives dehistoricise the questions of Africa's relationship with the rest of the world such as Africa's underdevelopment by Europe; colonial and cold-war injustice/brutality/liability; the role of Western corporations in African resource conflicts and aggravated human insecurity; the contribution of the policies of international financial institutions to instability and governance deficits in Africa; and the inappropriateness of justice models that consume infinite amounts of resources while accounting for little. We note that transitional justice often appears like a series of missionary projects by Western benefactors and their local NGO proxies to 'civilise' African politics or address their conviction that Africans have a pathological predisposition towards brutality. Arguably, transitional justice agenda setting in Africa is also about the production, distribution, legitimisation and ownership of knowledge about Africans and African societies. The knowledge produced can either reaffirm a sense of despondency and inferiority and an inherent brutish nature or can demonstrate that the monstrous conduct of a few hardly defines the character of Africa or Africans. Regrettably, the bulk of present approaches to transitional justice in Africa are largely Eurocentric and even when they purport to promote indigenous mechanisms, these mechanisms are viewed mostly through a European–American lens – a lens that focuses on the functional utility of such mechanisms to handle large volumes of cases as opposed to their normative and cognitive value in creating new knowledge about being, becoming and belonging to a reality called 'African'. Traditional mechanisms were never purely instrumental in orientation; they sought to reassert a sense of value and values. It was not so much the conclusion of the case that mattered, but the dialogic process that sought to re-establish relationships, mutual respect, recognition and social cohesion. African transitional justice practitioners must be careful not to reduce traditional mechanisms to the pervasive culture of bean-counting under the guise of measuring results in the delivery of justice.

That said, transitional justice is inconceivable, or at least unsustainable, without the reform and democratisation of the global governance system responsible for the manufacture of tyranny and impunity. Africa requires a nuanced transitional justice discourse that deliberately ensures that transitional justice is not fictionally separated from the broader global governance context. Starting with transient or current political, security or governance crises, or treating transitional justice as separate from African struggles against global economic, social and environmental injustice, is shortsighted. Those who sell blood diamonds are as culpable as those that buy them; those that sell small arms and light weapons as a business are as culpable as those that recruit child soldiers; those that pollute water and air are as guilty of genocide and crimes against humanity as those that wield machetes.

Within the African context, transitional justice is a discourse stuck between the failure or excesses of nationalism and the triumph of neoliberalism. As a result, the present transitional justice discourse unwittingly perpetrates two big lies. The first is that Africa has been independent for so long it can no longer justifiably blame colonialism, the cold war and apartheid for some of the ills experienced on the continent today. The same argument is certainly not applied to the Nazi criminals and collaborators still being hunted to this day for the genocide against the Jews. When the genocide against the Jews ended, not a single African country was independent. This attempt by the West at absolution from any liability for the current condition of Africa is baffling. The second lie is the attempt to conceptualise gross human rights violations, conflict and accountability outside their historical context. A variation of this is the revisionist approach to African history that truncates that history into a tale about the liability of African political elites for bad governance in the post-independence era. Indeed, there are many African tyrants and tin-pot dictators, but these are as much products of their times as they are children of the history that shaped them. An ahistorical transitional justice discourse refuses to, and is incapable of, accounting for the injustices done by the West to Africans for more than five centuries, including the slave trade, colonial plunder, the cold war and brutality and the new scramble for Africa under globalisation. Viewed through this tainted lens, Mobuto, Savimbi and others are depicted as caricatures of bad African leadership, not linked in any way to Western machinations and designs in Africa. This is an Afro-pessimistic view based on the belief that Africa is bad in and of itself, that it is ingrained in Africans to be tribalistic, brutish and corrupt, that Africans have a pathological pre-disposition towards inhumane and selfish behaviour, or are simply 'impish'. This in turn, confirms the historical characterisation by the colonialists of Africa as the 'heart of darkness'.

A historiography of injustice in Africa demonstrates the fundamental antithesis between current transitional justice narratives and global justice talk. It helps us to locate the role of African transitional justice actors within a broader narrative on global justice that is social, economic, environmental and political, a justice that has juridical and material dimensions, a culture of accountability that looks at internal mechanisms as well as external reparations by multinational corporations and developed nations complicit in Africa's conflicts, political repression and human rights violations. It looks at a broader continuum of violations that go beyond physical brutality to include socio-cultural, environmental, economic, generational and gender injustices. Such a narrative of justice is both developmental and restorative. What Africans yearn for is not just lives untouched by physical violence meted out by militia, the state or armed men; they want decent and prosperous lives and livelihoods free from fear, want and deprivation. Transitional justice should be about creating conditions where dignity and equality can be attained, decent work obtained, the right to development achieved, where the rights over public goods and natural resources are respected and fundamental rights and freedoms are addressed. The history of African conflict that hardly features in current debates about international justice and justice in situations of transition is briefly outlined below.

Historiography of injustice in Africa

The partitioning of Africa by European kings, princes and presidents in Berlin in 1885 occurred years after the continent had already been destroyed by many years of the trans-Atlantic slave trade. Black civilisations had been decimated across west, central and southern Africa. The slave trade resulted in the death of approximately 40 million African lives over the period 1450 to 1850 (Davidson 1961). Arguably, the European and North American industrial revolutions were built on the sweat, labour and blood of Africans. The slave trade almost totally destroyed African moral and social fibre. To understand the present conjuncture of African history, it is important to always recall how Europe underdeveloped Africa (Rodney 1972). Transitional justice narratives have to be situated within the historiography of the continuing domination, exploitation and plunder of Africa by Euro-American interests (Shivji 2007), whether through economic partnership agreements or unfavourable trade and investment terms. The famous Maori writer Linda Tihiwai Smith (1999: 34) observes that, despite the fact that our countries have been independent for close to half a century now:

> Our colonial experience traps us in the project of modernity. There can be no post-modern for us until we have settled some business of the modern. This does not mean that we do not understand or employ multiple discourses or act in incredibly contradictory ways, or exercise power ourselves in multiple ways. It means that there is unfinished business, that we are still being colonised.

Colonialism divided Africa into countries and nation states, cutting across 'natural' geographic, cultural and ethnic ties that had evolved historically. The boundaries that constitute modern day Africa were artificially drawn with dastardly consequences. New boundaries divided up peoples, cultures, natural resources and historical affinities. The newly created countries were ruled by different European powers with largely differing traditions of political rule, public administration, cultural outlooks, languages and systems of education. In reality, any talk of historical Africa is nonsensical because there was never an Africa, and colonialism simply turned the geographical area which is our continent into Arabophone, Anglophone, Francophone, or Lusophone (Shivji 2007) regions. These colonially defined differences have manufactured identities within and outside nation states that continuously feed and sustain so-called African conflicts.

Colonial economies were designed to serve the needs of the colonial powers that ruled each country. The African economies so conceived were largely export oriented and integrated vertically with the metropolitan centre. Africa provided raw materials and cheap labour while importing finished products from the metropolis. The prospects for African industrialisation were destroyed by both the slave trade and colonialism, which fore-closed any possibility of internal division of labour with mutual interdependence between craftsmen and cultivators, producers and merchants, industry and agriculture (Shivji 2007). This led to uneven development within and between countries (Kjekshus 1996). Colonialism fully exploited African natural and human resources, by keeping colonies as sites for generating surplus, while the metropoles were sites of accumulation (Shivji 1989). Colonial production processes were heavily dependent on the use of force rather than freedom of contract rules, e.g. forced labour in Mozambique, forced peasant production in Zimbabwe, enforced cash crop sales in Tanzania, restrictions on organisation and association in Kenya and the criminalisation of 'civil relations' in Nigeria. Breach of employment contracts often led to penal sanctions, as did the non-cultivation of minimum acreages of cash and food crops. Coercion was, therefore, an integral part of colonial production (Mamdani 1987).

To administer the colonies effectively, peoples were often divided into ethnic, religious and racial pockets. Missionary education was one of the tools of domestication and enlightenment of Africans (Switzer 1993). Colonial rulers sought to create an impression that Africans were lazy, dishonest, and incapable of learning and entrepreneurship. In some colonies traders and craftsmen and skilled labour were even imported: south Asians into East Africa, Lebanese into West Africa.

The white colonial rulers saw their obligation as one of ruling, disciplining, punishing, and suppressing supposedly savage African instincts. Religion and colonial education became vehicles for reproducing the notions of black inferiority and white superiority. It posited white men's beliefs as religion and black men's as 'witchcraft or black magic' (Fanon 1967a: 32). As Fanon observes:

> The native is declared insensible to ethics; he represents not only the absence of values, but also the negation of values ... The customs of the colonised people, their traditions, their myths – above all, their myths – are the very sign of that poverty of spirit and of their constitutional depravity. (Fanon 1967b: 32)

The colonial state was an implant; an alien apparatus imposed on the colonised society. It was a poor shadow of the metropolitan state without the latter's liberal institutions and politics. It was also a despotic state. Neither did the colonial social formation have its own civil society. The colonised were treated as heathens, criminals and natives, governed by force and regulated by custom. It was not a civil society made up of citizens with rights and duties regulated by law (Mamdani 1996).

The African elite that took over the reins of power at independence were faced with the herculean task of transforming brutalised colonial societies into national societies, citizens and rights-holders. As discussed above, this process seems to have faltered in a most dramatic way, partly, perhaps, because the African educated elite that led the anti-colonial struggle was nurtured in a system of education that reinforced black inferiority and affirmed white superiority. It was a middle class with a limited perception or at worst they were mere caricatures (Fanon 1967b). They were the chosen few who were allowed to have a white education, alienated from their own people, yet not fully accepted by their colonial masters. Jean-Paul Sartre, in the preface to Fanon's *Wretched of the Earth*, sums up the fate of this middle class thus:

> The European elite undertook to manufacture a native elite. They picked out promising adolescents; they branded them, as with a red-hot iron, with the principles of western culture; they stuffed their mouths full with high-sounding phrases, grand glutinous words that stuck to the teeth. After a short stay in the mother country they were sent home, whitewashed. These walking lies had nothing to say to their brothers; they only echoed. (Fanon 1967b: 7)

The contemporary discourses about transitional justice and economic, social and political reforms in Africa seem to have the potential to produce a civil society elite (civilocracy) that is manufactured out of a false consciousness insidiously rooted in Afro-pessimism. The real challenge is to imagine a transitional justice rooted in Afro-optimism, inclusivity and democratic Pan-Africanism. The attraction of universal principles of right and wrong should not be allowed to translate into intellectual slavery. We live in a world where Western leaders who attack another sovereign country under the pretence of destroying weapons of mass destruction do not end up at The Hague, but have the luxury of authoring self-congratulatory memoirs. For the same offences African leaders are imprisoned. Likewise soldiers of powerful nations who kill civilians merely plead collateral damage while their African counterparts who are guilty of the same evil become a public spectacle.

Democratic deficits versus democratic dividends

With the fall of the Berlin Wall and the break-up of the Soviet empire, a wave of political liberalisation reforms swept through Africa. This so-called 'second liberation' (Legum 2002, Olukoshi and Laakso 1996) of Africa, characterised by extensive political reforms, the demise of the single party and military dictatorships that had risen to power in the 1960s and 70s, seems to have resulted in higher levels of poverty, inequality and injustice for many African citizens. The Western media gleefully celebrated the rise of 'a new crop' of African leaders such as Meles Zenawi in Ethiopia, Yoweri Museveni in Uganda, Isias Aferworki in Eritrea and Frederick Chiluba in Zambia (Olukoshi 1998a). These leaders were better educated and their ascent to power was seen as a significant generational shift in the governance of African countries as well as potentially signalling the beginning of an African renaissance. As Adebayo Olukoshi observes:

> The end of the Cold War meant that the rival ideological blocs had less pressing geo-political reasons for obstructing domestic pressures for political reform and almost unconditionally propping up unaccountable client regimes on the African continent. This, together with the swing of popular international opinion in favour of political change in Africa even led many Western governments to introduce a new political conditionality into their relations with the countries of the continent. The spread of multi-party politics in those erstwhile socialist countries that made up the Soviet bloc in the aftermath of the collapse of the monopoly on power enjoyed by the communist parties served as a further boost to the local struggles within Africa for political reform. (Olukoshi 1998b: 15)

In many respects, the end of the cold war ushered in a 'new world order', which marked – according to Francis Fukuyama (1992) – 'the end of history' and the inevitability of liberal democracy as the only remaining viable option for the developing world. This new world order was characterised by superpowers abandoning their proxies such as Mobuto in Zaire and Jonas Savimbi in Angola (Adelman and Paliwala 1993). As noted above, this moment of political and economic liberalisation started off promising great hope for Africa, but has resulted in greater challenges for democracy, development and justice in the post-colony.

Ethnic and nationalist aspirations previously suppressed under communist regimes have broken to the surface, producing new levels of chaos and human carnage since 1989. The irreconcilability of a supposedly 'freer' people and increased brutality remains an enigma within contemporary African politics. Liberalisation created greater space for civil and political expression and association. By the same token, liberalisation exacerbated class, ethnic, gender, generational and racial tensions within most African countries. Thus democracy in Africa has not always been an integrative phenomenon; in many instances the highly liberalised countries are worse off than they were under oppressive and less liberal systems. Tragically, freedom has brought neither development nor real liberty. It is a difficult proposition to make, but the African experience demonstrates that there is no automatic correlation between democracy and the end of poverty. This may be because liberal democracy in Africa lacks the sociopolitical relevance, let alone key ingredients, that characterise its Western incarnation, namely a well-resourced and professional civil service; a functional culture of constitutionalism rooted in the rule of law and respect for human rights; a competitive and inclusive political system for selecting leadership; a stable domestic capital base or a productive and patriotic national bourgeoisie; and a system of ensuring universal social protection for the most vulnerable in society.

Equally, many of the desirable politics of pluralism have become a source of increased instability, conflict, corruption, ethno-nationalism and genocidal tendencies. State architecture has been configured to serve the specific interests of feuding ethnic elites, their sycophants and the looting agents of external capital. In many African countries, only three agents seem to have any influence on governance, justice delivery systems and the policy process: the political elite, political party activists and the rich who are able to pay bribes. Many Africans have resigned themselves to the belief that in order to get justice done – or anything for that matter – one has to align with or enlist the assistance of one or more of these agents. Most African systems do not seem to function without 'grease' or 'facilitation fees'. These are systems of co-conspirators from the watchman guarding office compounds to the highest echelons of the state. These co-conspirators are tied together by an umbilical cord of greed and short-term gain. Ordinary Africans are forced every day to pay double to middlemen and corrupt public officials for otherwise free services (birth certificates, passports, etc). The risk of non-compliance is always high: costly delays or forfeiture of one's rights. This concurrent institutionalisation of corrupt societies alongside 'normal' societies explains why many Africans distrust the law, justice delivery systems, politics and government generally. Law, politics and government have become vulgar words to the poor and excluded in Africa. To the enterprising political type, though, these same things are indispensable instruments for personal accumulation, consolidation of power, settling grudges and guaranteeing impunity.

African states – and indeed governments – have become havens for 'homeboys and homegirls', tribesmen, sycophants and xenophobes. Because of the high premium Africa places on politics and the state as a site of accumulation, the battle for the state is always likely to be replete with perils and contradictions. Tragically, civil society in many African countries suffers from the same malady as political parties. This ethnic civil society has also become a site of personal accumulation, consolidation of power and a waiting lounge for those who intend to enter government, or a retirement home for those who have unexpectedly exited government. The foreign and government control and financing problem is only a symptom of a larger African civil society challenge. It is often a mirror of the state's politics of incumbency or a debilitating donor-led missionary project of enlightenment. In this latter form, African civil society becomes a ghetto of failed Euro-American ideas, a proxy of imperial interests as it were. In the former incarnation, civil society becomes an accomplice in the culture of impunity, plunder and deception that permeates every aspect of African life. The latter often wears a progressive anti-imperial mask and the former a pro-democracy and good governance robe. Both are retrogressive, along with their coterie of hired intellectuals-cum-academics.

Today, hardly two decades after the beginning of the wave of reforms, it is apparent that the models of governance that emerged have not delivered to the expectations of most African citizens. This is as true for the quality of elections as it is for constitutional practice, multiparty political systems, social cohesion, citizen civil participation, poverty reduction and human development. Indeed, there are a lot more political parties being formed each day, more private media organisations, more churches and NGOs sprouting up, more access to cyber space, more TV and radio stations, fewer military forays into civil affairs and so on. However, the quality of African political systems measured by their inclusiveness, representativeness and accountability is perhaps worse now than in the 1980s. The levels of grand corruption have also increased, as has state repression of human rights defenders. In the final analysis, democracy as instituted through the golden age of liberal political reforms in Africa is failing to deliver the dividends expected by the citizenry. Some observers have gone on to suggest that not only has it failed to deliver but that it may even be disempowering Africans (Ake 1996) where replacing social movements with highly professionalised urban and internet-based NGOs makes the democratisation project in Africa a stillborn one (Bond 2005).

Democratic reform rituals have replaced substantive social and economic transformation agendas and struggles. Conversely, the wave of ethno-nationalism and xenophobia witnessed in several African countries can be characterised as anarchy born out of democracy (Chua 2003). The consequences of this failure have been widespread apathy and antipathy towards African politics and politicians. This disillusionment is not so much about the place and importance of democratic ideals, it is more about the ways in which democracy has been instituted and practised (Olukoshi 1998a). The 1990s liberalisation reforms failed largely because they were designed to serve and institutionalise a particular overarching framework of economic and social reforms that was neoliberal. The new systems of governance were conceptualised and/or operated to serve the requirements of a pre-determined orthodox economic agenda. As Adebayo Olukoshi argues, an economic agenda itself is neither the product of domestic democratic politics nor subject to full democratic accountability, and he insists that 'we cannot talk meaningfully about democratic governance and accountability if citizens cannot take an active part in policy-making and be confident that their active citizenry will help shape public policy (2011: 15).'

At a procedural and aesthetic level, the Western sponsors and local advocates of these reforms were in agreement regarding milestones for reforms in the security sector, judicial and financial services, parliament and the constitution. At a substantive level they were talking at cross-purposes. African local actors wanted a democratic state, which was accountable and developmental at the same time. Their Western sponsors conceived of a lean state that would facilitate the smooth operation of the market, employ fewer people and play a smaller role in the economy, in the redistribution and distribution of resources and opportunities.

The lean state was a sham as it could not address historical imbalances relating to resource ownership, social recognition and inclusion. In almost all African countries it became much easier to open a business than to get a child through school or feed one's family. The African state progressively became a mere handmaid of the ruling class and international capital and other strategic interests. Reform resulted in market friendly policies, higher economic growth, lower tax/GDP ratios, fewer jobs, deeper poverty and increased inequality. Across the continent, students, workers, peasants and the unemployed revolted against their governments, appalled by the decline in public services, the high cost of living and the poor quality of life. This context, with its contradictions, gave birth to new political contestations, new political movements, new ways of organising and new forms of state repression (Kagoro 2008).

Democracy is seen as a set of ideas and principles about freedom as well as a set of practices and procedures that have been moulded through a long and tortuous history of struggle. Democracy is, therefore, the institutionalisation of freedom with the presence of a constitutional government, respect for human rights and equality before the law (Kagoro 2008).

There are several ways to think about the development and democracy nexus. These include:

- The view that economic growth leads to democracy
- The argument that economic development leads to political decay – then the political system under instability moves towards democracy through and after institutionalisation (Huntington 1996)
- Using the case of China, the argument that advances the view that economic development will result in democracy because authoritarian regimes and autocracies show how people can enjoy the benefits of economic development while avoiding political liberalisation (de Mesquita and Downs 2005)
- The view of the 'Democracy first, development later' proponents, who argue that democracies always outperform non-democracies on most indicators of economic and social well-being so in the developing nations, promoting democracy should take priority over expanding economic development (Siegle et al 2004)
- The view that although politics influence economic performance, the impact of regime type is not significant on a state's economic growth so it is not possible to tell whether democracy improves or limits economic development.

Civil society tends to posit the following factors as either facilitating or hindering democratic development: legitimacy and performance, political leadership, political culture, social structure and socioeconomic development, state and society, political institutions, ethnic and regional conflict, the military and international factors.

However, the 2009 xenophobic attacks in South Africa against non-South African Africans demonstrate that democracy is only meaningful if it delivers what has become known as democracy dividends, i.e. socio-economic development. There is also an organic relationship between political freedom brought about by democracy, and the freedom from hunger, ignorance and disease that results from socio-economic development. In societies that have or are emerging from conflict or authoritarian/patrimonial rule, the previously oppressed tend to directly relate their poverty or deprivation to the privilege and/or affluence of those who historically benefited from the system of rule (the other tribe, race or nationalities). Poverty thus becomes a key consideration in both reconciliation and the political economy of transition or transitional justice.

Most African countries are in severe crisis over balancing the various interests of minorities and majorities; development and liberal democracy; peace and justice. The radical political short cuts to a better standard of living such as attempted in Zimbabwe between 2000 and 2007 do not always bear the desired fruits within the required or envisaged time.

In Africa more governments face citizen revolts over either poor or expensive social services (water, electricity, education, health, sanitation). Uneven economic development has generated fragmented socio-economic structures and divisive interests and has reduced previous class loyalties to the politics of ethnicity, religious fundamentalism and xenophobic identity politics. The orphans of South Africa's failed neoliberal, non-inclusive economic growth models are now criminals and xenophobes who murder African migrants in brutal attacks. In Kenya, these orphans of jobless growth constitute the numerous militia groups such as the Mungiki and Taliban, which are rented at will by unscrupulous politicians.

Africa's attempt over the last 20 years to transition to the European and American liberal-democracy models has faced many challenges. Almost all African states have formally adopted multi-party politics, without necessarily becoming more democratic. Even those countries like South Africa, Kenya, Uganda and Ethiopia that seemed to make strides in upholding the classic pillars of liberal democracy have tended to backslide within a decade. On the other hand, the tradition of radical popular political projects which are aimed at achieving democracy and development have been equally unsuccessful. Some of these radical projects have unwittingly bred dictatorships, famine and economic regress, as in Zimbabwe. This is partly because the mutations of radical popular projects largely tend to mobilise and manipulate the uneducated and dependent rural masses through elite-led parties and the state apparatus rather than through their own agency. Further, in most cases, radical populist projects do not prioritise democracy and human rights. Democracy and human rights are only tactfully 'respected' under pressure from the local middle classes, external actors (donors, bilateral partners) and, increasingly, regional economic communities.

There has emerged a belief among regional and international actors that external pressure and influence can compensate for the worst domestic obstacles. The Kenyan and Zimbabwean post-election violence and subsequent political settlements have created a dangerous precedent for democracy, development and justice generally. There seems to be a belief that if external actors intervene swiftly during periods of crisis, their major task is to swiftly craft alliances within the elite, stop violence and fashion the 'right' type of constitution and electoral system. This model cannot – and will never – yield sustainable democracy, development and security. It is important that we keep in mind the importance of the poorer members of society in any effort to establish lasting security, sustainable development and democracy. People power, that is, the power of organised and mobilised lower social classes, is key to genuine transitions and justice and development.

But what is even more perplexing is the paucity of definitions of the term 'justice' in transitional justice or the loose manner in which it is thrown about. Justice is a very complex political and legal term.

The paradox of justice

The concept of 'justice' is often symbolised as Lady Justice, blindfolded, with scales in one hand and a sword in the other. The blindfold symbolises impartiality, which is her principal feature; the scales represent the idea of balanced judgment and of equal considerations guaranteeing to each their own; the sword underscores the conclusiveness and authority of her judgment. In this sense justice is the highest political-moral virtue by which legal, political and social conditions as a whole – the basic structure of society – can be measured (Bratton and Van de Walle 1997, Schraeder 2000, Forst 2002).

This idealistic representation of justice confronts a reality that is mediated by history, politics, economics and the cultural contexts. Justice therefore takes different normative forms in different cultural, socio-economic, religious and political contexts. It is difficult to generalise about the existence of common, universalistic conceptions of morality.

The notion of blindfolded justice assumes impartiality without distinction of person, and equality of standing and entitlement for everyone. This conception of judgment and reason is distant from real human experience and risks being blind to the specific needs of human beings. The dilemma of justice is how to find a single standard for the complexity of conflicting claims that each community of individuals has, all the more so given that societal norms do not always enjoy absolute validity. Ideally, justice must avoid the context of blindness. It must also not resile into a relativism that fails to recognise certain universal conceptions of what is 'just'.

Bruce Ackerman (1990) proposes a dialogic model of justifying political and social distributions of power as a way of determining more concretely the criterion of 'neutral' norms and operationalising the same in political contexts. Central to Ackerman's conception is the principle of the legitimacy of norms that are to be justified generally. In this conception, the meaning of being a 'legal person with individual rights' is left to be determined within a democratic political community's institutionalised procedures of justification. Ackerman's theory is proceduralist in the sense that it grounds principles of justice in a general agreement of all citizens. Its potency lies in the three principles it assumes to be elementary, namely:

- The principle of neutrality, which reflects the pluralism of society, and which principle implies that only those norms that can be justified reciprocally and generally can claim general validity. The principle of neutrality therefore distinguishes a criterion for the justification of the validity of norms. The 'neutrality of justification', or 'neutrality of reasons,' or 'procedural neutrality' encompass and describe this principle. Neutrality in this sense refers to the moral impartiality of the justification
- The principle of rationality, which requires that social and political power relations be legitimated by good reasons and not by the exercise of crude power
- The principle of consistency, which imposes upon the participants of these dialogues the condition that the reasons they advance in various contexts do not contradict one another.

The above principle of neutrality presumes that there are specific 'good reasons'. In particular that no reason is a good reason if it requires the power holder to assert that their conception of good is better than that asserted by any of their fellow citizens; or, regardless of their conception of good, that they are intrinsically superior to their fellow citizens (Ackerman 1980).

In this regard the ends that the distribution of resources is to serve cannot therefore be controversial ethical ends; rather, they must be backed by generally shared reasons; the latter justify, as Ackerman (1980: 28) attempts to show, a state of formal equality before the law and an initially equal distribution of resources, which he calls 'undominated equality'.

Nagel (1970) advances the Kantian argument of reciprocity to the effect that only the reasons the other can accept grants one the right to treat the other in accordance with these reasons. In dealing with conceptions of justice we need to discard the fictitious separation between private and public. This is because what one considers to be right 'privately' one also defends 'publicly'.

The neutrality principle relates to the validity criterion of general norms. It therefore does not imply neutrality in the process of justification. Justice cannot be viewed as a neutral discourse especially in the context of former colonies, conflict, post-conflict and nations emerging out of crisis. What is important is that ethical arguments, when they propose values as a foundation for general regulations, be 'translatable' into universal arguments. They must be compatible with the principle of public justification; however, they do not therefore completely detach themselves from the ethical, social or political background from which they originate.

This conception of neutrality neither proposes nor defends the thesis of 'neutrality of effect' or a 'neutrality of consequences', at least not in the sense that the realisation and institutional implementation of norms within a legal system has the same effects on all life forms in the legal community and all conceptions of good present there. What neutrality does is simply to prohibit ethically motivated discrimination against forms of life; it does not guarantee that all are affected in the same way by the decisions and development of the political community and by social change (Forst 2002).

Liberal conceptions of neutrality require an observation of 'neutrality of aims' in the sense that the basic institutions and public policy are not to be designed to favour any particular comprehensive doctrine. This explains why the establishment of a state religion, state ideology or one-party state violates notions of a liberal state. A community can translate collective ends into valid law provided that this is done in a legitimate procedural way and the principle of strict generality is not violated (Habermas 1998). The principle of neutrality and impartiality does not mean that present conditions appear as justified in the sense of 'status quo neutrality' (Sunstein 1993). It also does not follow that a state that upholds the status quo is 'neutral'. 'Neutral' reasons have to be generally justifiable, whether they are for or against existing institutions (Ackerman 1990). It therefore follows that the concept of neutrality has implications for an understanding of equal treatment before and through the law. The dilemma, therefore, in societies emerging from conflict or authoritarian rule is that Lady Justice would have to remove her blindfold if substantive justice is to be achieved. In essence Lady Justice may have to go beyond existing law in order to achieve justice.

First there is the question of historical imbalances based on ethnicity, race, gender and class that are in some instances constitutionally sanctioned. As MacKinnon (1989: 231) notes, liberalism's claim that a general law guarantees equality is faced with a twin dilemma. The first is the argument that opposes special treatment of, say, minorities, persons with disabilities, the poorest of the poor, blacks and women on the grounds that such special treatment essentially underpins existing differences; it affirms them symbolically and can in reality turn out to the disadvantage of its intended beneficiaries. Hence the proposition that the goal of legal equal treatment should be preferred over explicit special treatment (Kaminer 1991). The alternative argument objects to the simplistic pursuit of legal equal treatment. It insists that such an approach does not understand the special problems of historically disadvantaged groups and their identity. Accordingly, equal treatment of unequals can be achieved only through unequal treatment. In this regard, the 'gender, ethnicity or race-blindness of the law' is dissolved in favour of special rights and regulations. Thus, in the context of societies in transition, justice must necessarily have a historical (retrospective), present and futuristic characteristic or dimension.

In the discussion of ethnicity, race and gender we subconsciously grapple with a further dilemma. Martha Minow (1990: 42) describes this dilemma thus: 'Governmental neutrality may freeze in place the past consequences of differences, yet any departure from neutrality in governmental standards uses governmental power to make those differences matter and thus symbolically reinforces them.' In essence, this dilemma rests in the question of how the law can achieve justice to particular identity groups without enslaving them to traditional role patterns, on the one hand, or branding them as 'different', on the other. Forst (2002) posits these questions thus: how can 'difference' be preserved and at the same time not have disadvantageous effects? How can it be recognised? How can impartiality do justice to particular and unequal parties? Although this is not an academic paper about justice per se, as practitioners and activists we do need to wrestle with the nuances peculiar to the subject under discussion: transitional justice.

The reciprocal and general justification of laws and procedures, however, requires that particular claims to legal recognition be justified generally, that is, that it be possible to draw upon a reinterpretation of the norms of equal treatment. Historical exclusion of certain groups from political, economic and social life determines whether the special consideration required by the equality principle can be stretched so as to grant – at the risk of violating formal equality – special treatment to members of a particular group, in contradistinction to other persons (as members of non-discriminated groups). In other words, does a given socio-economic or politico-legal context justify positive discrimination? What might this mean in the contexts of countries like South Africa and Kenya, faced with multi-layered racial and ethnic legacies of exclusion, respectively?

In the quest to make societies more just, a political community must deal with the substantive rights claims of discriminated minorities; these minorities themselves must have a voice. This presupposition encompasses the right to participate in political processes as well as the means (education and social communication) necessary for such inclusion and participation. Rawls (1971) argues that without a certain degree of social equality there cannot be equal political participation or formal legal equality. Equal 'value of political liberty' requires that minorities (or historically excluded groups) be first of all able to articulate their interests before a political community decides what measures are justified. In practice, it is useful to reflect what this might mean for constituencies such as women, youth and children participating in peace agreements and post-conflict reconstruction. Within the context of transitional justice the identity of minorities shifts on a case-by-case basis and through time.

Justice may also be conceptualised as the forum in which groups raise their voices to protest against exclusions and to question power relations (operative in how 'private' or 'national sovereignty' is defined, for instance). Thus in the context of justice, the status of the 'citizen' not only requires formal equal opportunities to participate but also includes material conditions, which make personal and political autonomy possible. In practice this establishes the linkage between economic empowerment, development and political participation in transitional justice processes. To secure and determine these is the task of a political community. Notably, citizenship is in itself a discussion of the place and role of free associational life (civil society) in the life of the state.

As demonstrated above, the concept of 'justice' is premised on the idea of impartiality on the one hand and of balanced judgment and of equal considerations on the other hand. In this sense justice is underscored by conclusiveness and an authoritativeness of judgment

Finally, it seems that in the context of African transitional justice, we need to strike a balance between being alive to the context within which we practice and yet avoiding the kind of relativism that causes us to neglect universalistic conceptions of what is 'just'.

This makes the employment of the term transitional justice conceptually problematic as the justice required by societies emerging out of crises or conflict goes beyond more laws or redressing the manifest excesses of a repressive order. It relates to the construction of socially inclusive, economically equitable relations of equality, fairness, dignity, respect and recognition. In practice, the question is always: who presides over this process of transitional justice and how are they held accountable?

In the quest to make societies more just, a political community must deal with the substantive rights claims of discriminated minorities: these minorities themselves must have a voice. This presupposition encompasses the right to participate in political processes as well as the means (education and social communication) necessary for such inclusion and participation (Rawls 1971). Without a certain degree of social equality there cannot be equal political participation or formal legal equality.

Within the context of African countries under consideration in this chapter, the identity of minorities shifts on a case-by-case basis and through time. Such minorities may be viewed as antagonistic to the establishment. Siding with them attracts the tag 'enemy of the state'. In these instances legitimacy can only be rooted in the values of a given society, particularly because the question of whether the matter has been finally resolved is much more a socio-cultural and politico-economic issue than a legal process of ascertainment of guilt or determination of appropriate punishment. Achieving best outcomes, has – in some situations – less to do with impartial, even-handed dispensing of just processes. Modern African societies present a huge dilemma given their enclave nature or division between the rural and urban. This division is much more than geographic or just demographic. It is a distinction related to world views, access to information, influence by global mass media, Westernisation, interaction with other cultures and religions, cultural perspectives, life-styles, conceptions of right and wrong as well as justice, and so on.

We cannot, therefore, without the benefit of prior rigorous research, ascribe an opinion, views, aspirations or claims to a universe defined simplistically as 'Kenyans, Zimbabweans, Congolese, Sierra Leoneans, Liberians, and so on'. This is even more complicated by the dramatic diversities based on gender, culture, race, ethnicity and religion in these African countries. It is also insincere to talk of a nationalistic conception of justice devoid of a keen understanding of the anthropological views of each ethnic community. In multi-ethnic communities, what is just for one society might be a travesty of justice for another. At the very least, research should give attention to how major and a sample of minor religious and ethnic communities deal with issues such as murder, arson and rape. This would help achieve an understanding of how questions of guilt, confession, forgiveness, reconciliation or punishment are processed by different nationalities within the nation state. For instance, if one were to take Zimbabwe as an example: among the Shona peoples, if someone commits murder, guilt is ascribed to the murderer's entire clan. It is believed that an avenging spirit (*ngozi*) follows that clan to kill and destroy everyone in it unless the clan offers the offended clan a young virgin girl as atonement. In short, the Shona traditionally believed in a life-for a-life as the basis of forgiveness or reconciliation.

Key to both Ndebele and Shona cultures is the belief that the spirit of the dead will cause unrest within the family unless their dead are laid to rest according to the culture and usages of the ethnic group or clan. This entails the sacrifice or slaughter of a cow or goat, communion with the ancestors and instruction to the dead man's spirit to join the world of long-gone wise-ones, the ancestors. It is a plea to the ancestors to console and comfort the dead spirit. It is also a process of inviting the dead to join the guardians of the clan, the protectors from the other world of the 'know-ers', the see-ers'. This process (*umbuyiso* in Isindebele or *kurovaguva/nyaradzo* in Shona) is carried out at least a year after a person's death. It does not matter how much a murderer confesses; unless the body or bones of the deceased are brought home for this process, forgiveness is not possible among the rural communities.

This practice was highly discriminatory against women, who were reduced in this transaction to the equivalent of modern-day damages. While among the Ndebele there was belief in the avenging spirits (*ingozi*), the offending clan had to offer damages in the form of cattle and goats as well as sacrifice either a sheep or cow as part of the atonement. The assumption was that the murderer's clan had the means or livestock to undertake this process. The default position within both the Ndebele (inclusive of the Kalanga, Sotho, Venda, Fengu, Nambia, Tonga, etc) and Shona (inclusive of the Karanga-Rozvi, Zezuru, Kore Kore, Manyika, Shangani, Remba, etc) was retribution by the avenging spirits instigated by the offended clan. Blood shedding was also associated with mental illness. The offender was often cursed and seen walking around the streets as a mad man. These belief systems acted as social constraints against would-be murderers. What constitutes forgiveness for the majority of Zimbabweans who reside in the rural areas would, therefore, not simply be court trials, confessions of the truth, the imprisonment of offenders or the building of memorials for the dead. These feel-good, borrowed perspectives are viewed in Zimbabwean society outside the urban areas, at least among the aforementioned major ethnic groups, as being neither justice nor transitional.

The African Union and transitional justice

In establishing the AU through the Constitutive Act of 2000, African heads of state and government clearly recognised the need to discard the 1963 compromise and radically set the AU apart from the Organisation of African Unity (OAU). The new Commission of the AU, in particular, benefits from clear-cut executive competence; additionally, the continent's political and economic integration is explicitly indicated as the ultimate objective of the union.

These changes are underpinned by eight key ideas emanating from the Constitutive Act. The first of these is that political integration should be the raison d'être of the AU, the objective being to achieve a United States of Africa (federation or confederation) in the long run. This key idea is fully in line with the theses advocating political integration – among the minority in 1963 and of whom President Nkrumah was the most ardent proponent. However, those advocating the immediate establishment of a United States of Africa without any intervening stages did not prevail, nor did the idea of achieving unity on the basis of mere cooperation. What won the day was the idea of building African unity on the foundations of regional groupings. This is the distinctive feature of the AU when compared to the OAU. The disintegration of authoritarian regimes offered the hope that political integration would be progressively achieved between democratic states which were respectful of human rights and keen to forge equitable societies that shunned exclusion, racism and any form of discrimination, particularly discrimination against women.

The second key idea is that the struggle for the continent's political liberation, accomplished formally and legally with the liquidation of the apartheid regime in South Africa in 1994, should be invigorated by substantial economic development. As a matter of fact, in the context of globalisation and intense regionalisation both in the North (European Union, NAFTA) and in the South (MERCOSUR, ASEAN), regional integration should be placed on Africa's priority agenda. The Abuja Treaty adopted by the OAU summit in 1991, which made regional integration the strategic model for the transformation of African economies, thus regained legitimacy, as the AU founders passed on to the AU the responsibility for speeding up this integration.

The third key idea is that the integration process should be geared to stimulating or re-energising the role of states. This role should be re-evaluated in the light of the experience of the Asian countries where it has been recognised that the state contributed significantly to the economic success achieved by the countries of the region. Moreover, the inter-African solidarity which was paramount in achieving the continent's political liberation should be intensified more than ever, not only for countries emerging from conflicts but also those that are victims of natural disaster. To this end, the integration process should pay special attention to humanitarian action and civil protection.

The fourth key idea is that, though predicated on strong leadership, integration should be anchored on an enlarged, popular base, culminating in a democratic AU since it would have been sustained by a union of the people. Thus, regional integration should take on board not only government representatives but also parliamentarians, political parties, economic operators and civil society representatives. It was with this in view that the Pan-African Parliament and the Economic, Social and Cultural Council (ECOSOC) of the AU were established. Moreover, the integration drive could be championed by groups of countries acting as the engine of integration within and among the regional economic communities. In other words, it is not necessary for all countries to be ready at the same time to embark upon the integration train. Integration at variable speed should be conceivable.

The fifth key idea is that the policies and strategies to be implemented would have no meaning unless they are human-centred. Humans in Africa – over 50 per cent of whom are women – must, in all circumstances, be both the actors in and beneficiaries of the structural changes engendered by development; and development should enable humans to accept their identities and conditions, rather than fall victim to them. In this regard, development should focus on the rural world and the middle class. Disadvantaged people, particularly the disabled, should be given special attention and taken on board at all levels. Africa cannot move forward unless the situation of women is corrected, particularly those who are victims of violence. Gender should therefore be mainstreamed into all the activities and all the organs of the union, thereby creating an irreversible momentum for the recognition and emancipation of women; more so as women are becoming increasingly involved in economic activities both in rural and urban areas. Furthermore, respect for individuals and the collective rights of the human person within the context of universal values and the peculiarities of Africa's human and peoples' rights should be taken on board. The right to water and food forms an integral part of these values.

The sixth key idea is that African youth should, more than ever before, be mobilised around the ideals of African integration. Accounting for the majority of the continent's population and becoming increasingly active in political and democratic processes at national level, the youth could serve as a driving force both in the political advancement of the continent and in the attainment of the objectives and goals enshrined in the Constitutive Act of the AU. If they are to do this, their need for education, health and basic infrastructure will have to be met to shield them from the mistake of delving into conflicts and wars. Furthermore, the fight against child labour, child trafficking, and the use of child soldiers needs to be intensified.

The seventh key idea concerns the African diaspora. The Constitutive Act of the AU calls for the total mobilisation of all segments of the African population to accomplish the set objectives. Undoubtedly, the diaspora is a particularly important and vital segment as it is in a position to mobilise, for the continent, the requisite scientific, technological and financial resources and expertise for the successful management of the programmes of the AU Commission. Besides, it can form an abiding bedrock of support in the partnership which Africa would like to see develop with industrialised countries and other countries of the South. On this score, the immigration issue and the question of return to, and retention of, African human resources on the continent, will continue to claim the attention of the AU.

The eighth key idea is that integration policies and strategies need time to yield results and for their full impact to be felt. They have to be situated within specific time frames, given the fact that the apathy, rigidities and constraints to be combated cannot disappear overnight. For this reason, the policies and strategies must be inspired by a long-term vision which could serve as guide, and facilitate strategic management of development in a context characterised by numerous uncertainties.

Relevance of transitional justice to the AU

The difficult progress of the continent towards democracy is evidenced by the reluctant recognition of the rights of opposition parties and opposition forces, press freedom as well as the right of civil society to participate in decision making and to express its opinion. Disputes over election results, especially presidential elections, with the attendant allegations of fraud sometimes degenerate into a show of force and often culminate in outright nullification of election results.

Africa has made significant progress beyond the classical Western media image of a continent synonymous with violence and long-standing conflicts. Where progress has been minimal, women and children pay the heaviest price for this state of affairs, while the spiralling number of refugees and displaced persons poses a real threat to human security on the continent. Judicial and legal insecurity derails the basic principles of a state of law, undermines the environment for investment and renders precarious the legal protection of citizens. In such a context persistent corruption considerably compromises sustainable development.

African leaders are increasingly conscious of the numerous negative factors standing in the way of the continent's progress towards economic and social development. They all recognise the interdependence of peace, security, stability, political and economic good governance and respect for human rights. They are aware that unconditional opposition to unconstitutional changes should necessarily be backstopped with deliberate efforts to organise transparent, free and fair elections. Similarly, African leaders understand that unless the imperatives of peace and good governance are taken on board, the continent's economic integration will remain illusory and its economic progress fragile.

These ideas have been energetically articulated by Africans themselves at many continental (the Cairo Agenda, the CSSDCA Process) and international (TICAD Process, China–Africa Forum, United States–Africa Conference and Africa–Europe Partnership) forums; and there is currently wide consensus that, like in other regions of the world, peace and development in Africa go hand-in-hand; that peace is another name for development, and that respect for the cultural, sociological, ethnic and linguistic diversities that characterise the countries of the continent is a number-one prerequisite for development. Significant progress has been made since the 1990s with political transitions towards democracy in Africa. However, the process of nurturing and consolidating democratic systems remains a daunting task. Evidence suggests that democratic transition has been relatively easier than building and sustaining democracy. The numerous transitions from apartheid (South Africa), genocide (Rwanda, Burundi), authoritarian rule (Malawi, Kenya, DRC, Senegal, Togo, Liberia, and Sierra Leone) and military dictatorship (Nigeria, Guinea) bear testimony to the challenges of democratic transition, nation building, development and reconstruction.

The struggle to build more inclusive, democratic, accountable and developmental states has been complicated by the desire to address past wrongs, purge impunity and maintain cohesion among the different interest groups and class formations within the nation state. In this regard the nature of the African state, its weaknesses and excesses, has been a central issue of great debate and friction. Fulfilling the aspiration to transform the nation state (as well as the behaviour and attitudes of bureaucratic and military elites) has been a disintegrative process bounded by two extreme solutions, namely appeasement of such elites as the ultimate price of peace or vilification/prosecution as the ultimate marker of justice and an end to impunity.

It is one thing to jettison authoritarian rule and quite another to build the institutional and cultural foundations for peace, democracy, truth and justice. The short history of democratic transitions in Africa since the 1990s aptly demonstrates that there cannot be democracy without democrats; peace without truth and justice; development without national consent and consensus; national healing without inclusion of all stakeholders; accountable leadership without capable institutions; new values without home-grown democratic constitutions, and so on. This struggle to build or reinforce democratic values, institutions, leadership and citizenship as the premise of post-conflict reconstruction or re-alignment after periods of repression is now part of the industry of transitional justice.

The AU recognises this challenge, which partly explains the numerous declarations and decisions that it has adopted as it strives to institutionalise political, economic and social governance. The AU is attempting to consolidate the gains of the OAU in governance by re-asserting and codifying Africa's shared governance values. The main instruments for this consolidated codification have been the African Charter on Democracy, Elections and Governance (ACDEG), the African Governance Architecture and the Human Rights Strategy for Africa. These instruments are yet to be fully ratified and domesticated by AU member states. ACDEG has the broadest reach within the governance arena.

In adopting the ACDEG, the AU and its member states sought to consolidate all past commitments made on democracy, elections, human rights and governance, as embodied in past declarations and decisions. The preamble sets the stage by establishing the foundational principles of ACDEG. It reiterates the linkage between ACDEG and previous OAU/AU commitments with deliberate emphasis laid on the rejection and condemnation of unconstitutional changes of government. Chapter 2 (objectives) highlights the main objectives of the charter, which are the 'need to promote democracy, rule of law, human rights, constitutionalism etc'. Chapter 3 presents the key principles that the charter upholds, including the 'promotion of democratic and participatory democracy, separation of powers, holding of regular, credible and transparent elections, gender equality, and rejection of acts of corruption, related offences and impunity'.

Chapter 4 on democracy, the rule of law and human rights commits AU member states to:

- upholding the supremacy of constitutions
- imbuing a culture of constitutionalism and the rule of law

- protecting fundamental freedoms, human security, human and people's rights
- inculcating a culture of popular participation
- eliminating all forms of discrimination and intolerance and in the process respecting all forms of diversity.

Chapter 5 on democracy and peace exhorts AU member states to establish, promote and consolidate a culture of democracy and peace, which the charter suggests should be done through, inter alia:

- ensuring transparent and accountable public administration
- strengthening governance institutions
- providing civic and voter education and through the formal educational curricula
- multi-stakeholder political and social dialogue within member states.

Chapter 6, on democratic institutions, emphasises the importance of robust and effective institutions for democracy to prevail and endure. The chapter, therefore, encourages AU member states to continuously institutionalise democratic governance through, among other means:

- constitutional civil control over the security forces
- the establishment and resourcing of democracy protection
- institutions such as ombudsmen, human rights commissions and electoral commissions
- cooperation at both regional and continental levels among AU member states through exchange of best practice and lessons learnt in governance.

Chapter 7 (democratic elections) underscores the centrality of democratic, credible and transparent elections for governance, peace and development. The chapter commits AU member states to

- the establishment of independent and impartial national electoral bodies
- ensuring fair and equitable access to public resources by parties and candidates contesting elections

- the establishment of national mechanisms for constructive management of electoral disputes
- ensuring respect and enforcement of a binding code of conduct for electoral stakeholders
- the provision of technical assistance to AU member states by the AU Commission
- election observation and monitoring by the AU in member states holding elections.

Chapter 8 (unconstitutional changes of governments) is certainly the anchor chapter of ACDEG. If all the other chapters form the body of ACDEG, chapter 8 is its very heart. Its primary focus is on sanctions when there are unconstitutional changes of government. The chapter starts off with a five-pronged definition of what exactly constitutes an unconstitutional change of government:

- a military coup
- replacement of an elected government by mercenaries
- replacement of an elected government by armed dissidents or rebels
- refusal by an incumbent government to relinquish power to a winning party following democratic, credible and transparent elections
- an amendment of the constitution which infringes on the democratic change of government.

The chapter goes on to articulate steps that the AU Commission, through the Peace and Security Council (PSC), will take if there is an unconstitutional change of government in any AU member state. These are wide-ranging measures that apply to the perpetrators of unconstitutional change themselves, the government of the country concerned and any AU member states supporting unconstitutional change of government in another member state. The chapter ends by encouraging AU member states to conclude bilateral extradition treaties so as to be able to cooperate fully in cases of unconstitutional changes of government where perpetrators flee to neighbouring states.

Chapter 9 (political, economic and social governance) is unique in that it establishes the importance of the role of state parties in advancing governance in its broad sense. It also provides for engagements with traditional authorities and the decentralisation of governance. The AU's New Partnership for Africa's Development (NEPAD) and the African Peer Review Mechanism (APRM) are seen as important milestones in Africa's democratisation path. The pursuit of the developmental vision of NEPAD and achievement of the Millennium Development Goals (MDGs) are considered crucial if Africa's socio-economic governance is to complement its political governance in a mutually reinforcing fashion. This chapter is particularly innovative as it creatively establishes the important linkages between governance, development and peace. It is in this chapter that the issue of gender equality as a key pillar for the consolidation of democratic governance features prominently.

Women's rights in transitional justice

There is a wide array of issues pertaining to women and their human rights within transitional societies. There are less-than-obvious questions around gender roles, culture, tradition and religion within the context of post-war societies. There are also the expectations that male combatants and activists have of their female counterparts to keep the moral and social fabric of the movement intact and then there are questions relating to violence against women and girls.

Violence against women and girls is a widespread and serious problem and is an obstacle to the achievement of equality, development and peace across the globe. It endangers women's lives and impedes full development of women's capabilities. According to the UN Study of the Secretary-General, 'Ending Violence against Women: From Words to Action' (2006) it interferes with the exercise of their rights as citizens, it harms families and communities and reinforces other forms of violence throughout societies, often with deadly consequences. Violence against women is a violation of human rights, rooted in historically unequal power relations between men and women and the systemic discrimination against women that pervades both the private and public sectors.

Violence against women takes many forms informed by patriarchy, socio-cultural norms and practices that perpetuate gender-based discrimination and economic inequalities. Addressing these factors requires a broad perspective that seeks to end all forms of discrimination against women, advance gender equality and the empowerment of women and create societies in which all women enjoy their human rights. The wide range of settings in which women experience violence include the family, the community, state custody, armed conflict and refugee situations. Such violence occurs in a continuum across the lifespan of women, cutting across both public and private spheres and reinforcing each other. This violence may take the form of physical and psychological abuse or economic deprivation. In recent conflicts as in Kenya, DRC, Sierra Leone, Liberia and Zimbabwe, attempts have been made to compile comprehensive data to establish the scope and magnitude of the various forms of such violence. This data remains largely inadequate.

The forms of violence to which women in any given society are subjected and the ways in which they experience the violence are often shaped by the intersection of gender with factors such as race, ethnicity, class, age, disability, nationality, legal status, religion and culture. It follows that taking cognisance of these different manifestations as well as dynamics calls for diverse intervention strategies. Since the end of the cold war there has been significant progress in defining and enacting international, continental and regional standards and norms to address violence against women. These form the baseline of commitments by the states as well as other stakeholders (including the AU and UN systems) in the struggle to end impunity for violence against women and girls. The obligations encompassed in the existing international protocols and other legal instruments are concrete and clear and include violence committed both by state agents and non-state actors. States have a duty to prevent acts of violence against women; to investigate and prosecute such acts when they occur and punish perpetrators; and to provide remedies and redress to victims or survivors of such violence. In all the countries under review, these obligations are not being met. The consequence of impunity for violence against women is both the denial of justice to the individual victims, but also the reinforcement of unequal and inequitable gender relations.

In the discussion of gender justice within the context of

transitional justice in Africa, one of the stark realities is the huge gap between the international standards on violence against women and the actual commitment of political capital and resources to implementing these standards. The specific nature of state obligations may vary from context to context. Arguably, varying circumstances and constraints allow for different actions to be taken by individual states, but do not excuse state inaction. The obligation of the state to prevent, punish and eliminate violence against women is one that it cannot delegate to other actors. The development of state strategies to address violence should be based on women's experiences and requires their active and effective leadership, control and involvement. The women's movement has played a key role in identifying a broad range of ways in which women experience violence as well as bringing these to national and international attention, for example with DRC.

Violence against women is very complex and diverse in its forms and incarnations. It is not, however, immutable or inevitable. The enabling conditions for violence against women are socially produced and as such the processes by which this social pathology is produced can be altered. This requires a huge investment of political will and resources, so securing gender equality and ending violence against women must not be treated as optional or marginal tasks. A coordinated, cross-cutting and multi-sectoral response is required to effectively address violence against women in times of both peace and war. The response must be backed up with strong institutional mechanisms at the local, national, regional and international levels to ensure effective action, coordination, monitoring and accountability. Detailed recommendations for action on violence against women are contained in the Beijing Declaration and Platform for Action and the numerous studies, reports and guidelines produced by UN agencies.

Conclusion: development as Justice?

The notion that in a country as vast and expansive as DRC, Sudan or Kenya, it is possible to make reparations for historical injustices to a finite set of victims/survivors is unrealistic. Equally so, the idea that development or community development projects would suffice as reparations is replete with difficulties. The following contrasting views of development explain the general nature of this difficulty:

> Development in human society is a many-sided process. At the level of the individual, it implies increased skill and capacity, greater freedom, creativity, self-discipline, responsibility, and material well-being ... The achievement of any of these aspects of personal development is very much tied in with the state of society as a whole. The relations which develop within any given social group are crucial to an understanding of the society as a whole. Freedom, responsibility, skill have real meaning only in terms of relations of human beings in society. At the level of social groups, therefore, development implies an increasing capacity to regulate both internal and external relationships. (Rodney 2012 [1972])

There is hardly ever consensus amongst scholars – let alone practitioners – about meanings of basic terms such as development and poverty. The rights-based approach to development views development as having the following constituent elements:

- a process that starts from within individuals, communities and the nation
- the realisation of the potential for self-support and contributing to society
- the building of self-confidence
- the aim to lead lives of dignity, which include gainful employment that assists individuals to meet basic needs, security, equity and participation, thereby leading to self-fulfilment
- freedom from fear of want and exploitation
- freedom from political, economic and social exploitation
- freedom from discrimination and exclusion on the basis of gender, social class, ethnic origin, race, religion, age, political affiliation and other forms of identity

- the continuous struggle for the right, and access, to decision making that affects the life and livelihood of the individual, the community, the nation and the region.

In this sense, development is both a process of self-empowerment and an outcome of the struggle for liberation from structures of domination and control. It is also a struggle against particular mental constructs, knowledges, uses of language and culture, etc. This struggle is waged between nations, within communities, within organisations, and even within households and perhaps within oneself as well. Transitional justice processes cannot – on their own – deliver this kind of development.

Thus development from this perspective might be anti-imperial economic exploitation, anti-colonial or anti-national oppression. It assumes the following:

- the essential well-being of the people epitomised by freedom from want, fear, discrimination, exclusion and exploitation – this is what some scholars refer to as the social factor
- the fundamental right of people to participate in the decision making that affects their rights, interests or legitimate expectations commonly referred to as lives and livelihoods – the democratic factor
- the right of a people, community or nation to freely determine their aspirations, visions, development goals and approaches without prior or subsequent restraint from external forces – the self-determination factor (Tandon 2008).

Taking all these factors into account, for most historically marginalised groups development must consider and satisfy the material and social needs of the most vulnerable in a society. It might do this through systems of government that are fair, inclusive, transparent and accountable, thus increasing self-determinination and minimising alienation from external interventions in developing societies.

Development, therefore, is much more than 'economic development'. It is not simply a matter of the combination of given 'factors of production', namely land, population, capital, technology, specialisation and large-scale manufacturing. These factors are undoubtedly relevant, but would engender uneven and unequal development if they are not complemented by human freedoms; elimination of all forms of exploitation; full employment and just wages; an engaged labour sector and citizens invovled in fashioning and implementing development. We have to consider and acknowledge the full human, historical, and social dimensions of development in addressing transitional justice concerns. Essentially, a dialogue about national development strategies that focus on practical and effective ways to combat 'underdevelopment' would be the most ideal perspective to adopt when discussing transitional justice within the context of the African Union.

References

Ackerman, B. (1980) *Social Justice in the Liberal State*, New Haven, Yale University Press

Ackerman, B. (1990) 'Neutralities', in Douglass, R.B., Mara, G.M., and Richardson, H.S. (eds) *Liberalism and the Good*, New York, Routledge

Adelman, S. and Paliwala, A. (1993) 'Law and crisis in the Third World', *African Discourse*, Series 4, London, Hans Zell Publishers

Ake, C. (1996) *Democracy and Development in Africa*, Washington DC, Brookings Institution

Bond, P. (2005) *Fanon's Warning: A Civil Society Reader on the New Partnership for Africa's Development*, Trenton, NJ, Africa World Press

Bratton, M. and Van de Walle, N. (1997) *Democratic Experiments in Africa: Régime Transitions in Comparative Perspective*, Cambridge, Cambridge University Press

Chua, A. (2003) *World on Fire. How Exporting Free Market Democracy Breeds Ethnic Hatred and Global Instability*, New York, Anchor Books

Davidson, B. (1961) *The African Slave Trade*, Oxford, James Currey

de Mesquita, B.B. and Downs, G. (2005) 'Development and democracy', *Foreign Affairs*, 84(5): 77–86

Fanon, F. (1967a) *Black Skin, White Masks*, London, Grove Press

Fanon, F. (1967b) *The Wretched of the Earth*, London, Penguin Books

Forst, R. (2002) *Contexts of Justice: Political Philosophy Beyond Liberalism and Communitarianism*, Berkeley, CA, University of California Press

Fukuyama, F. (1992) *The End of History and the Last Man*, New York, Free Press

Habermas, J. (1998) *The Inclusion of the Other: Studies in Political Theory*, Cambridge, MA, MIT Press

Huntington, S. (1996) *A Clash of Civilisation and the Remaking of World Order*, New York, Simon and Schuster

Kagoro, B.B. (2008) *Chaos and Transition in Zimbabwe: Transformation or Mirage*, Harare, Prestige Books

Kaminer, W. (1991) *A Fearful Freedom: Women's Flight from Equality*, Boston, Addison-Wesley Publishing Company

Kjekshus, H. (1996) *Ecology Control and Economic Development in East African History*, Oxford, James Currey

Legum, C. (2002) *Africa Contemporary Record, 1996–1998*, New York, Holmes and Meier Publishers

MacKinnon, C. (1989) *Toward a Feminist Theory of the State*, Harvard University Press

Mamdani, M. (1987) *Some Considerations on the National Question and the Democratic Struggle in Uganda*, Makerere, Makerere Institute of Social Research

Mamdani, M. (1996) *Citizen and Subject: Contemporary Africa and the Legacy of Late Colonialism*, Princeton, NJ, Princeton University Press

Minow, M. (1990) *Making All the Difference: Inclusion, Exclusion, and the American Law*, Ithaca, NY, Cornel University Press

Nagel, T. (1970) *The Possibility of Altruism*, Princeton, NJ, Princeton University Press

Olukoshi, A. (1998a) *The Politics of Opposition in Contemporary Africa*, Uppsala, Nordic Africa Institute

Olukoshi, A. (1998b) 'The democracy debate in Africa', in Kayizzi-Mugerwa, S., Olukoshi, A. and Wohlgemuth, L. (eds) *Towards A New Partnership with Africa: Challenges and Opportunities*, Uppsala, Nordic Africa Institute

Olukoshi, A. (2011) *Democratic Governance and Accountability in Africa*, Uppsala, Nordic Africa Institute

Olukoshi, A. and Laakso, L. (1996) *Challenges to the Nation-State in Africa*, Uppsala, Nordic Africa Institute

Rawls, J. (1971) *A Theory of Justice*, Cambridge, MA, The Belknap Press of Harvard University Press

Rodney, W. (2012 [1972]) *How Europe Underdeveloped Africa*, Oxford, Pambazuka Press

Schraeder, P.J. (2000) *African Politics and Society: A Mosaic in Transformation*, New York, Bedford/St Martin's

Siegle, J., Weinstein M., and Halperin, M. (2004) 'Why Democracies Excel', *Foreign Affairs*, 83 (5): 57–71

Shivji, I.G. (1989) *The Concept of Human Rights in Africa*, Dakar, CODESRIA

Shivji, I.G. (2007) *Silences in NGO Discourse: The Role and Future of NGOs in Africa*, Oxford, Fahamu Books

Smith, L.T. (1999) *Decolonizing Methodologies: Research and Indigenous Peoples*, Auckland, Zed Books

Sunstein, C.R. (1993) *After the Rights Revolution*, Cambridge, MA, Harvard University Press

Switzer, L. (1993) *Power and Resistance in an African Society*, Madison, University of Wisconsin Press

Tandon, Y. (2008) *Ending Aid Dependence*, Oxford, Fahamu Books

United Nations (UN) (2005) *In Larger Freedom: Towards Security, Development and Human Rights for All, Report of the Secretary-General*, New York, UN, http://daccess-ods.un.org/TMP/3577583.13417435.html, accessed 23 April 2012

United Nations (UN) (2006) *Ending Violence against Women: From Words to Action*, *Report of the Secretary-General*, New York, UN, http://www.un.org/womenwatch/daw/vaw/publications/English%20Study.pdf, accessed 23 April 2012

2

A conflict-sensitive justice: adjudicating traditional justice in transitional contexts

Stephen Oola

Introduction

The role of traditional or customary justice principles and the potential of these traditional time-tested mechanisms for promoting transitional justices in the context of African challenges remain ambiguous. The current transitional justice discourse lacks an 'African' perspective in addressing continental challenges of peace, justice, reconciliation and good governance.[1] Scholars have highlighted the disconnect arising in transitional justice implementation when local contexts challenge perceived international justice models.[2] This chapter presents a way to overcome this challenge by taking into account traditional justice norms and principles when adjudicating in formal criminal justice mechanisms. There exist core traditional customary principles of justice across communities on the continent that could help to address some of the contemporary peace and justice challenges.[3]

The transitional justice discourse today treats traditional/ customary justice mechanisms as last resort alternatives: an addition to the many recognised pillars of transitional justice but one with lesser weight.[4] In most literature, traditional justice mechanisms are treated with significant suspicion: as homogeneous, local, archaic, static, pre-colonial, Afro-centric practices that have remained stagnant, and thus have no place in the modern era. Adopting a strategic peace-building lens that questions some of these assumptions of justice as court based can help.

Increasingly, there is need to promote an integrative approach to justice that resonates with people's senses of justice but also promotes the rule of law.[5] For transitional justice discourse and processes in Africa to resonate with people's justice needs, they must draw from principles embedded in customary/traditional African justice mechanisms and ways of life. Today, customary justice mechanisms continue to play an integral role in many rural areas. Adjudication of such principles complements the effective administration of formal criminal justice.

Background to the laws and customs

Laws are binding norms and customs within a given society. Such norms vary from society to society depending on social, political, economic and cultural contexts. International customary laws and international criminal laws are also known to have evolved according to changing situations.

In Uganda there are still a large percentage of people whose access to formal justice is limited and informal mechanisms are their only forum for seeking redress.[6] International criminal justice advocates and transitional justice actors must recognise this reality. The 2011 Traditional and Cultural Leaders Act in Uganda, despite its shortcoming, acknowledges the importance of upholding cultural practices and beliefs. This provides a basis for making further use of informal mechanisms to maintain local harmony and build communal reconciliation. Harmonising local and national legal practices is important in sustainable peace building and national reconciliation.

There are many instances in Ugandan legal developments where formal courts have evoked the fundamentals of local customs as a basis for their often very judicious verdicts. The principles of acknowledgment, apology, forgiveness and compensation ingrained in *mato oput* and other local practices can be equated to concepts such as ubuntu, *gacaca,* the *magamba* spirit and *bashingantahe* throughout Africa. In essence, applying principles of African traditional justice mechanisms when adjudicating serious crimes and violations of human rights has significant foundation in Africa.[7]

The reality, however, is that such an undertaking faces several challenges. The most obvious of these is the retarded growth of most customary laws and justice principles owing to colonialism. The other challenges include the nature of legal training for lawyers and judges, and the growing influence of a Western notion of justice that is highly funded and yet largely inaccessible. By drawing on the core principles of traditional justice mechanisms in adjudicating justice, transitional processes overcome some of the above challenges.

This approach complements what Lyandro Komakech, Tim Murithi, George Mukundi Wachira, Brian Kagoro and other commentators have said about the core principles indispensable to addressing transitional justice challenges in Africa. Komakech's chapter illustrates some of the previously documented mechanisms of African local justice dispensed through the various mechanisms like *mato oput, ailuc, kayo cuk, tonu ci koka* practised among communities in northern Uganda. Murithi, Mukundi and Kagoro have outlined the key pillars of the pre-colonial African perception of justice. While traditional justice mechanisms often go by different names and practices, there are core principles in each. These include the cessation of hostility, truth telling, voluntary participation, societal harmony, communal participation, consensus building, accessibility, and affordability. These are considered as indispensible ingredients of justice, however, many of these values are taken for granted in the contemporary prosecutorial international criminal justice paradigms.

In Uganda, the Juba peace agreement on accountability and reconciliation declared that traditional justice mechanisms must play a central role in any accountability and reconciliation process. The proposed transitional justice policy should enable stakeholders to consider traditional justice mechanisms and practices in all processes. This means that even the International Criminal Court, War Crimes Division/International Crimes Division should uphold and honour a preference for certain traditional justice alternatives when it serves the interest of justice.

A 2010 survey, *Transitioning to Peace,* is indicative of people's attitudes towards the role of traditional justice mechanisms in addressing the human rights violations during the northern conflict between the Lord's Resistance Army and the Ugandan government. It found that about 53 per cent viewed traditional ceremonies as useful for transitional justice;[8] 39 per cent said it was useful to help community reconciliation; and about 25 per cent said it would help to forgive wrongdoers even though a similar percentage wondered whether it could change anything.[9] These findings, combined with the overwhelming majority in society favouring peace with amnesty, confirm that formal court processes cannot ignore the importance of appealing to local perceptions of justice and the application of their ritual for meaningful transitional justice outcomes.

The demand for traditional justice practices

Formal criminal justice systems administered by courts are failing to deliver meaningful justice to both the survivors and alleged perpetrators, as seen in the case of Thomas Kwoyelo. Very few Ugandans are aware of the system, and therefore remain unengaged in it. The 2010 study mentioned above found that over 49 per cent of the respondents have no knowledge of the formal justice system and about 29 per cent have very little knowledge.[10] This means the bulk of the population continue to interact with informal mechanisms. According to the report, over 33 per cent believed the formal justice system is corrupt.

Many ordinary Ugandans view the court system as detached from their plight for justice. The alien nature, unclear judgements, complicated court processes, delays, foreign language, costs, inaccessibility and perceived corruption have severely discredited the formal criminal court system. Only a few learned and wealthy citizens can access formal courts for justice in Uganda. Over 11 per cent of the people surveyed responded that the formal court system was for the rich and educated.[11] Accordingly, the bulk of the predominantly poor rural folk still invoke communally based mechanisms: family heads, clan courts and the local councillors. Their justice is through the traditional rituals and settlements and a system devoid of such principles can never satisfy their justice needs in transition.

In many parts of rural Uganda, clan courts continue to dispense justice parallel to the legal system. For example, on 14 September 2010, *New Vision* reported that Mr Otemo, a suspected witchdoctor in Alebtong, was killed during a clan meeting to air grievances over witchcraft. The meeting was presided over by Peter Okello, a clan chief, and was attended by over 243 clan members. Mr Otemo was accused by the villagers of witchcraft and related deaths. He was arrested and taken to a police post at Angwetangwet before being referred back to the clan chief. He confessed to killing people using witchcraft and was sentenced to death by beating. The police then arrested six people in relation to the incident. This kind of incident indicates that, while some of the clan-based practices are legally 'repugnant', the forum can still be used to dispense community justice.

Part of the reason the police initially referred the case back to the clan chief is that they believe such matters are better handled at the local court level, but the fact that these courts have been suppressed and not developed meant that they ignored the clear constitutional prohibition of the death sentence. Under Uganda's constitution no death penalty can be executed unless it is confirmed by the highest court of appeal, which is the Supreme Court. Transitional justice processes provide an opportunity to tap into these local courts, update them with new laws and practices and improve their efficacy. Opportunities exist to harmonise clan forum practices with state laws in order to promote rights-based communal-justice sentencing while addressing people's justice needs, for example, the nature of penalty imposed and manner of execution, without overstepping their jurisdictions. It is therefore evident that these local forums, with all their shortcomings, still embody people's sense of justice, and by alienating them, we obstruct the course of peace and justice in Uganda.

Customary laws and criminal justice systems in Uganda

Underlying transitional justice discourse is the maxim that 'to move forward, we must look back'. This maxim is equally pertinent to understanding the future of international criminal justice in Uganda today. The duality of formal criminal justice approaches and traditional justice principles is a product of colonial inequality. Local customs were deliberately suppressed in favour of foreign values that were alien to people's senses of justice. Prior to the declaration of a British protectorate in 1885, communities within the region that became Uganda followed their own body of established rules, which were unwritten customary norms and practices for peace and justice. These practices for dispute settlement and stability had strong consistencies across tribes and ethnic groups in the region.

Within a decade of the introduction of colonial rule, local customs and laws were forcefully abolished (abolished in practice, but not in the hearts and minds of the natives) in favour of British and Indian legal systems. The colonial government made very little effort to strengthen local customs but instead opted to subject all natives to colonial laws. Under the Foreign Jurisdiction Act, and the African Order in Council (OIC) 1889, British laws became applicable to all its colonies.[12] A consular court was established applying English laws alongside village courts, which continued applying customary laws albeit on a smaller scale.

The local council courts retained jurisdiction to enforce customary laws, but the consular court had overriding jurisdiction. It was required to exercise this jurisdiction 'as far as circumstances permitted with principles of and in conformity with, the substance of the law for the time being in force in England'. By 1889 conformity or complementarity was already in place.

In Uganda, the 1900 Buganda agreement that acknowledged the Buganda kingdom acted as a launch pad for imperial conquest in other parts of Uganda. The agreement became the first law regulating rights with separate applications for natives and settlers. For over a decade, colonial laws operated side by side with local court systems within Uganda. But each maintained its jurisdiction.

In 1902, another OIC was passed to set up a high court in Uganda with full jurisdiction over all persons and matters in Uganda. Its jurisdiction was to exercise 'as far as circumstances permitted, in conformity with the Civil Procedure, Criminal Procedure and Penal Codes of India, except so far as might otherwise be provided by law'. Ordinances could be passed by the Governor subject to the Secretary of State rights of disallowances. In effect, all Ugandans became subject to Indian laws. By virtue of this same OIC, Indian laws had priority over Uganda customs and norms, which were to be abolished. It amended the 1889 OIC and provided that, 'where other provision was not made by ordinance, any law, practice or procedure established by law or under the said African Order in Council of 1889 should remain in force until other provision was made'.

In 1911, another OIC was enacted with the effect that in so far as the Indian codes did not apply, jurisdiction was to be exercised in conformity with the substance of the common law, doctrine of equity, and the statutes of general application in force in England on 11 August 1902 and with the powers vested in and according to the procedures observed by and before courts of justice and justices of the peace in England.

This officially marked the beginning of the imposition of English values and precedents on Ugandans. But even here the imposition recognised the peculiarity of local circumstances. It added that 'the common law, the doctrines of equity and statutes of general application were to be in force in Uganda so far as the circumstances of the people permit and subject to such qualification as local circumstances render necessary.'

Political independence and legal dependence

The 1902 OIC, as amended in 1911, constituted our current formal justice framework and remained even after independence. The whole of legal education and post-independent legislation simply removed the words 'Indian' or 'English' but added nothing African or, for that matter, Ugandan.

The Judicature Statute No. 62 of 1962 (later Cap 34, now Cap 13 of the Laws of Uganda) operationalised colonial laws in independent Uganda and simply localised imperialism to date. It provides that:

> the High Court shall exercise jurisdiction in conformity with the written laws in force and, subject to such laws and so far as they do not extend or apply, jurisdiction is to be exercised in conformity with the substance of the common law, doctrine of equity and the statute of general application in England on August 11, 1902

Throughout these ordinances, the adjudication of customary laws was left ambiguous. The imperial government recognised its importance in dispensing justice and maintaining peace and tranquillity, but it needed a system that better served imperial interests. The legal imposition meant that the local customs did not die, but also could not grow to prevent colonial exploitation. As a result the application of customary laws was subjected to statutory laws and 'traditional justice would be enforced by courts unless declared repugnant to justice and morality or inconsistent with the general law'.

The judges who administered the repugnancy test prior to and immediately after independence were foreign English or Pakistani judges, who ended up declaring as repugnant most of cherished customary norms and practices as evident in rulings such as the infamous *Rex vs Amkeyo* case. This ruling declared African marriages as mere wife purchases and not legally binding. Such precedents characterise the nomenclature of the contemporary formal criminal justice system and its perception as being alien to local contexts. In the light of these imposed justice principles, therefore, the current transitional justice discourse offers new opportunities to rekindle some of the superior African values and customs to reform our administration of criminal justice. Inculcating such values within formal courts and mainstream transitional justice discourses offers an opportunity for sustainable peace, justice and reconciliation.

Towards an African transitional justice framework

The appointment of the African Union High Level Panel on Darfur (also known as the Mbeki Panel) was a bold step by the AU to promote 'Africans' solutions to Africa's problems'. It was recognition that imposed colonial solutions were not working and that there was a need to invest in Africa's own values and traditions of peace building and dispute resolution if meaningful transition was to take effect.

The Mbeki Panel submitted a report which highlighted the need to address the objectives of peace, reconciliation, and justice as interconnected, mutually dependent and equally desirable. The report highlighted that justice and peace must be pursued in a manner consistent with the need to achieve democratic and socio-economic and cultural transformation. It emphasised that local ownership and inclusive participation of affected communities and the implementation of appropriate mechanisms are vital for success.

The report espoused a number of key transitional justice principles relevant to the African context, including the urgency of pursuing peace through inclusive negotiations rather than by force or through military struggles. This should include acknowledgement of past and ongoing suffering by victims and attention to regional and international dimensions. It emphasised the need to investigate serious crimes and establish measures to prevent the commission of future crimes, as well as the need to preserve evidence for later proceedings, and to adopt measures of witness protection to encourage victims of sexual crimes to come forward.

The report supported the suspension of hostilities and the protection of civilians to enable participation in dialogue and the search for meaningful peace and justice, including a permanent ceasefire, demobilisation and comprehensive security arrangements. It also called for a broader understanding of justice to encompass processes for achieving healing, equality, reconciliation, obtaining compensation and restitution, and establishing the rule of law.

The Mbeki Panel's recommendations are important for transitional justice initiatives in Africa. They add to the other core principles of justice and reconciliation which balance the demands of peace and justice. This provides a benchmark for the adjudication of transitional mechanisms. It enables hybrid courts and tribunals to consider whether the proposed alternative traditional justice mechanism seeks to restore communal reconciliation and harmony or promote local peace building as imperative to justice. In other words, if a party invokes the willingness to engage with a victim in a traditional ritual with the manifest intention of achieving the stipulated goals of transitional justice, as given above, then the court could consider and grant such requests.

Conclusion

The inclusion of traditional justice norms in transitional justice mechanisms has a firm foundation in African history. It is simply a refocusing of the lens through which we view justice.[13] Because the criminal legal system and the punishment it metes out cannot by itself fulfil all the ends of justice, we need to tap into the restorative component that is prominent in traditional justice discourse.

By combining prosecutorial justice processes with traditional justice principles, transitional justice mechanisms will promote legal reforms and become part of the growing movement to reform the administration of criminal justice globally, as is evident in the restorative justice movement.[14]

Criminal prosecution constitutes an important element in combating impunity and building sustainable peace, but to facilitate meaningful justice there must also be legislation and institutions to provide effective accountability for the different levels of criminal participation.[15] At a practical level, a conscious effort should be made by transitional justice interveners to promote locally led solutions.

Complementary peace-building measures will enhance local transformations that are consistent with the constitution and norms addressing international perspectives on penal sanctions. There is a need to enhance procedural and evidential provisions with traditional justice values to enable the effective and timely delivery of justice, as well as the participation of witnesses and victims in local judicial processes. Necessary reforms in the traditional courts may include adopting special measures for dealing with serious rape and other sexual crimes at all stages of the proceedings, such as the protection of witnesses and victims in serious cases. The risks of participating in traditional court proceedings are far fewer than in formal legal courts. Both systems still require capacity building to handle sexual and gender-based violence effectively. Also needed is a clear procedural rule for coordination between the different courts and functions within the criminal and traditional justice systems, as well as between traditional justice mechanisms and other institutions of accountability and reconciliation.

Notes

1   For the potential role of adjudicating traditional principles see O. Oko Elechi (2006) *Doing Justice Without the State: The Afriko (Ehugbo) Nigeria Model*, New York, Routledge.
2   Roselind Shaw and Lars Waldorf, with Pierre Hazan (eds) (2010) *Localizing Transitional Justice: Intervention and Priorities After Mass Violence*, Stanford University Press.
3   Lucy Hovil and Joanna R. Quin (2007) 'Peace first, justice later: traditional justice in northern Uganda', Refugee Law Project Working Paper 17: 1–59.

4 Richard L. Goldstone, Leslie Vinjamuri and Anthony Dworkin (2007) 'Do war crime trials do more harm than good?', dialogue at the Centre for the Study of Human Rights, London School of Economics, 27 May, http://www2.lse.ac.uk/humanRights/articlesAndTranscripts/WarCrimeTrials.pdf, accessed 30 March 2011.

5 Daniel Philpott (2010) 'Reconciliation: an ethic for peace building', in Daniel Philpott and Gerald F. Powers (eds) *Strategies of Peace: Transforming Conflict in a Violent World*, Oxford, Oxford University Press: 91–114.

6 P.N. Pham, P. Vinck, M. Wierda and A. di Giovanni (2005) 'Forgotten voices: a population-based survey of attitudes about peace and justice in northern Uganda', ICTJ and Human Rights Center, University of California, Berkeley.

7 Tim Murithi (2006) 'Practical peacemaking: wisdom from Africa', *Journal of Pan African Studies*, 1(4): 25.

8. Phuong Pham and Patrick Vinck (2010) 'Transitioning to peace: a population based survey on attitudes about social reconstruction and justice in northern Uganda', Human Rights Centre, University of Berkeley: 1–47.

9 Ibid: 40.

10 Ibid.

11 Ibid: 40.

12 For more about legal history in Uganda, see H. F Morris and James S. Read (1974) 'Indirect rule and the search for justice', *Journal of African Law,* 18(2).

13 Rama Mani (2002) *Beyond Retribution: Seeking Justice in the Shadows of War*, Cambridge, Blackwell: 3–22.

14 Eirin Mobekk (2011) 'Transitional justice in post-conflict societies – approaches to reconciliation', http://www.bmlv.gv.at/pdf_pool/publikationen/10_wg12_psm_100.pdf, 8 March, accessed 20 January 2012.

15 Mariam J. Aukerman (2002) 'Extraordinary evil, ordinary crime: a framework for understanding transitional justice', *Harvard Human Rights Journal*, 15: 39–53.

3

Traditional justice as a form of adjudication in Uganda

Lyandro Komakech

Is nation building a Western game or African nightmare?

In Europe, the English and Irish have differences; Irish Protestants and Irish Catholics have conflicts; so too do the Bosnians and Serbs, the Czechs and Slovaks, the Georgians and Russians, and so on. On the other hand Africans are dominated by ethnic conflicts – or are they? Kikuyu vs Kalenjin, Luo and Luya in Kenya; Shona vs Ndebele in Zimbabwe; Zulu vs Xhosa in South Africa; Tutsi vs Hutu in Rwanda; Yoruba vs Igbo in Nigeria, Luo vs Bantu in Uganda, and so on again. Are these different nations and peoples who were forced to coexist within the borders of nation states, under one master, one flag, one national anthem and one currency without their consent?

What we often characterise as ethnic conflicts are actually unresolved national questions, superimposed on even more complex economic, agrarian and industrial questions. As Ugandans, Kenyans, Rwandans, Burundians, Congolese, Nigerians and Sierra Leoneans, we have never decided whether we want to live together as one and if so on what terms. Until we seriously address the national question with its regional, continental and international dimensions, no amount of transitional justice will deal with the sense of dissatisfaction that the imposed nation state generates. We must in doing this think globally whilst acting locally. Our meaning of local is in our traditions, values and belief systems.

Traditional justice – the new common sense?

There is a growing trend internationally to integrate traditional justice mechanisms into the mainstream administration of justice. Truth-telling exercises such as the one instituted in South Africa cannot address the sense of restoration and reconciliation largely experienced by rural communities in the rest of Africa. Guilt in most conflicts where mass atrocities have been committed is attached to whole groups identified by their ethnicity or race. A penal system anchored in individual guilt and punishment is by nature out of sync with community perceptions of guilt, responsibility and fair outcome. There is a disconnect between the juridical outcome (e.g. imprisonment) and social relevance (such as reparations and healing). Most Africans are deeply spiritual and issues of mass atrocities are processed by communities within the context of their belief systems. Forgiveness based on biblical principles or outright amnesty often falls short of the community expectations that great loss requires reparations as a necessary outflow of repentance. Memorialisation by the construction of statues and structures does not address memorialisation in most African traditions, which involves bringing the souls of the dead to a place of rest in the homestead through specific rituals. International prosecutions such as those witnessed in Sierra Leone and Rwanda have not had the desired impact. They are too expensive – and elitist in nature. They have attracted very little African media attention and little public participation.

Uganda – a case study

Uganda's attempts at a transitional justice process have never been conventional ones. Most transitional justice theory contemplates an examination of past wrongs going hand in hand with a political transformation. Yet in the Ugandan context, all such prior attempts were initiated by the regimes in power and were not accompanied by wide-ranging systemic reforms in governance. The first attempt was initiated in 1974 by Idi Amin and subsequently in 1987 through the human rights commission under the National Resistance Movement. These attempts never resulted in reports with recommendations for action. In Uganda, the current transitional justice process is being contemplated and initiated in an extremely complex political context, without corresponding regime change and in the presence of a precedent-setting amnesty for all armed groups who renounce rebellion, including perpetrators of international crimes. The conceptualisation of the north as being the only part of the country in need of transitional justice is itself symptomatic of many Ugandans' mistaken view that the north alone has suffered the consequences of war. Uganda's transitional justice process is now at a crossroads. It has the potential to either transform the country or plunge it back into conflict. The Juba peace talks between the government of Uganda and the Lord's Resistance Army (LRA) created a window of opportunity. The signing of a number of agreements, including an agreement entitled 'Agenda Item 2 on Comprehensive Solutions to the Conflict'[1] and 'Agenda Item 3 on Accountability and Reconciliation'[2] (and its annexure), lays down a broad framework for a transitional justice policy.

Traditional justice practices could play a role in a transitional justice process concerning conflict legacies that communities feel require redress. A history of conflicts and failed peace agreements has left a multiplicity of legacies that are far from uniform in Uganda, and even vary between the Acholi, Lango, and Teso sub-regions in the north. A common trend among these legacies is the trail of human rights violations that remain unacknowledged in any comprehensive way. At the core of these legacies lies a complicated and multidimensional set of mutual resentments, all of which need some address if full reconciliation is to be achieved.

Efforts to address accountability, reconciliation, reparations and even the legitimacy of the current government have been sorely wanting. Uganda's current legal regime emphasises formal justice mechanisms directly derived from the British colonial common law model. Given the complex history of Uganda and its rich and numerous cultural heritages, there is a compelling need to explore opportunities for a comprehensive legal framework that addresses and reflects the sense of justice of the peoples of Uganda. Widespread perceptions that there is some kind of parity between the abuses committed by the government and those committed by the LRA have vital implications for any reconciliation process. Any reconciliation process will have to include the victims along with both LRA and Ugandan government perpetrators.

Policy options

Policy debate has emerged since peace talks between the Ugandan government and the LRA began in July 2006. Agenda item 3 and the annexure propose a framework for accountability and reconciliation that carves out a potentially vital role for traditional justice practices. Clause 3.1 of the agenda states that 'traditional justice mechanisms such as *culo kwor, mato oput, kayo cuk, ailuc, tonu ci koka* and others as practised in the communities affected by the conflict shall be promoted, with necessary modifications, as a central part of the framework for accountability and reconciliation'. The Peace, Recovery, and Development Plan's (PRDP) Strategic Objective 4, 'Peace Building and Reconciliation',[3] broadly proposes a place for traditional justice practices, calling for a focus on 'building informal leadership among men and women to engage with local authorities and civilians in the reconciliation process' through 'localised conflict management mechanisms'.[4]

The call for an appraisal of traditional justice may in part relate to the limited responsiveness of existing national and international formal justice mechanisms in addressing Uganda's numerous legacies of conflict, and to the way in which the broader colonial legacy of Ugandan law alienates much of the country from the existing justice system.[5] Although both Juba and the PRDP acknowledge that traditional justice practices have a role to play, the nuances of their operation and applicability remain unclear. Moreover, the ability of these mechanisms to address injustices committed in the course of decades of violence is increasingly challenged by the conflict's own state of flux. These issues are heatedly debated in the Justice Law and Order Sector, tasked as it is with the responsibility to design a fitting transitional justice policy for the country. This policy debate is part of a broader narrative currently being charted in Uganda as the country struggles to confront a history of conflicts, and moves toward national reconciliation. While the whole enterprise of traditional practices in addressing 'modern' injustices may go unresolved, there is evidence that tradition still enjoys a degree of local application in areas affected by conflict and that the values and principles embodied in these practices have a future role to play in national transitional justice mechanisms.

Jurisprudence of traditional justice

The objective of traditional justice systems in African communities is to seek assistance from the community leaders to facilitate, acknowledge (account) and resolve (reconcile) conflicts arising from violations or abuses or in support of healing. The process creates a socio-cultural context that allows individuals and communities to refrain from violence and re-establish broken relationships.

Our recent research findings show that traditional justice practices exist among the Acholi, Lango and Teso and include *tolu koka* (Madi), *kayo cuk* (Lango), *ailuc* (Teso), *mato oput* and *gomo tong* (Acholi).

The traditional justice practices from the Acholi, Lango and Teso vary considerably. The study found that five fundamental principles seem to be at the centre of each of them: material compensation, reconciliation and forgiveness, truth telling and responsibility, cleansing and welcoming, and punishment (retributive aspects). While the relationship between abuses that arose from wars and related conflicts and those that do not remains unclear, the overall traditional justice principles are similar in both situations and express the values of each of these groups.[6]

These principles found expression in a sequence of practices which are designed to result in reconciliation between the parties and their clans. The process normally begins with one of two principles. If the individual who committed the abuse has been absent from the community for an extended period of time, there is a welcoming or cleansing ceremony. Otherwise, the first step is to identify the responsible party and learn about the damage caused. The next step begins with retributive action such as caning. Truth telling in the form of a dialogue to discuss the events and to ask the offending party to accept responsibility follows. This dialogue helps establish the reparations due to the victim. Finally, an act which expresses reconciliation and forgiveness takes place. These principles are based on collective community responsibility and find relevant benchmark space with international standards.

Traditional justice practices place on the individual and society conscious engagement in processes through which the victims may come to terms with, emotionally respond to, and actively remember and discuss the events of the past. These practices have specific features that include:

- Reconciliation and restoring social harmony
- A belief that crime is a community problem, not solely an individual responsibility
- Processes that are voluntary
- Selected traditional arbitrators based on status and lineage
- A high degree of public participation
- Discussions confirmed through rituals aimed at reintegration
- Flexible procedural and evidence rules as set by the customs
- Restorative penalties
- Penal enforcement secured through social pressure.

Figure 1 Traditional Justice cycle

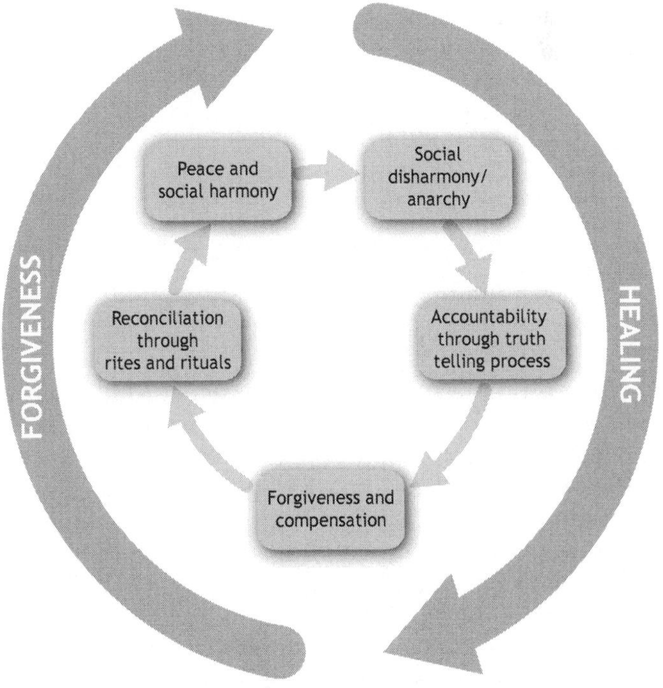

Source: Justice Law and Order Sector Sub-Committee on Traditional Justice Report 2008

Benefits of traditional justice practices

The traditional justice cycle provides a quick snapshot of how simple though complex the process might be. It is noticeable that these practices have numerous advantages that merit contemporary application:

- Accessible to local and rural people and within walking distance
- Proceedings carried out in the local languages
- Simple procedures that do not require language translation services
- None of the delays associated with the formal system and its bureaucracies
- Easy to educate all members of the community about the rules to be followed
- Non-custodial sentences, so effectively reducing prison overcrowding, allowing prison budgets to be diverted towards social development purposes
- Offenders continue contributing to the economy and paying reparations to victims
- Economic and social dislocation of the family avoided.

These benefits of traditional justice practices offer domestic credibility.

Cleansing, cooling and welcoming

Cleansing practices are an important element of traditional practices among the ethnic communities of Uganda. For example, throughout the Acholi, Lango and Teso regions, these practices form the core of reintegration processes after conflict. They are most commonly practised as part of a process of welcoming, but also remain integral to response mechanisms for a killing or other act properly understood in the community as an abomination. Cleansing also functions as part of a final reconciliation process to normalise relations between a victim and a perpetrator. Cleansing is most prominently connected with welcoming practices for individuals who have been absent from a community for a prolonged period of time. Cleansing ceremonies remain integral to major reconciliation practices among local communities in Uganda. Community members often give expression to cleansing as part of the reconciliation process in the slaughtering of a bull, sheep or goat. For example, in northern Uganda the communities closely associate cleansing with the idea of cooling one's temper after becoming hot or disturbed. Others view cleansing as important in restoring balance, both mentally and emotionally, which serves as a necessary preparatory step in readying both individuals and the community for a further process of reconciliation. Cleansing is also framed as welcoming individuals back into the community. This principle of welcoming and cleansing should be part of the national transitional justice process to facilitate the restoration of a national community.

Punishment and retributive aspects of traditional justice

It would be an error to entirely ignore the role of punishment in the practice of traditional justice. Caning was the most common form of punishment and was ubiquitous across the three regions. The retributive aspects of traditional justice are often part of an initial community response to a given abuse, then followed by mechanisms that embody the justice system's other elements. The intended purpose of punishment is primarily focused on deterrence. Importantly, punishment is a largely individualised element of traditional justice, unlike the communal nature of much of its other elements. The individual who committed an offence is caned, not the clan as a whole.

Truth telling, dialogue and responsibility

Truth telling is integral to achieving justice in traditional communities in all three regions, but should be understood more accurately as a process of interactive dialogue between the offended and offending parties rather than a one-sided public declaration. Chronologically, a truth-telling dialogue takes place after both an initial welcoming and cleansing process and after retributive action. It is fundamental to traditional justice practices in the three regions that both the wronged party and the perpetrator need to agree on an account of the events that transpired in the committing of an offense. Truth telling has been widely discussed as a potential element in the post-conflict transitional justice process in Uganda. It should be noted that there still remains the question of whether commanders from the various parties to the conflicts, including the LRA, the Uganda People's Army and the Uganda People's Defence Force, among others would be willing to participate in any form of dialogue or truth telling in any future process in Uganda.

Material compensation as reparations

Compensation for losses incurred is the most important issue when considering the subject of reconciliation. Whether the loss is suffered due to war or through normal criminal behaviour (cattle theft, as an example), compensation for the loss must occur first. For example, the military is seen as being mostly responsible for the loss of cattle in Teso in eastern Uganda and to a lesser extent in Acholiland in northern Uganda. While there was little direct discussion of compensation as a means of punishment, the motive and intentions of the crime were considered in the amount to be rewarded, suggesting that there were at least some retributive aspects to it. An often-cited example was the differing compensation awarded for intentional as opposed to unintentional killings. Multiple purposes of material compensation suggest several things for the creation of a contemporary reparations framework in the overall transitional justice process in Uganda. A contemporary reparations framework in essence should seek to address the financial impacts of the legacy of conflicts in various regions of Uganda. There may be several ways of fashioning reparations, including larger infrastructure projects aimed at restitution, as has already been called for in the Peace, Recovery and Development Plan (see Chapter 9), though seeing these reforms through will be a challenge of the utmost importance. A contemporary reparations framework will also need to be related specifically to the abuses committed throughout the conflicts, and should reflect the gravity of those offences in recognition of what transpired. This would aid in reconciliation and could provide a level of consolation to those who suffered in the conflicts. The challenges will be how to accurately identify victims within the conflict, and how to identify the resources for their compensation. It should be noted that there exists a potential disconnect between this notion of contemporary restitution and the traditional understanding of compensation, directly linked to the nature and severity of a given abuse. While restitution might fulfil the purpose of compensation, which is intended to address the economic impact of an abuse, it may or may not be able to address the reconciliation process at a local community level.

Reconciliation and forgiveness

Reconciliation in essence refers to a normalisation of relations between the offended and offending parties to a conflict. Reconciliation practices are seen as being required for a wide range of abuses, including sexual offences and assault, but are most commonly discussed in the context of killings. The restoration of a relationship between the offending and offended parties is strongly connected to a process of shared eating and drinking, often after slaughtering an animal. Reconciliation is also expressed most clearly through a particular practice in each of the three districts: *mato oput* in Acholi, *kayo cuk* in Lango, and *ailuc* in Teso. These three practices have become symbolic of the broader systems of traditional justice and often combined several of the other principal elements of traditional justice. While it appears that the practices are still widely understood, instances of their use are fairly rare, particularly in relation to abuses committed during contemporary conflicts in the regions. And yet there exists a substantial desire for a role for them in addressing the legacies of these conflicts, though there are reservations about the feasibility.

The notion of reconciliation as a means of ending cycles of violence and achieving normal social relations remains, perhaps, the most widely appreciated aspect of traditional justice. An abuse of any sort between clans, or even within a clan, was a disturbance in the relationship between the offended and offending party. In the case of differing clans, they would no longer be allowed to eat or drink together, get water from the same well, or intermarry.

It would be important to address this in order to restore a social harmony that allowed for the proper functioning of day-to-day life. Reconciliation was only possible when cleansings, truth telling and compensation had either already taken place or were part of the final reconciliation. Any contemporary application of the practices and principles of traditional justice would have to include all of these elements. In addition, it would be important to create a space for celebration at the conclusion of the national transitional justice process to recognise the new peace.

Potential challenges for traditional justice practices today

The principles and the practices from which traditional justice mechanisms were derived find contemporary use and are considered highly relevant today. Nonetheless, there exist major obstacles to their current use as well as their potential role in the national transitional justice process in Uganda.

At present, the clan elders' loss of their relative economic power within the community poses a serious gap in decision-making processes. The youths are becoming higher income earners than their elders, and the latter's ability to garner support through patrimony has declined. The rise in education levels of the younger generations means they no longer see the elders as the ultimate figures of authority or wisdom. In something of an amalgamation of the first two points, along with other economic and social effects, the broader force of modernisation increasingly pushes the elders' social role into the background.

Western religious beliefs are at times interwoven with traditional justice practices in the Acholi and Teso regions of Uganda, although this was not the case in Lango, where religion appeared to have deeply altered or in some cases entirely eliminated some elements of traditional justice practices. Religion most often came into conflict with traditional practices when it came to notions of cleansing and in particular the slaughter of animals.

The issue of how women and youths are involved (or not) in traditional justice poses one of the greatest challenges to any contemporary use of the practices as part of a broader transitional justice strategy. Women's roles in traditional justice processes are minimal and although this is changing, the pace of change is slow. Women were predominantly not allowed to administer the practices, though there were exceptions over welcoming practices. The youths have had virtually no distinct role in the administration of traditional justice. Noticeable changes were claimed, but without attesting evidence. Perhaps the most immediately challenging aspect of women's participation in traditional justice practices had to do with how they were treated as complainants in cases. There is a widely held belief that women cannot directly receive compensation if they have married a man from a clan different from their own. This was rooted in the belief that a woman was not a full member of her husband's clan.[7]

Although rural citizens understand the need for a formal justice system, they do not understand how it relates to the traditional one. Significant wariness continues to be voiced by rural communities about the effectiveness and desirability of the formal justice process and about members of the court system. The most common frustrations are corruption in the police force, the confusion and legal expenses of navigating the court system, and the fact that reported cases either took a long time to resolve or did not result in conviction. On the whole, members of rural communities believed the formal justice system was not competent to handle judicial matters. In trying to understand how traditional justice principles and practices may relate to the formal justice process in the future, it is vital to understand how the two relate to one another now, and what models already exist for their relationship.

Recent research by the Refugee Law Project[8] certainly confirmed that traditional justice practices have been historically used to address 'ordinary' or daily criminal and civil conflicts – both large and small – and not conflicts arising from war. While many of the elements of 'war' crimes are the same as for crimes committed outside of war (murder, arson, rape), the motives and gravity of the offenses are often very different in war. Traditional justice practices do not appear to be designed to address crimes in which only the victim or only the perpetrators are known, a common reality for many of the communities who have suffered losses during contemporary conflicts. There are also concerns about the complexity of the abuses committed. For example, contemporary conflicts have involved three or four parties, with the

Lord's Resistance Army, the Uganda Peoples' Defence Force, local militias and the general population all playing a role. Defining any of these groups as victims or perpetrators remains difficult, and often individuals may be both. The question of whether traditional practices can deal with war-induced crimes remains a central debate within the local community. Several respondents, however, assert that traditional justice practices potentially serve as a confluence for complementarity with formal justice practices.

The traditional justice part of the equation essentially has three components: one part will need to address the clan-to-clan needs, another the community-to-community needs and the third to respond to the nations' broader needs, addressing the government's relationship with the various rebel groups and the responsibilities of all for the conflicts. Current national justice structures appeared unresponsive to local needs and values, and the void left by the shortcomings of these structures is being filled by locally practised, traditional mechanisms. Inter-ethnic tensions in the various regions of Uganda continue to brew just below the surface of seemingly placid relations, indicating that further dialogue is still vital for achieving a lasting peace in the region.

Traditional justice practices should therefore be used to establish the principles of a national system, while also being practised directly in local communities affected by the conflict. The legacies of conflict discussed in this chapter are far from local in nature. They are dynamic at regional and national levels, and are connected to a national pattern of cyclical violence that has produced a tenuous peace through pacification rather than reconciliation. Moreover, the need for a national set of transitional justice structures is highlighted by the fundamental question of how abuses committed in a particular region by an individual from another region should be addressed. All these should be placed within the framework of a national reconciliation law and national policy framework on peace building and conflict prevention. These are new challenges that require effective national responses.

Traditional justice practices need to be a major part of this transitional process. Of necessity the traditions of Uganda's informal justice system will need to change if they are to assist in the healing from years of conflict. Moving from its historical role of resolving individual conflicts within a clan or village to a role that complements the formal justice system in addressing war crimes will be the next challenge. The respect that traditional practices continue to have in rural areas underscores the need to use them in the coming transitional justice environment.

Conclusions

Traditional justice practices have local, national, regional and international relevance in contributing to a comprehensive international jurisprudence on redressing the complex balance between retribution and restoration after mass atrocities. Within the conflict-prone Great Lakes region, traditional mechanisms could contribute to addressing both the legacies of the major conflicts in the region and day-to-day issues of crime in a multi-dimensional way. Traditional mechanisms would be a starting point for addressing today the lingering national questions in the broader East African community. Traditional justice practices will need to play a multifaceted role in both the transitional justice process in Uganda and in future reforms to the broader legal system. Rather than attempt to codify the specific practices of different ethnic groups, legal reform should focus on how to apply the emerging cross-cutting principles which are shared across the different regions of northern Uganda as the beginning.

Bibliography

Allen, T. (2005) 'War and justice in Northern Uganda: an assessment of the International Criminal Court's intervention' (draft), Crisis States Research Centre, Development Studies Institute, London School of Economics

Bloomfield, D., Barnes, T., and Huyse, L. (eds) (2003) *Reconciliation After Violent Conflict: A Handbook*, Stockholm, International IDEA

Collaborative for Development Action, Inc. (1999) 'Case study: an overview of initiatives for peace in Acholi, Northern Uganda', The Reflecting on Peace Practice Project, Cambridge, MA

Dolan, C. (2000) '"Bending the Spears" – Notes on Denis Pain's report to International Alert: "The Bending of the Spears" Producing Consensus for Peace development in Northern Uganda', COPE Working Paper 31, ACORD

Finnström, S. (2004) 'Reconciliation grown bitter? Amnesty, ritual, and war in northern Uganda' (July 2005 version), paper originally presented at the African Studies Association (ASAUK) biennial conference, London, September 2004

Harlacher, T., Okot, F.X., Aloyo, C., Balthazard, M. and Atkinson, R. (2006)

Traditional Ways of Coping in Acholi: Cultural Provisions for Reconciliation and Healing from War, Kampala, Caritas Gulu Archdiocese

Hovil, L. and Lomo, Z. (2005) 'Whose justice? Perceptions of Uganda's Amnesty Act 2000: the potential for conflict resolution and long-term reconciliation', Refugee Law Project Working Paper 15

Hovil, L. and Quinn, J.R. (2005) 'Peace first, justice later: traditional justice in Northern Uganda', Refugee Law Project Working Paper 17

Hovil, L. and Okello, M.C. (2007) 'Partial justice: formal and informal mechanisms in post conflict West Nile', Refugee Law Project Working Paper 21

Human Rights Focus (2007) *Fostering the Transition in Acholi-land: From War to Peace, from Camps to Home,* September

International Center for Transitional Justice and the Human Rights Center (2010) *Forgotten Voices: A Population-Based Survey on Attitudes About Peace and Justice in Northern Uganda,* University of California, Berkeley

Justice Resources (2004) 'Law and Disorder: The Impact of Conflict on Access to Justice in Northern Uganda'

Komakech, L. and Sheff, A. (2009) 'Tradition in transition: drawing on the old to develop a new jurisprudence for dealing with Uganda's legacy of violence', Beyond Juba Project Working Paper, 1, revised edition, May

Lederach, J.P. (1997) *Building Peace: Sustainable Reconciliation in Divided Societies,* Washington DC, United States Institute of Peace Press

Liu Institute for Global Issues (2005) '*Roco Wat I Acholi*: restoring relationships in Acholi-land: traditional approaches to justice and reintegration', Gulu District NGO Forum, Ker Kwaro Acholi

Molenaar, A. (2005) 'Gacaca: grassroots justice after genocide', Research Report 77, Leiden, African Studies Center

Pain, D. (1997) *The Bending of the Spears: Producing Consensus for Peace and Development in Northern Uganda,* London, International Alert and Kacoke Madit, http://www.kmnet.org/publications/spear.doc, accessed 8 June 2009

Penal Reform International, Research on *Gacaca* report, Report IV 'The guilty plea procedure, cornerstone of the Rwandan justice system', http://www.penalreform.org/publications/reports/gacaca/rep-ga4-2003-guiltyplea-en.pdf, accessed 13 May 2012

Uganda Joint Christian Council (2007) *A Framework for Dialogue on Reconciliation and Peace in Northern Uganda*

UNOCHA Report (2007) *Making Peace Our Own: Victims Perceptions of Accountability, Reconciliation and Transitional Justice in Northern Uganda*

Notes

1 Refer to the Agreement on Comprehensive Solutions to the conflict between the Government of the Republic of Uganda and the Lord's Resistance Army/Movement, Juba, 2007.

2 Refer to the Agreement on Accountability and Reconciliation between the

Government of the Republic of Uganda and the Lord's Resistance Army/ Movement, Juba, 2007.

3   Refer to the report on Peace, Recovery and Development Plan for Northern Uganda, Government of Uganda, 2007.

4   Refer to Peace Recovery and Development Plan (PRDP) (2007): Strategic Objective 4: Peace Building and Reconciliation, Article 4.4.1: Public Information, Education and Communication (IEC) and Counseling Program.

5   This and the following paragraph draw on Briefing Note No. 1 (2008): Conflict, Justice and Reconciliation in Teso: Obstacles and Opportunities.

6   See section on Traditional Justice and the challenges of Mass Conflict.

7   Interview with an LRA Delegate to the Juba Peace talks, Gulu Town, 16/09/08.

8   'Tradition in transition: drawing on the old to develop a new jurisprudence for dealing with Uganda's legacy of violence', (revised edition) (May 2009) Beyond Juba Project Working Paper No.1.

4

Culture, customs, tradition and transitional justice

David Kaulemu

Introduction

It is now generally accepted that major societal transitions cannot adequately be handled without dealing with the local people's cultures, customs and traditions. Some analysts even suggest that local cultures and traditions provide key solutions to the requirements of transitional justice. Whatever solutions can be found to the challenges of transitional justice, their understanding and implementation will have to deal with local cultures, traditions and customs. People who experience political transitions and people who need to go beyond conflict situations are always embedded in specific customs, cultures and traditions which can either facilitate the movement towards peace or become part of the problem. Any framework for transitional justice will have to take this into account.

In this chapter, I argue for a critical treatment of the social artefacts that we call culture, custom and tradition. To declare them as artefacts is not to demean their importance. It is, however, to recognise that as human creations, they can be re-created, deepened and expanded in order to be used as tools for transitional justice, social justice, development and peace. I recognise and emphasise the potential productivity that cultural traditions and customs can deliver in the interest of transitional justice. Yet the potential dangers of the same social and historical artefacts producing oppression, conflicts and injustice have been demonstrated. This deeply ambivalent and reflexive relationship between tradition and justice – between customs and justice – calls for more self-conscious handling of both traditional cultures on the one hand and social and political transitions on the other.

Culture, customs and traditions

The definitions of the concepts of 'culture', 'custom' and 'traditions' are intricately linked to each other. This family of three concepts tends to confuse many people for any attempt to define one of them implicates the other two. This gives the impression that the three concepts mean the same. Enthusiasts of logic are quick to point out the circularity in many attempts to define these concepts. Any decent attempt to define these concepts will surely lead to some form of circularity, but I think that the circularity is more virtuous than vicious. Each of the concepts emphasises a different aspect of the same human and social phenomenon.

Culture, customs and traditions deal with human habits and how human beings organise life. These are habits of thought, behaviour and actions and ways of organising socially, politically and economically. It is therefore not surprising that culture, customs and traditions are different aspects of humans' ways of organising themselves. Customs are a set of socially agreed, generally accepted rules or norms that are socially enforced. Customs refer to the rules of what we do and what we expect others and succeeding generations to follow. However, we often forget that what we do is developed over periods of time and that the rules change from time to time. We also sometimes forget that the rules of what we do are developed as responses to human needs, aspirations and strategies for solving concrete social problems. We tend to repeat those actions that give favourable results. Thus customs initially are repeated for their results. Yet after a period, actions can be repeated as a matter of custom – that is we say to ourselves, 'This is what has always been done.' Sometimes when we do this, we follow customs automatically without thinking of what problems they are meant to solve. We therefore sometimes forget the origins of our customs. We are, therefore, sometimes trapped by customs whose origins and usefulness have been forgotten. The African philosopher, Kwasi Wiredu, called these customs anachronisms. Anachronisms are customs that have outlived their usefulness. In many situations of transition, people can be distracted by outdated customs. Sometimes people want to apply customs which do not have the capacity to solve the problems before them. And yet in some cases, local customs can in fact be helpful in bringing divided societies together.

Culture, on the other hand is generally understood as a way of life. When we talk of culture, we tend to focus more on the integrated patterns of knowledge, beliefs and behaviour that are passed on from one generation to another. Culture combines customs, social practices, values, relations and institutions that we value and wish to pass on to coming generations. Hence, when we talk about culture, we focus on the cultivation of a way of life. Cultivation suggests conscious and deliberate encouragement of certain ways of organising and doing things. Cultures teach us what to think and how to feel in specific circumstances. Cultures suggest efforts for the improvement and refinement of social performance and human relations. Hence, culture emphasises the cultivation of virtues (e.g. courage, respect, justice) and the discouraging of vices (e.g. cruelty, corruption, injustice). In this sense, virtues are qualities that are seen as positive and therefore need to be encouraged and cultivated in children, adult individuals, families, communities and organisations. Culture, therefore necessarily involves the use of moral values and ideals to determine social direction. Usually, morality of culture encourages liberation, freedom, respect for life and dignity and self-fulfilment. Yet different cultures may emphasise different sets of values. These differences are sometimes at the centre of cultural, political and social conflicts.

When we talk of traditions, we tend to focus on beliefs, customs and values that are passed on from one generation to another. Traditions emphasise the preservation of values and customs through this passing on from generation to generation. Traditions are usually the ways of doing things that are developed and preserved over a long period of time. Normally, traditions develop as the established responses and ways of proceeding that are accepted without consciously remembering the moral values that justify them and the historical conditions that triggered them. When we talk of traditions we tend to emphasise their conservative aspects: the preservation of values, practices, institutions and knowledge. This sometimes creates some blind spots about the usefulness of what is being conserved.

Traditions are normally seen as clear and cast-in-stone. Yet they are always constructed by human beings and not machines. As Bourdillon points out:

> We think of culture and tradition as coming from the past, something proven and stable on which we can rely. In fact, tradition and culture constantly change according to the choices we make. We choose things from the past that serve our present needs. (Bourdillon 1993: 9)

People make choices about what to preserve and how. Because of this, traditions, customs and cultures always involve ambiguity and ambivalence. Attempts to banish ambiguity in traditions result in oppression, cruelty and marginalisation. Traditions and cultures are essentially ambiguous because they are human. They possess possibilities for both oppression and liberation.

Deconstructing approaches to customs, culture and tradition

While culture and traditions are usually presented as clear and cast in stone, in this chapter I emphasise a sense of ambiguity and ambivalence in the development and practice of culture, customs and traditions. Because culture and traditions are human, they are always historical and social. Even if culture and traditions were cast in iron and therefore unambiguous, following them would always raise ambiguities and ambivalences. As Wittgenstein postulated, there are an indefinite number of ways in which any rule can be followed and in which traditions and cultures can develop. Cultural rules are always ambiguous because human beings are human beings and not machines. Human beings have feelings, memories, relationships and aspirations that always inform how they follow rules, practices and principles. Attempts to banish ambiguity have been the major drive towards modern forms of oppression. The rationalisation of modern social and political life, understood as being in direct opposition to human feeling, has been seen as the basis of immense suffering in the modern world.

The colonial project as a rationalising project that involved imperialism, colonisation and colonialism caused much human suffering in Africa. The patriarchal projects to define women and their roles have been at the core of the oppression of women in most traditions and religions. Definitions of citizenship in colonial and post-colonial societies have led to social conflicts. The apartheid system, for example, which led to one of the longest conflicts on the African continent, was an attempt to enforce a certain exclusive definition of citizenship. The modernising forces that led to the invention of modern ethnicity in Africa helped to create some of the deepest conflicts that any continent has experienced. The modern politicisation of ethnicity in places like apartheid South Africa, Rwanda, Burundi, Sudan, Nigeria, Kenya and Zimbabwe has been at the centre of the major conflicts in Africa. Politics, people's needs, power, access to resources, corruption and greed are some of the factors that influence the development of cultural traditions.

If pre-colonial cultures, traditions, customs and identities are understood to be ambiguous, then they must also be understood as having possessed possibilities for both the suppression and the liberation of women and Africans in general. The colonial experience helped to push African cultures in more monarchical, hierarchical, patriarchal and authoritarian directions. This was possible because the local cultures had the potential of developing in those directions. In many ways they already had their own hierarchies, forms of oppression, prejudices and exploitation. But they also had the potential to develop in many different, liberating directions. Mamdani (1996) describes this process clearly in his book *Citizen and Subject* on the legacy of colonialism in contemporary Africa.

African traditions and cultures need to be understood in the context of modernity. It is in this context that we can fully appreciate the major ambiguities of modern African societies. As Mudimbe (1988) has demonstrated in his book *Invention of Africa*, African traditional society is a modern creation as much as it is an African response to the forces of modernity. The creation of modern Africa was only possible because there were enough people both in Europe and Africa prepared to invest in the creation of modern African societies. It is therefore not surprising that when Africans successfully waged struggles against colonialism, their leaders did not call for the abolition of colonial boundaries and institutions. The Gramscian insight that political hegemony implies both coercion and consent is clearly demonstrated in the context of African social and political development (Hoffman 1984: 32). Therefore, African identities, traditions and customs are partly constructed by modernising forces. This is true of African customary law and the invention of ethnicity, for example. But for these forces to succeed, Africans have to appropriate aspects of these dominant forces. As Africans we are more than mere victims and beneficiaries of dominant cultures and traditions. We contribute to the building of our cultures by the choices we make – even if those choices are made in the context of struggle. As Mamdani points out:

> The form of colonial rule shaped the form of revolt against it. Indirect rule at once reinforced ethnically-bound institutions of control and led their explosions from within. Ethnicity came to be simultaneously the form of colonial control over natives and the form of revolt against it. (Mamdani 1996: 24)

Post-colonial theory has recognised the different strategies that Africans have used to survive the colonial period. A look at some of the strategies clarifies how African customs, cultures and traditions are social constructions full of ambiguities and ambivalences. We can consider the strategy of cultural appropriation, for example. Explaining this strategy, Bill Ashcroft, Gareth Griffiths and Helen Tiffin point out the meaning of 'appropriation' in post-colonial theory. They point out that 'appropriation' is:

> A term used to describe the ways in which post-colonial societies take over those aspects of the imperial culture – language, forms of writing, film, theatre, even modes of thought and argument such as rationalism, logic and analysis – that may be of use to them in articulating their own social and cultural identities ... the dominated or colonised culture can use the tools of the dominant discourse to resist its political or cultural control. (Ashcroft et al 1998: 19)

Sometimes appropriation takes the creative form of what Gayatri Spivak calls catachresis. 'Catachresis is the process by which the colonised take and re-inscribe something that exists traditionally as a feature of imperial culture' (Ashcroft et al 1998: 34). Catachresis is a legitimate, creative and empowering strategy that Africans and other subordinated and marginalised peoples have used in their various struggles. What is important in this context is to recognise how customs, cultures and traditions are not cast in stone. This recognition opens up ways of reinventing the same cultures to move people beyond periods of violent conflicts. This can only be achieved when customs, cultures and traditions are not only understood, but respected and appreciated. But to respect a culture is not to cling to it, even when it ceases to help resolving contemporary conflicts. Respect for culture, customs and traditions must mean the need to keep them alive by expanding, deepening and extending them. Our respect for culture is therefore always tested in social transitions.

Important assumptions when dealing with transitions

Transitions in the context of human conflicts are complex. Yet, because we want to deal with them in order to solve conflicts, we tend to simplify them. In many ways this is inevitable. To understand is always to find a way of making sense of conflict. Usually we make sense by simplifying complex conflicts. One way we have done this is by making assumptions about the agents involved in the conflict. Many conceptual frameworks used in conflict analysis assume that the people engaged in any conflict are rational, egotistic individuals. This is a wrong assumption. We should never, in any conflict analysis, start with idealised rational, egotistic individuals the way modern economics or modern liberal theory does. We should always start with real human beings who are embedded in customs, cultures and traditions.

In conflict analysis there is also a tendency to present the conflict in terms of binary oppositions that are moralised. This is the tendency to reduce the conflict to two sides – the good side and the bad one. Using this type of binary opposition, we rush to praise the good side and condemn the bad one. This rush, which is usually facilitated by our commitment to universal human rights, justice and the rule of law, makes us blind to the cultural context of the conflict. This blindness, in turn, forces us to miss real opportunities and useful cultural and traditional tools that could help transform or solve the conflicts. This blindness also makes us insensitive to the injustices that may be committed against those we see as being on the wrong side. We also tend to be blind to the injustices committed by those we see as being on the right side. It is important to appreciate that no culture or tradition deliberately teaches its people to be bad people. Yet it is also true that customs, cultures and traditions are characterised by both possibilities of oppression and of transformation and liberation; possibilities for conflicts and for peace. Understanding these possibilities is critical to conflict transformation and conflict resolution. This is part of what it means to treat human beings as human beings and not to demonise them or treat them like angels.

Oversimplifying transitional justice in Africa

Transitional justice is often oversimplified by assuming that it can be realised in simple, clear social or political transitions. We often talk about the simple transition from conflict or war to peace and social harmony; from a bad situation or injustice to a good situation or that of justice. Simple, clear single transitions hardly take place anywhere in the world. Every transition is actually a complex bundle of separate, multiple, social, political, cultural and economic transitions that may or may not interact. For example, the African transition from tradition to modernity is a series of very complex processes that include transformation in education, change of health care systems, Christianisation, urbanisation, bureaucratisation, development of market systems, industrialisation, liberation struggles and many other developments. Any history of any conflict reveals that transitions are not simple.

Transitional justice is also oversimplified by presenting it in terms of simple 'victim–perpetrator' dichotomies. In real transitions the story is more complex than this. Today's victims may have been yesterday's perpetrators and the other way round. In many conflict situations, individuals and groups of people are both victim and perpetrator at the same time.

Another way of oversimplifying transitional justice is to present it as if it brings about the end of politics. There is a general tendency to think that in order to solve a situation of conflict, parties must forget their political interests or that once the conflict is solved, everybody should be on the same side. Politics never ends with transitional justice. The very process of conflict transformation or conflict resolution is a political process.

Justice in transitions

Culture, customs and traditions have social tools, political resources for handling new conflicts and challenges that come from within themselves. They also develop tools for dealing with conflicts with other communities and are capable of appropriating new strategies for handling old and new conflicts and challenges. Yet every society meets with new challenges that require new approaches, new tools and strategies. It is therefore not obvious that traditional cultural practices can solve the challenges of mass killings, genocide, modern liberation struggles, secessions and modern national conflicts. Yet we ignore them at our own peril.

One of the fundamental aims of transitional justice has been to somehow maintain the focus on justice in a situation of fluidity. How can societies in conflict situations uphold social justice and to what extent? This is important because conflicts have a tendency to undermine justice. Part of what it means to be in transition is to challenge established practices, enforced rules and preserved values. People who are in conflict tend to ignore or suspend their sense of justice and respect for moral principles. Hence as conflicts escalate, ordinary members of society are more and more sucked into acts of violence and killing. This is why it is always amazing to see how ordinary people are transformed into brutal killers during tribal, racial, gender or class conflicts. In the situations of political violence and genocide that we have seen in Rwanda, Kenya, Sierra Leone, Democratic Republic of Congo and Zimbabwe it has been quite shocking to see what cruelty ordinary, otherwise good people have been able to show to their fellow humans. In many of these places, even church-going citizens, including priests and nuns, have been implicated in acts of violence and genocide.

Transitional justice is an attempt to minimise the undermining of justice that occurs in social and political transitions. To appreciate the complexity of this process, it is useful to look at two ways of understanding justice. 'Conservative justice' aims at preserving the existing order of rights and possessions in a society or community. It also works to restore the rights when undermined. In situations of transition, this may be very complicated, for some of the rights and possessions may, in fact, be contested and be the reason for the existing conflicts. It is challenging for conservative justice to be realised when an established order of rights is being challenged. Hence, the popularity sometimes of another form of justice – 'ideal' or 'prosthetic justice', which aims at modifying the status quo. Ideal justice gives the ideal criteria not for what is the case but for what ought to be. It therefore gives the basis of working to transform social relations, rights and the system of possessions. This, again, works better in a stable situation. In a situation of transition, the process is a big challenge. How can there be agreement on criteria for transforming society when people are in conflict? In many cases, the criteria for transformation are themselves sources of conflict.

It is a legitimate question to ask whether transitional justice is not a form of accepting the impossibility of justice in a situation of transition. Is transitional justice a way of accepting and indirectly justifying the existence of injustice during the period of transition? Is transitional justice a modern cultural invention that helps us to live with injustices during periods of transition? It may, in fact, appear to be the lowering of our standards for demanding justice. What, really is the difference made by qualifying justice as 'transitional'? What is the reason for not insisting on justice – period?

Politics of transitional justice

The questions above raise the issue of transitional justice itself as a modern cultural political form. What do we want to achieve with the social/political invention called transitional justice? What new traditions, cultures and customs do we want to invent through it? In asking these questions, we want to know what social imaginary is behind the promotion of transitional justice. Charles Taylor defines social imaginary as:

> the ways people imagine their social existence, how they fit together with others, how things go on between them and their

fellows, the expectations that are normally met, and the deeper
normative notions and images that underlie these expectations.
(Taylor 2004: 23)

How have people imagined their social existence? How have
we imagined the way we relate to each other? What stories and
images about ourselves and about others inform the values and
attitudes that determine our systems of governance? What metaphors do we live in? In short, what have been our imaginaries of
governance? Imaginaries are important because they determine
how we treat each other and how we respond to each other. They
inform our friendships, enmities and modes of governance. If
we imagine our nation to be like a small village with chiefs and
headmen, that imagination will inform how we conduct our business and how we treat each other. If we imagine our society as
characterised by divisions, hostility and war, this imagination will
shape our attitudes and emotional responses to issues of governance and social justice.

We have had different social imaginaries being assumed in
situations that call for transitional justice in the African context.
If we take the transition from African traditional societies to
modernity, we can see a number of different responses available. There has been total hostility to modernity, total embrace of
modernity and various attempts at combining African traditions
with modernity. These various responses to modernity have, over
time, developed into customs, traditions and cultures meant to
guide us on how to proceed in situations of transition. Since colonialism, we have developed customs, cultures and traditions that
are exclusivist. We also have examples of responses that have led
us into inclusive customs, cultures and traditions. These strategies
have influenced us as we deal with conflicts on the continent. In
deciding what cultural traditions we will use in future, we must
assess the reality of our situation. More and more writers are
pointing out that certain approaches we have used in the past will
have to be abandoned. Jeffrey Sachs makes the following point:

The defining challenge of the twenty-first century will be
to face the reality that humanity shares a common fate on a
crowded planet. That common fate will require new forms of

global cooperation, a fundamental point of blinding simplicity that many world leaders have yet to understand or embrace. For the past two hundred years, technology and demography have consistently run ahead of deeper social understanding. Industrialisation and science have created a pace of change unprecedented in human history. Philosophers, politicians, artists, and economists must scramble constantly to catch up with contemporaneous social conditions. Our social philosophies, as a result, consistently lag behind present realities. (Sachs 2008: 3)

Writing earlier but on the same point Reagon points out, more dramatically, the brute facts about our contemporary reality:

We've pretty much come to the end of a time when you can have a space that is 'yours only' – just for people you want to be there ... we've finished with that kind of isolating. There is no hiding place. There is nowhere you can go and only be with the people who are like you. It's over. Give it up. (Reagon quoted in Sandercock 1993: 117)

Reagon here points out to the need to reinvent our social imaginaries and the cultural traditions that will influence our contemporary conduct in transitional societies. We have all the resources that we have used in the past, but we must also be aware that new situations demand new responses. This situation of ambiguity can never be abolished. It can only be bridged by human creativity as we search for new forms of governance.

Traditional metaphors in governance

One of the major challenges of societies in transition in Africa is how to construct a system of governance that guides us on living with our political opponents. Traditional metaphors of governance could suggest useful insights for contemporary Africa. Our political leaders should have big hearts and wide minds, capable of helping all of us to live together but without attempting to abolish politics. In African traditional societies that role seems to have been played by the 'Old Man' and the 'Old Woman' – grandfathers and grandmothers. This role is critical in the system of social governance. Part of what it means 'to grow old' or 'to mature', is to give up close involvement in the narrow or day-to-day political fights. When someone says, 'You have met me when I am now old,' it may mean, 'You have met me after I have matured, mellowed and grown to be more responsible.' The suggestion is that 'to grow up' and to grow old is to develop into a more responsible, socially sensitive and politically mature person. The old man and old woman are given the socially responsible role of looking at the big picture – reconciling people, defending the weak and helping the powerful to be responsive to the needs of others, especially the marginalised. *Sekuru* and *ambuya*[1] are people who are considered to have lived their lives and are now ready to help the young live their lives too. In modern terms, *sekuru* and *ambuya* are the retired, those who do not compete with the young on the job market, those with few direct vested interests, those unlikely to be vexed by the clash of selfish political and business interests. They are the people who are supposed to have given up the old grudges partly because most of their peers will have died and partly because some of the issues they fought for will have been taken over by others using new techniques and approaches. This is why they are people to whom even murderers, political malcontents and social transgressors turn to for advice and support. They play the role well because they have a lifetime of experience, which protects them from being shocked by any transgressions referred to them. They tend to play the role well because they know everyone and so they can talk to anyone in ways that can help resolve difficult issues. In contemporary times, this should be the role of eminent persons, retired presidents and other political and social leaders.

The African leaders who led us to political independence tried to imagine the new nation states in what they thought were traditional terms. They helped to build social imaginaries informed by 'traditional' experiences to justify their modes of governance. Unfortunately, many of them tried to play double roles. They tried to be eminent persons while also acting as revolutionaries with many direct, vested political and economic interests that brought them into confrontation with fellow citizens. They wanted to be respected as eminent persons yet they were still deeply engrossed in live combat with fellow citizens. They either failed or refused to defend their own citizens because those citizens had different political opinions from theirs. One-party states were defended by images of African traditional societies. In this discourse, nation states were conceptualised as cattle kraals with only one bull, or chicken runs with only one cock. What we were not told, however, is that cattle kraals and chicken runs were human constructs and not natural institutions. Humans prescribed that there be only one bull in the kraal. Hence the kraal paradigm could not act as a moral ideal to guide humans. Yet this simple and false idea inspired many good people and inspired them to hate, fight and sometimes commit murders in its name.

Much imagination was invested by those who invoked 'African socialism' in conceptualising the nation state as an African family governed through the African court, which is said to have relied on the building of consensus. What we were not encouraged to question were the moral legitimacy and power dynamics of the African court itself. Could it adequately work as a metaphor for an ideal family or a morally adequate system of social and political governance and conflict resolution at the level of the nation state? If you were African, you were supposed to accept and defend this understanding of African traditions without asking whether this paradigm was the best that we could use to handle contemporary African social, political, economic and technological challenges. In this way, oppressive African customs and traditions were being constructed.

But these African traditions were presented as if today's African people had no role in interpreting them and selecting what was relevant to them and in their context. Our ancestors were intelligent people who reflected on their situation and tried to provide answers to their own live social and political questions. They were not perfect. They did not always agree with each other. They sometimes even fought with each other. But they tried to be rational about their traditions. In other words, they rationally selected values, systems, and attitudes from their elders to solve their own challenges. They debated about the best ways of following their respective traditions. Yet some of our modern African traditionalists present our ancestors as if they never cherished debates on the meaning of their traditions. Hence, we now have exclusive, self-appointed interpreters of African traditions, ubuntu, African liberation struggles and African governance traditions. We now end up with African traditions being forced down our throats.

Someone now appoints himself to be the arbiter of what it means to be fully and authentically African. This has been a source of some of the deepest conflicts of the post-colonial era.

For example, some of these leaders have suggested that African participatory governance could be inspired by the African court system. Others have suggested that the African family system could be a paradigm for contemporary African political governance. Experiments inspired by the African court and the African family system were rife and spearheaded by liberation movements – Nyerere's ujamaa, Moi's *nyayoism*, Kaunda's humanism. African victims of these experiments have a clear view of the experiments' moral limits. The philosopher Kwame Anthony Appiah has talked about how his father suffered harassment and arrests perpetrated by 'the father of African liberation', Kwame Nkrumah. Women have raised serious issues about some of the ways that participatory governance has been conceptualised by the dominant political leaders on the continent. Serious questions have been raised about the blindness of these paradigms to the rights of many Africans. These political efforts, inspired by invented African traditions, struggle to handle the complex multi-tradition, multicultural, multi-religious character of modern African states. The ideas of the village court and that of the African extended family system have many good points to inspire us. Yet the irony is that many Africans have suffered and lost their lives in the name of African traditions of participatory political governance and conflict transformation and resolution. It is tragic when Africans persecute other Africans in the name of making them more African.

Most of our invented political traditions and governance frameworks still rely on binary oppositional paradigms of us/them, friend/enemy, local/foreigner, insider/outsider etc. We still do not know how to handle ambiguities. Our social imaginaries are yet to handle adequately the question of citizenship. Many Africans still suffer persecution at the hands of fellow Africans. Even within the same country, compatriots kill each other. Our political emotions still cannot handle the possibility of a white child being fully African. The white child in Africa struggles to see herself as African. Deep down in our hearts, the idea of a woman president still appears ridiculous in the way that Americans used to scoff at the idea of a black president. For as long as we only want to be with the people who think, talk and look the same as us, we will continue to fail on social participatory governance. Just as Hitler caused much suffering by embarking on a project to eliminate difference and banish ambiguities in people's identities, we find ourselves, as essentially good people, plunged into horrible human tragedies for trying the same.

Transition and the expansion of social imaginaries

What we imagine good governance to be informs our sense of who will participate in it and how. Our various historical traditions and cultures have informed our imagination, conceptual frameworks and emotional responses to the issue of participation in governance. We conjure up images, metaphors and vocabularies from our various traditions to express our understanding and prescriptions on governance. However, situations of transition destabilise these social imaginaries and social frameworks. Contemporary multicultural societies demand the expansion of our various historical and social imaginaries. In the past, each group, steeped in its traditions, has tried to universalise its particular values. Each group has closed itself in its fort – starting with the white settler communities, followed by the various ethnic groups, classes, and other social and political groups. This has made it difficult to establish universal participatory governance. Yet, as Jeffery Sachs has pointed our in the passage quoted above, this is what we need.

Our societies in Africa have been undermined by the narrowness of our social imaginaries. We have been let down by the sorts of things people imagine governance to be and how that imagination informs and guides our respective values, attitudes and conduct. We must learn from our various moments of madness that certain emotions and attitudes can be dangerous to the nation when fed into the national psyche. Certain political slogans which cultivate emotional responses geared towards turning political opponents into enemies and political debates into wars are based on narrow visions of our various societies. Africans must develop inclusive systems of governance that recognise that politics cannot be banished, disagreement cannot be wished away and neither should political opponents be silenced by intimidation or elimination. Inclusive systems of governance plan for and deliberately develop respectable spaces for political opponents. They cultivate appropriate emotional responses towards them, always treating them as human beings.

Modern institution of elders

It was on the basis of seeing the usefulness of the institution of the grandfather and grandmother in African traditional society that the modern institution of 'The Elders' was reinvented. The elders are respected global leaders brought together by Nelson Mandela to use their influence to assist in peace building and promote human rights and consist of: Martti Ahtisaar (Finland), Fernando H. Cardoso (Brazil), Jimmy Carter (USA), Gro Brundtland (Norway), Graça Machel (Mozambique), Kofi Annan (Ghana), Mary Robinson (Ireland), Lakhdar Brahimi (Algeria), Desmond Tutu (South Africa), Ela Bhatt (India), Nelson Mandela (South Africa) and Aung San Suu Kyi (Burma).

The modernised institution has adopted the following principles:

- The elimination of discrimination by age, race, gender
- The move towards a multi-ethnic, multicultural, multi-religious society
- Developing an inclusive and nuanced sense of history
- Respecting ambiguity, ambivalence and the reality of people's multiple identities.

The lessons that have been learnt by using the institution of elders in contemporary Africa include the importance of:

- Developing genuinely inclusive social imaginaries and social and political virtues that encourage peace
- Recognising the reality of politics and conflict
- Encouraging and reinventing customs, cultures and traditions of politics that do not deteriorate into violent conflicts
- When dealing with transitions, to always gravitate towards

human liberation, freedom and fulfilment that is consistent with economic prosperity and environmental sustainability; solidarity (never losing sight of the humanity of others); and respect for human dignity and human rights.

The modernised and expanded institution of elders seems to be an example of how an African traditional institution can be updated to contribute to the challenges of transitional justice in the contemporary world. What is fascinating about this example is that it challenges some past African customs and traditions on age, ender, ethnicity and race. Yet, in important ways, Africans can still feel proud that they have contributed to the development of the modern culture of justice in periods of transition.

Conclusions

Anthony Giddens defined for us what it means to be human in the contemporary world:

> We begin from the premise that to be human is to know, virtually all of the time, in terms of some description or another, both what one is doing and why one is doing it. All human beings continuously monitor the circumstance of their activities as a feature of doing what they do, and such monitoring always has discursive features. (Giddens 1991: 35)

To understand customs, cultures and traditions is to increase our opportunities for expanding our social imaginaries. To do so is to choose to actively participate in the construction of a better, more peaceful, prosperous world. It is to open ourselves to the question, 'What choices can we make for transitional justice?' This chapter has offered the beginning of an answer to such a question. I have argued that we gain a lot by seeking opportunities for justice in our cultures, but to say this does not restrict us only to the world we know. We gain confidence by listening to Bourdillon when he points out:

> Our culture gives us a framework within which we think and live. But we are not slaves to custom. We often cite culture and custom to support the actions which serve our interests. But, in fact, we often pick and choose from our culture those aspects

which best help us to cope with our present circumstances. (Bourdillon 1993: 11)

We must therefore ask ourselves what choices we shall make for justice in the context of transitions in a globalised world.

Note

1   Shona terms for 'grandfather' and 'grandmother'.

Selected bibliography

Ashcroft, B., Griffiths, G. and Tiffin, H. (1998) *Key Concepts in Post-Colonial Studies*, London and New York, Routledge

Bourdillon, M.F.C. (1993) 'Where are the ancestors? Changing culture in Zimbabwe', University of Zimbabwe

Giddens, A. (1991) *Modernity and Self Identity: Self and Society in the Late Modern Age*, Cambridge, Polity Press

Gyekye, K. (1997) *Tradition and Modernity*, New York, NY, Oxford University Press

Hoffman, J. (1984) *The Gramscian Challenge: Coercion and Consent in Marxist Political Theory*, Oxford, Basil Blackwell

Hope, A. and Timmel, S. (1984) *Training for Transformation: a Handbook for Community Workers*, TfT, South Africa

Mamdani, M. (1996) *Citizens and Subject: Contemporary Africa and the Legacy of Late Colonialism*, Princeton, NJ, Princeton University Press

Mudimbe, V.Y. (1988) *The Invention of Africa: Gnosis, Philosophy and the Order of Knowledge*, Bloomington and Indianapolis, IN, Indiana University Press

Nusbaum, M. and Glover, J. (eds) (1995) *Women, Culture and Development*, Oxford, Clarendon Press

Ranger, T. (1985) *The Invention of Tribalism in Zimbabwe*, Zimbabwe, Mambo Press

Sachs, J. D. (2008) *Common Wealth: Economics for a Crowded Planet*, Penguin Books

Sandercock, L. (1998 [1993]) *Towards Cosmopolis: Planning for Multicultural Cities*, Chichester, John Wiley and Sons

Taylor, C. (2004) *Modern Social Imaginaries*, Durham and London, Public Planet Books, Duke University Press

5

The politics of truth commissions in Africa: a case study of Kenya

Davis M. Malombe

Introduction

> When violent conflict ends or a harsh totalitarian state
> collapses, the perpetrators and victims of violence must
> often resettle together in their communities. This can be
> immensely difficult when neighbours and even family mem-
> bers have fought on opposite sides of a conflict or attacked
> each other. The sheer numbers of participants in the vio-
> lence, the various perceptions of who was in the 'right' or in
> the 'wrong' and the presence of struggling state institutions
> make the pursuit of justice and reconciliation quite complex.
> Nonetheless it is important to have some means with which
> to acknowledge crimes committed during a period of totali-
> tarian rule or violent conflict.[1]

Truth commissions have for the last 20 years become a key man-
tra in transitional justice processes in Africa and other countries
emerging from conflicts or despotic regimes.[2] Many scholars and
practitioners have written on the extent to which these commissions have realised both their specific mandates and the objectives
of transitional justice programmes. Key gains, challenges and recommendations have been postulated in order to provide positive
lessons for other commissions.

The extent to which these lessons have informed the ongoing
work of Kenya's Truth, Justice and Reconciliation Commission
(TJRC) is worth analysing before the commission concludes the

thematic hearings (due to be in April 2012) and submits the final report the following month.

Conceptual perspectives on truth commissions

Truth commissions should uphold the right of victims of past human rights violations to obtain truth, justice and reparation. To this end, truth commissions should: clarify as far as possible the facts about past human rights violations; feed the evidence they gather into continuing and new investigations and criminal judicial proceedings; and formulate effective recommendations for providing full reparation to all the victims and their relatives.[3]

Truth commissions are defined as 'official, temporary, non judicial, fact-finding bodies that investigate a pattern of abuses of human rights or humanitarian law, usually committed over a period of time'.[4] According to Priscilla Hayner, the central elements of a truth commission's work are usually: (1) statement taking, through which individual victims are invited to give their story, generally one-on-one, in private, to a staff member who has been trained in statement-taking skills; (2) research and investigation, by which investigative staff look into individual cases, try to establish the roots of the violence and the patterns of abuses, document locations where torture took place and so on; and increasingly, (3) holding public hearings, to give some victims and witnesses a chance to tell their story in public.[5]

Pundits have argued that the object of their inquiry (a pattern of human rights violations, rather than a specific event) distinguishes truth commissions from other commissions of inquiry. Their temporary character distinguishes truth commissions from many national human rights commissions and other national institutions for the promotion and protection of human rights, which are permanent monitoring and enforcement bodies. Truth commissions are established by national authorities, generally during a political transition.

Louis Bickford adds to this discourse in his argument that truth commissions are part of the transitional justice strategy, focus on human rights, emphasise the value of knowing the truth, focus on the recent past and on systemic and ongoing patterns of abuses, listen to victims' voices, are temporary, submit final reports, and are officially sanctioned by the state and other official parties.[6] Thus the commissions, being part of the wider project for truth telling in transitional justice, have an obligation to victims' rights to truth, justice, reparations and reconciliation as envisaged under international human rights and humanitarian laws.[7] The duty to ensure the protection, promotion and respect of these rights needs to be assessed against four benchmarks.

First, the right of individuals to know the truth about mass atrocities and violations, and the reasons for and circumstances within which they occurred, is recognised and accepted as a critical component of any transitional efforts that seek to address past abuses and guarantee their non-repetition. Second, the right to justice entails investigating past violations and, if enough admissible evidence is gathered, prosecuting the suspected perpetrators.

Third, the right to reparations entails creating initiatives to restore and foster the human dignity and development of the victims and banish the culture of impunity through such programmes as restitution, compensation, rehabilitation, satisfaction and guarantees of non-repetition. Finally, and though not explicitly captured as a rights issue, victims and suspected perpetrators are expected to engage in reconciliation, which requires reconstructing their relationships and attitudes towards each other, and building state institutions towards genuine healing, integration and development in the society.[8]

While these official truth-telling mechanisms are critical, experts and practitioners have also called for 'unofficial truth projects' or 'peoples' truth commissions'. According to Louis Bickford, these are initiatives driven by civil society, victim groups and other non-state actors at two levels:

1 Commission-like efforts that often share most of the attributes of official truth commissions – even though they may not have similar bureaucratic structures to commissions (e.g. they may not have 'commissioners'), they are comparable in a number of ways, and represent the majority of case studies examined here.
2 Projects within documentation centres or other existing NGOs – these emphasise confronting the legacy of past human rights abuses by revealing the truth.

Finally, Bickford captures three relationships (purposes) between official truth commissions and unofficial or people's truth projects:

- To pave the way for or precede a truth commission, either by specific design or because of contingent and unanticipated developments
- To provide complementary initiatives working in symbiotic ways to get at multiple truths about the past
- To replace truth commissions especially when civil society organisations see a need for a truth commission but do not expect or trust the government to establish one. The same may apply when they are opposed to truth commissions.

The political and historical context of truth commissions

We agree that transparency and accountability in the affairs of the government, together with the fight against impunity, are essential if the country is to make progress in addressing all the challenges mentioned above. Indeed, transparency, account-ability and the fight against impunity and corruption must underpin the entire reform agenda. In addressing these issues, it will be particularly important to ensure that the recommen-dations of the Truth, Justice, and Reconciliation Commission are implemented.[9]

David Easton is credited for the famous definition of politics as the study of authoritative allocation of values in a society.[10] He went further in defining the political system responsible for that allocation as: 'that system of interactions in any society through which binding or authoritative allocations are made'.[11] Authoritative allocations may be roughly defined as the govern-ance processes responsible for policy or decision making in a society. UNDP defines governance as: 'The exercise of economic, political, and administrative authority to manage a country's affairs at all levels. It comprises the mechanisms, processes and institutions, through which citizens and groups articulate their interests, exercise their legal rights, meet their obligations and mediate their differences.'[12]

Rather than protect the interests and rights of citizens, and moderate the obligations and differences between the state and its citizenry, the colonial and post-colonial regimes in Africa, as in other developing countries, were and still are governed by retrogressive and repressive political systems which are responsible for gross human rights violations, economic crimes and vicious conflicts. For many years, these states lacked progressive transitional justice or governance mechanisms to create accurate historical records for society; effective remedies to the victims; accountability to perpetrators; reformation and reconstruction of the state; and coexistence and sustainable peace.[13]

However, following the global wave of democratisation in the 1990s, a number of processes have been initiated ranging from institutional, legal and constitutional reforms to memorialisation, prosecutions, documentations, community or traditional justice, reparations and truth commissions among others. Truth commissions seem to be one of the major initiatives within transitional justice programmes in Africa and the world in general.

Studies indicate that from 1974 to 2011, at least 37 truth commissions were established in more than 30 countries, with at least 14 in Africa.[14] There are also ongoing debates on either the formation or the re-establishment of truth commissions in Burundi, Rwanda, Madagascar and Democratic Republic of Congo among others. Despite this recognition, critics are quick to point out that although the earlier investigative commissions, such as Uganda's 1974 Commission of Inquiry into Disappearances,[15] fit the definition, the most internationally significant truth commissions began in 1984 with the Argentine National Commission on the Disappearance of Persons (CONADEP) and the Chilean Truth and Reconciliation Commission (1991), followed by commissions in Guatemala and, perhaps most famously, South Africa, to name only a few.[16] Most of the modern commissions have attracted both local and international candidates in order to increase their expertise and legitimacy.

According to Africa's Centre for Open Governance (AfriCOG), the quest for truth and justice in Kenya goes back 100 years.[17] For from colonial times, successive governments in Kenya have appointed various commissions of inquiry to look into a myriad of issues considered to be matters of public interest. Between the

Native Labour Commission of 1913 and the Kiruki Commission of 2006, Kenya has had 31 commissions of inquiry.[18]

The AfriCOG report, which looked at the efficacy of the commissions of inquiry in Kenya, found that they had been created for varying reasons, including in response to public pressure, to pacify the public, to re-examine national policies and as political exit strategies. The report adds: 'The history of the commissions also reveals a common thread running through almost all the commissions – the failure or lack of enthusiasm by the Government to implement recommendations of reports of the Commissions.'[19]

The Kenya Human Rights Commission (KHRC) corroborates this situation in its report entitled *Lest we Forget: The Faces of Impunity in Kenya*. KHRC notes that the failure to ensure justice for victims of human rights violations and corruption has not resulted from a lack of information on the nature and extent of the violations, nor on the perpetrators of such violations and crimes. Many official reports in Kenya make adverse mention of the key political leaders and administrators who have allegedly been involved in human rights violations and corruption. These reports have been derived from a number of 'truth and justice-based' or transitional justice mechanisms. What has been lacking has been the political will to follow up on the recommendations made in these reports – to investigate and call to account those found responsible for the violations.

The demand for a TJRC began in the 1990s as the citizenry pushed the then repressive Kenya African National Union (KANU) regime under President Daniel Arap Moi to initiate pro-people reforms and accountability processes. Mwai Kibaki took over the mantle of leadership under the National Rainbow Coalition (NARC) on a platform of reform and justice in December 2002.

From February 2003, discussions between the NARC government, civil society and victims organisations led to the formation of a task force in April 2003, whose mandate was to establish the viability of a truth commission in Kenya. The task force, comprising mainly civil society actors, published a report in October 2003. The report recommended the formation of a TJRC by June 2004.

The mandate of the commission was to deal with both the human rights violations and the economic crimes which had been committed between 12 December 1963 (independence day) and 31 December 2002 (the day NARC took over). However, between the June 2004 deadline and December 2007 (when general elections were due), the government totally betrayed or abandoned the agreed agenda for transitional justice partly due to the political contest with NARC. This pitted the National Alliance for Change party (NAC), led by President Kibaki, against the Liberal Democratic Party (LDP), led by Raila Odinga, then road minister. This forced President Kibaki to form a government of national unity in June 2004, which brought on board members of parliament from KANU. Ironically, the KANU regime (1963–2002) was to form the core basis for the investigations by the TJRC at that time.

This failure to deal with the historical injustices and NARC polarisation lay behind the contested December 2007 presidential elections, which again pitted Mwai Kibaki's Party of National Unity (PNU) against Raila Odinga's Orange Democratic Movement (ODM).[20] The disputed election results led to post-election violence, which resulted in the displacement of 663,921 people, more than 1,300 deaths, the massive destruction of property and the polarisation of the state.

The timely intervention of the African Union (AU) through the Kenya National Dialogue and Reconciliation (KNDR) process, chaired by Kofi Annan, ended the violence and led to the signing of various agreements in February 2008. As a result, the TJRC returned to the national agenda through the agreement signed on 14 February 2008 and Agenda Item 4 of the KNDR.[21] Finally, a national accord was signed between Mwai Kibaki (as president) and Raila Odinga (who later became the prime minister) on behalf of their disputing parties on 28 February 2008.

The drafting of the TJRC Act started immediately, but the speeded-up legislative process reduced the room for national consultations. The act was finally adopted by parliament on 23 November 2008, granted presidential assent five days later and came into force on 9 March 2009. The recruitment of commissioners began in April 2009, and in July and August 2009 they were finally appointed and sworn in. The TJRC has since continued with its work under very challenging and difficult circumstances. These circumstances form the basis for this paper. At the time of writing (March 2012), the commission is finalising its thematic hearings. The final report is due to be published in May 2012.

Critique of the progress of Kenya's TJRC

My assessment of the establishment and effectiveness of Kenya's TJRC compared to other truth-telling and transitional justice programmes will be based on ten indicators, which are measurable and derived from international human rights standards and best practice.[22]

1 Political context, justice and accountability

Ideally, democratic elections and peace accords provide the transitional moment within which transitional justice is considered. However, most of the countries do not go through complete transitions that provide a total break with the past. Analysts indicate that in Kenya and other transitional societies, truth commission processes were undertaken while the systems and personalities associated with impunity remained unchanged:

> The politics of accommodation and the continued influence of such persons on the national stage render truth commissions ineffectual as mechanisms for countering impunity. In Kenya, the findings and recommendations of previous commissions implicating some of the people in the positions of influence were ignored thus raising the possibility or even likelihood of the TJRC findings/recommendations being equally ignored.[23]

This also points to the fact that all along the political elite in Kenya have been averse to the truth and justice agendas due to their possible complicity in the violations or crimes being targeted. This puts the TJRC and other transitional justice mechanisms into direct confrontation with perpetrators who still wield political and economic power. The confirmation of charges in January 2012 by the International Criminal Court (ICC) against four out of the six suspects[24] accused of having perpetrated the 2007–08 post-election violence has occasioned unnecessary political polarisation and mobilisation in Kenya. This has created two camps within the political class – those supporting versus those opposing the ICC process. This confirms the perception that most of the Kenyan political elite does not believe in justice and accountability.

2 Clarity of focus, mandate and timeframe

According to the United Nations *Tools on Truth Commissions*, the commission's mandate should in some areas be specific and relatively detailed, but it must remain flexible enough to allow interpretation and definition by the commissioners. In most cases, the commissions cover serious human rights abuses and sometimes, egregious economic crimes are added.

The terms of reference should also establish the start and end dates for the operation of the commission. These dates can be flexible, allowing for one or more extensions. Experience indicated that a period of one-and-a-half to two-and-a-half years of operation is generally desirable.[25]

A broad mandate enabled the Truth and Reconciliation Commission of South Africa to identify the systematic nature of the violations and abuses committed by the state and by opposition groups. However, such a broad mandate was criticised because it did not include some of the violations perpetrated by the apartheid regime (in particular forced removals).[26]

Kenya's TJRC has a mandate to investigate human rights violations and economic crimes committed between 12 December 1963 (independence day) and 28 February 2008 (the day the national accord was signed). The injustices committed before this period will be addressed as antecedents. It is one of a few commissions to be given the tripartite components of 'truth, justice and reconciliation'.[27]

While this mandate is clear and broad enough, it poses the challenge of focus and effectiveness for it makes the commission the home for virtually all the gravest injustices in Kenya's history. This happened because the act establishing the commission borrowed heavily from the TJRC agreement signed on 14 February 2008. This agreement had erroneously inherited the mandate proposed in the October 2003 task force report, which had recommended that all the past atrocities should be addressed by the TJRC because it was the first and the only major transitional process operating then. Moreover, the commission has spent most of its time fighting the credibility issues below, and may therefore not have had adequate time to realise the expectations of Kenyans.

3 Soundness of the legal framework

The legal framework establishing the commission (whether through legislation, presidential decree or other legal regime) should be progressive in its mandate, functions and other operational and policy issues and processes. There is also a need for related laws to be supportive and to work in tandem with the transitional justice mechanisms of the country in question. While this may be the case with Kenya's TJRC, some legal bottlenecks have been identified. First, the act provides for amnesty for various crimes including greed and corruption. Second, it has very weak provisions on reparations to victims. Finally, the Indemnity Act may be an obstacle especially in pursuing the perpetrators responsible for the atrocities committed in the Northern Frontier District in the 1960s.[28]

Responding to a petition submitted by the Kenya Transitional Justice Network (KTJN) on some of these flaws, the TJRC concurred as follows:

> With respect to the first flaw, we note that the Commission only has the power to recommend amnesty. This is of course, a weak power compared to the South African TRC, which had the power to grant amnesty for acts that included gross violation of human rights. With respect to the second one, the act only allows the Commission to recommend reparations. We agree with the network that this is a weak provision, though we note that this limited power to recommend reparations is no different than the reparation powers given to most, if not all, truth commissions, including the South African one.[29]

4 Political goodwill and financial and operational independence

A commission is likely to be more successful if there is a genuine political will for rigorous investigation and truth seeking. This entails access to public resources, allocation of adequate funds and the ability to carry out work without political interference. The TJRC Act provides for immunity of the commissioners, and the operational and financial independence of the commission.

In 2010, the commission used to complain of a lack of authority to incur expenditure, inadequate funds and other support from the state. However, in a 2011 report by the commission, Tecla Namachanja, the acting chair, pointed out that there is political goodwill on the part of the government, and the commission was financially comfortable. In a media briefing meeting held in February 2011, she argued thus: 'Our original budget was (K)sh1.2 billion. We have so far received (K)sh190 million and we expect an extra (K)sh500 million in the supplementary budget'.[30] Clearly, even this pledge was far below what had been budgeted for.

Finally, and in the final stages of its work, the commission is still facing calls from state and non-state actors for disbandment. The minister for justice, national cohesion and constitutional affairs has also advocated this a number of times. This is critical given that he is the minister responsible for policy matters affecting the commission.

5 Support from the victims, civil society and the international community

It is critical for truth commissions to garner the greatest public and international support across the board. Stakeholder consultation and liaison enables partners to build and sustain contacts from the beginning through to the end of the TJRC process.

According to the UN *Tools on Truth Commissions*, the very decision to establish a truth commission should be based on a broad consultative process to seek, in particular, the views of victims and survivors, and make clear the functions, strengths and limitations of the commission. This should enable the commission to enjoy widespread moral, financial and technical support from those partners. The TJRC has faced a number of challenges as regards support.

First, there were inadequate consultations during the initiation and institutionalisation of the TJRC project. This could be attributed to the need to fast track the reform and justice agenda after the post-election violence. This was also based on the erroneous assumption that Kenyans had already given their opinion during the 2003 task force hearings, but a number of amendments were required given the later political developments. Moreover, the TJRC has performed dismally in awareness creation and media mobilisation. The commission in its media updates on 21 December 2011

(*Daily Nation*) attributes this to lack of resources. This has partly contributed to its waning public support and attention.

Second, support from key actors within civil society has waned from 2010 to 2012 owing to the legal and credibility issues affecting the commission. For those years, we have witnessed a situation where key civil society and development organisations within the transitional justice sector have disengaged with the TJRC. During the National Dialogue Forum organised by the KTJN for the civil society and victim organisations on 3 September 2010, members said that:

> While acknowledging the democratic right of some victims to engage with the process, we the Kenya Transitional Justice Network, totally disengage with the TJRC until the credibility crisis has been resolved. We commit ourselves to pursue other options of truth, justice and reparations, including using the newly created Constitutional and Agenda 4 organs on historical injustices such as the National Land Commission, the National Human Rights and Equality Commission, the Kenya Anti Corruption and Integrity Commission and the revamped judiciary.[31]

The TJRC in its update to members of the public dated 16 December 2011 acknowledges that civil society groups, including women's groups, did not engage with the commission. As a result, the number of statements initially taken from women did not meet expectations.

The victims' organisations in Kenya are also divided in their support for the TJRC. While a group called the National Victims Network, with members mostly employed by the TJRC, is cooperative, another group under the auspices of Kenyans Against Impunity (KAI) went to court seeking the reconstitution of the commission due to what it called conflicts of interest among the commissioners and the flawed legal frameworks. KAI subsequently lost its case.

6 Competence, independence, accessibility

The membership of truth commissions is particularly important, indeed vital, for their effective functioning, as the actions and personal qualities of the commissioners frequently set the tone for the activities of the commission as a whole. Members of a truth commission should be selected on the basis of their competence in human rights, proven independence and recognised impartiality.

Moreover, and according to the United Nations *Tools on Truth Commissions*, 'ideally, these should be widely respected members of the society (or internationals) who are accepted as neutral by all sides of the conflict (or the group as whole should be seen to be representative of a fair range of views)'.[32]

The tools provide that a commission should take great care in hiring its staff, especially its most senior staff, as the politically sensitive environment will require sharp administrative and managerial skills, good political instincts and an ability to work effectively under great pressure. Finally, the commission should ensure effective public outreach and accessibility. Indeed, Section (20)(5)(a) of the TJRC Act provides that the commission shall, after its inauguration, inform the public of its existence and the purpose of its work.

The TJRC is composed of nine commissioners (six national and three international) with great professional and academic credentials on human rights, gender, justice, security reforms, peace and conflict among others. In the first three months, the commission successfully finalised its organisational structure and formulated policies, including a code of conduct for commissioners.[33] In September 2010, the Office of the High Commissioner for Human Rights (OHCHR) in Kenya, the Ministry of Justice, National Cohesion and Constitutional Affairs and the KTJN organised a training and orientation workshop for commissioners on what was expected of the operationalisation of the commission.

However, the biggest challenge has been the legitimacy and credibility crisis occasioned by questions around possible conflicts of interest among the commissioners and the alleged involvement of the commission's chair, Bethwel Kiplagat, in the past human rights violations. According to the different petitions developed by civil society, victims' organisations and the TJRC, Bethwel Kiplagat is accused of untruthfulness with regard to the murder of Robert Ouko; complicity in the Wagalla massacre; and the alleged grabbing of public property through illegal and irregular allocations.[34] On 19 April 2010 the commission's vice-chair, Betty Murungi, resigned, three days after the commission presented its petition to the chief justice, calling for the investigation of the chair. On 29 October 2010, the chief justice established a tribunal to investigate these allegations against Kiplagat but it remained moribund until 10 February 2011. Kiplagat finally resigned on 5 November 2010.

The Kenya National Commission on Human Rights observes thus:

> Before the tribunal could embark on its work, Kiplagat challenged its jurisdiction. The tribunal ruled against him. He however proceeded to file an application in the High Court in Miscellaneous Civil Application No. 95 of 2011 where he sought an injunction to bar the tribunal from inquiring into his conduct. The court issued a stay preventing the tribunal from investigating him. It was during the life of the latter suit that the tribunal's mandate lapsed by reason of effluxion of time. Kiplagat then voluntarily withdrew his petition in December 2011. In January 2012, the TJRC filed a judicial review application seeking to compel the CJ to establish a tribunal to investigate Mr. Kiplagat and to bar him from undertaking any duties as chairperson. The TJRC's application was dismissed in February 2012. An appeal is pending in court.[35]

The commissioners within the TJRC have vowed to legally and administratively block his return and the operations at the commission pending the resolution of these issues.

These developments have created three problems for the commission. First, we have a commission struggling to proceed and conclude with its work when its chair is the subject of investigation by a related truth-telling process. Second, there are fears that Kiplagat may interfere with the final stages of the commission's work given that the he is alleged to be among the perpetrators. Third, the resignation of both the commission's chair and vice-chair may have deprived the commission of a much-needed quorum in committees and hearings in addition to expertise in peace and conflict (Kiplagat) and gender and human rights (Murungi). The fourth problem is the lack of support from the key state and non-state actors, as indicated earlier in this chapter.

On staffing, the December 2010 report by the commission indicates that the TJRC has established eight departments, each headed by a director, and has recruited 77 staff members of the projected 101, which puts the commission's strength at approximately 78 per cent. The TJRC has further recruited, trained and deployed countrywide 305 statement-taking officials and set up regional offices in Mombasa, Garissa, Kisumu and Eldoret, each headed by a regional coordinator.

Moreover, hearings have generally gone well, starting with individual sessions in every region, before institutional and thematic hearings are conducted. The commission was expected to submit its final report in 3 November 2011, two years after it started its work.[36]

A number of glaring challenges have emerged. First, it is clear that the commission is completely behind schedule: it sought and received a six months extension in November 2011. Second, it is facing staffing (a 22 per cent shortfall), outreach and accessibility challenges owing to its inadequate credibility and resources. Finally, many questions have been raised about the quality of the statements taken so far.

According to the statement released by Bethwel Kiplagat at his resignation, at least 5,000 statements had been taken. In a statement released by the commission's acting chair, Tecla Namachanja, on 2 December 2010, barely a month later, she averred thus:

> So far, over 10,000 statements have been recorded and about 71 memoranda received, and the process will continue until the end of January 2011 when TJRC will have had direct engagement with at least 30,000 Kenyans through the statement-taking process.[37]

By January 2011, the statements had doubled to over 20,000. According to the *Daily Nation*[38] the statements received by 16 December 2011 included 23,853 from male victims, 14,878 from female victims, with 39,286 statements received in total.

Logically and practically, it was virtually impossible to collect 5,000 quality statements in a month given the operational, financial and political constraints facing the TJRC. Statement taking determines the most critical stages of truth seeking for it forms the basis for further research, investigations and the determination of window cases for hearings. As a result, civil society observed:

113

The statement-taking process by the TJRC has outrightly been found wanting, incompetent, compromised and not credible hence cannot form a basis for public hearings. Public hearings based on the statements with the TJRC shall lead to double jeopardy on the part of victims whose expectations shall be raised to no avail.[39]

7 Mechanisms to support victims, witnesses and alleged perpetrators

A truth commission is expected to be victim-centred. This entails providing victims with opportunities to tell their story, treating them with humanity and dignity, providing them with effective protection, and ensuring support and special units for witnesses, child victims, victims of sexual violence, persons with disabilities and other vulnerable groups.[40] A truth commission should also provide a fair procedure in which alleged perpetrators and individuals can participate. Principle 10 of the UN basic principles on the right to a remedy and reparation states:

Victims should be treated with humanity and respect for their dignity and human rights, and appropriate measures should be taken to ensure their safety, physical and psychological well-being and privacy, as well as those of their families. The State should ensure that its domestic laws, to the extent possible, provide that a victim who has suffered violence or trauma should benefit from special consideration and care to avoid his or her re-traumatisation in the course of legal and administrative procedures designed to provide justice and reparation.[41]

It is important to note that there has been good progress on the arrangements to support the vulnerable victims and to provide training to commissioners to equip them with skills and information to enable them to effectively communicate with victims. However, the following gaps have yet to be addressed, thus creating a major threat to the work of the TJRC. First, is the lack of a witness protection programme. According to the TJRC, the problem of witness protection does not lie with the powers granted to the commission, but rather with the limitations of state capacity. While the TJRC plans to work with the Kenya National

Commission on Human Rights (KNCHR) to address this gap, this creates other fears given the allegations by the suspects who are being investigated by the ICC that they are in frequent contact with the witnesses being hosted by the KNCHR.

Second, it is on public record that the TJRC hired many victims to be statement takers, among other roles. While this may be good for according victims opportunities to engage, drive the justice agenda, grow professionally and benefit economically, it may compromise the quality and outcome of the process. This may give the suspected perpetrators a feeling that the process was prejudicial, unfair and geared towards victor's justice for victims. While the commission holds that it has put measures in place to militate against the possibility of subjectivity, negative perceptions on the credibility of the process may persist.[42]

Finally, the fact the commission is yet to develop a comprehensive framework for reparations and amnesty may occasion compromises on justice for both the victims and perpetrators.

8 Coordination with other transitional justice and reform processes

According to the *UN Tools on Truth Commissions*, truth commissions are only one part of a comprehensive transitional justice strategy, and should be considered together with other initiatives such as prosecutions, reparations, vetting and other accountability and reform programmes. Wachira and Kamungi[43] add to this debate by observing that truth commissions have been established rather casually in post-conflict or newly democratised societies without due consideration being accorded to the unique justice and reconciliation needs of such societies and with little regard for ongoing state and extra-state reforms and reconciliation processes. This approach risks intercepting and displacing ongoing, locally driven processes while raising expectations that the truth commission eventually cannot fulfil.

While Kenya's TJRC was established alongside commissions and accountability processes under Agenda Item 4 of the National Accord (February 2008) and the August 2010 Kenya constitution, its broad mandate seems to cut across other institutions, thus the need for clarity, specificity and complementarity. For instance, the

TJRC substantially overlaps with the National Cohesion and Integration Commission (on aspects of reconciliation), the Ethics and Anti-Corruption Commission (EACC) (on economic crimes), the Land Ministry and Commissioner, expected to be replaced with the National Land Commission (NLC), (on land grabbing and injustices), the KNCHR (on broad human rights violations), the courts (over finalised and pending cases brought by victims) and the ICC (on the post-election violence, especially on the February 2008 deadline).

This raises the following issues: 'the fact that the TJRC is operating at the same time as some of these issues are being addressed … suggests poor sequencing and lack of a distinctive and realistic role of a truth commission. Therefore the question: What is the unique role that only a truth commission can best fulfill?'[44]

Thus, while the commission has strived to partner with the relevant ministries and commissions, there is a need to ensure an effective coordination that guarantees forward and backward linkages on related thematic issues and processes.

9 Absence of ongoing conflict, other security threats and repressive acts

Truth commissions are expected to operate in a context where there have been adequate changes of attitude and systems of governance. However, save for some of the policy, legal and institutional reforms in the implementation of the 2010 constitution the culture of impunity in Kenya reigns supreme. This is partly attributed to retrogressive values, practices and mindsets which are not in tandem with the ongoing or envisaged reforms.

10 Implementing the recommendations of the commission's report[45]

To avoid secrecy and non-implementation of the truth commission reports, the constituting act has provided a clear schedule for the publication, implementation, and monitoring and evaluation processes. Section 48 of the TJRC Act provides that the commission will submit a report of its work to the president at the end of its operations.

The report will summarise the findings of the commission

and make recommendations for reforms in various sectors; prosecutions; reparations for the victims; and the mechanisms and framework for the implementation of its recommendations. Upon submitting the report to the president, the commission will publish the report in the official gazette and make copies of the report and summary widely available to the public in at least three local newspapers with wide circulation.

On the implementation and other follow-up processes, sections 49–50 of the act provide that the minister for justice and constitutional affairs will operationalise the implementation mechanism six months after the report is published. The implementation committee will publish the reports of the government in the appropriate form and submit its own quarterly report to the public evaluating the progress made. The minister will report to the National Assembly within three months of receipt of the report of the commission, and twice a year as to its implementation. The National Assembly can also require the minister to furnish it with the reasons for any non-implementation.

While the law is clear on this process, the main challenge could arise from the quality of the report given the constraints highlighted above and the limited time between the conclusion of the hearings and the finalisation of the report. Moreover, the implementation of the recommendations may be frustrated by the vested interests of those in power.

Recommendations

Acknowledging and atoning for the systemic abuse of human rights and for the violation of international humanitarian law is arguably one of the most controversial, complex and unpredictable processes undertaken by citizens in societies transitioning from a violent past.[46]

A number of issues emerge from these discussions.

First, the political systems in Africa are mostly responsible for the gross human rights violations and economic crimes which have bedevilled the continent for more than a century.

Second, truth commissions tend to be the commonest transitional justice instruments for dealing with these acts of impunity. The question is whether they are really the best option.

Third, where the truth either seems to be available or have been captured in other forms through other official or unofficial truth-telling projects, the questions remains about what would have been the best entry point, for example for Kenya's TJRC.

Fourth, while we have the international human rights standards and best practices on truth commissions, there has been very little to apply and contextualise them and ensure proper sequencing or complementarity with other reforms and justice and accountability processes available nationally and internationally.

Finally, Kenya seems to have squandered a golden opportunity to learn from the mistakes committed by the other more than 30 truth commissions in the world.

Based on these issues, I would suggest several recommendations.

I advocate strengthening the protection and support mechanisms for the victims, witnesses and perpetrators within the current work of the TJRC. For whether the process is effective or not, this is a critical human rights obligation for all actors.

Moreover, and since Kenya's TJRC has moved on, albeit under many constraints, there is a need to assess the veracity of its findings and recommendations and ensure implementation. However, given the potential gaps to its work, there is a need to have the National Cohesion and Integration Commission, the NLC, KNCHR, EACC, ICC, courts and civil society (especially through the National Victims Network and KTJN) among other actors to conduct further investigations and ensure timely response and remedies over both the past and emerging violations.

Related to this is a need for having a clear transtional justice matrix or roadmap for our countries and region. While the Agenda Item 4 matrix to the national accord and the constitution of Kenya provide the general policy framework on transtional justice, the national trajectory is still unclear. A national roadmap will help to sequence and coordinate the related processes at all levels.

We advocate the adoption of the regional convention on truth commissions or other forms of remedies. This has happened before, for example when the African Union adopted the UN Guiding Principles on Internally Displaced People into a regional convention.

We should conduct a study of the other possible options for truth telling and seeking in Africa, which could replace, complement or precede truth commissions or the intervention of the ICC.

In future, we should ensure that all the legal and operational frameworks relating to truth commissions and other transitional justice interventions are above board. The policy and legal framework should be a product of genuine and legitimate consultations with the state and non-state actors (including victims). Operationally, such bodies should have adequate funding and extremely competent, committed and credible commissioners and staff. Commissioners and senior staff should be appointed through a thorough and stringent public vetting process. There should be room to have such officers removed from public offices if information is found over any past questionable practices.

Finally, we need to adopt what pundits call the 'justice balance' approach in the entire truth-telling project. According to Tricia D. Olsen and colleagues:

> A justice balance approach assumes that truth commissions on their own tend not to achieve human rights goals as a result of the imbalances they introduce. On their own, truth commissions tend to emphasise either accountability or impunity. Accountability alone can jeopardise stability, a crucial factor for the transition from authoritarian rule. Impunity meanwhile fails to create the legal framework, political and moral environment necessary to deter future human rights violations.[47]

Thus, combined with amnesties and trials, truth commissions can achieve human rights by promoting a balance between stability and accountability. Sequencing within a comprehensive national transitional programme or roadmap is critical.

Notes

1 S.N. Anderlini, C.P. Conaway and L. Kays (2004) 'Transitional justice and reconciliation', in International Alert and Women Waging Peace, *Inclusive Security, Sustainable Peace: A Toolkit for Advocacy and Action,* Washington and London, Hunt Alternatives Fund and International Alert: 2.

2 The term 'truth commission' here includes truth, justice and reconciliation commissions (TJRC) and/or truth and reconciliation commissions (TRC).

3 Amnesty International (2007) *Truth, Justice and Reparations: Establishing an Effective Truth Commission,* London, Amnesty International.

4 D. Orentlicher (2005) *Updated Set of Principles for the Protection and Promotion of Human Rights Through Action to Combat Impunity, Addendum*

to the Report of the Independent Expert to update the Set of Principles to Combat Impunity, Geneva, Office of the United Nations High Commissioner for Human Rights: 6.

5 P. Hayner (2003) 'The truth commission as an institution for transitional justice: lessons and challenges from other countries', a presentation in Nairobi, Kenya at a conference hosted by Transparency International-Kenya and the Kenyan Human Rights Commission: 3–4.

6 Louis Bickford (2005) 'Unofficial truth projects (draft)': 4–5, subsequently published at http://www.zarekom.org/uploads/documents/2010/11/i_182/f_10/f_105_0.pdf, accessed 15 March 2012.

7 See the United Nations General Assembly *Basic Principles and Guidelines on the Right to a Remedy and Reparations for Victims of Gross Human Rights and Serious Violations of International Humanitarian Law; Updated United Nations Principles for the Protection and Promotion of Human Rights through Actions to Combat Impunity*; Office of the United Nations High Commissioner for Human Rights (OHCHR) (2006) *Rule of Law Tools for Post-Conflict Societies: Truth Commissions*, Geneva, OHCHR; and the Human Rights Commission Resolution 2005/66 on the Right to Truth; and precedent on the right to know, truth and information as established by international human rights bodies including the Inter-American Court on Human Rights.

8 This also includes the realisation of the broad objectives of the transitional justice programmes for ending the culture of impunity, and establishing the rule of law in the context of democratic governance.

9 Kenya National Dialogue and Reconciliation (mediated by H.E. Kofi Annan, Chair of the Panel of Eminent African Personalities) (July 30, 2008) 'Statement of Principles on Long-term issues and solutions': 4, http://tinyurl.com/c3tubkh, accessed 11 April 2012.

10 D. Easton (1953) *The Political System*, New York, Alfred A.Knopf.

11 D. Easton (1965) *A Framework for Political Analysis*, Englewood Cliffs, NJ, Prentice Hall: 50.

12 United Nations Development Programme (UNDP) (1997) *Governance and Sustainable Development*, New York, UNDP: 2–3.

13 D. Malombe, D. Kawira and K. Chadianya (2011) *Lest We Forget: The Faces of Impunity in Kenya*, Nairobi, Kenya Human Rights Commission: 8–10.

14 Amnesty international (2007). The ones in Africa are: Burundi (International Commission of Inquiry, 1995); Chad (Commission of Inquiry on the Crimes and Misappropriations Committed by the ex-President Habré, his Accomplices and/or Accessories, 1991); Democratic Republic of Congo (Truth and Reconciliation Commission, 2003); Ghana (National Reconciliation Commission, 2002); Liberia (Truth and Reconciliation Commission, 2005); Kenya (Truth and Justice Commission, 2008); Morocco (Equity and Reconciliation Commission, 2004); Nigeria (Human Rights Violations Investigation Commission, 1999); Sierra Leone (Truth and Reconciliation Commission, 2002); South Africa (Truth and Reconciliation Commission, 1995); Togo (Truth, Justice

and Reconciliation Commission, 2008); Uganda (Commission of Inquiry into the Disappearance of People in Uganda, 1974, and Commission of Inquiry into Violations of Human Rights, 1986); Zimbabwe (Commission of Inquiry, 1985).

15 J. Quinn (2004) 'Constraints: the un-doing of the Ugandan Truth Commission', *Human Rights Quarterly*, 26(2): 401–27.

16 L. Bickford (2005): 3.

17 Africa's Centre for Open Governance (AfriCOG) (2008) *Commissions of Inquiry in Kenya: Seekers of Truth or Safety Valves*, Nairobi, AfriCOG.

18 1913 – The Native Labour Commission, 1914 – The Coconut Commission, 1919 – The Land Settlement Commission, 1921 – The Public Works Department Commission, 1950 – The Kenya Meat Commission, 1956 – The Nairobi City Council Commission, 1959 – The Television Commission, 1959 – The Teachers Salaries Commission, 1962 – The Economic Commission, 1963 – The National Anthem Commission, 1963 – The Lutta Commission, 1964 – The Ominde Commission, 1965 – The Maize Commission, 1967 – Agricultural Education Commission, 1967 – The Muller Craig Commission, 1967 – The Commission of Inquiry into the Law of Marriage and Divorce, 1967 – The Commission on the Law of Succession, 1971 – The Ndegwa Commission, 1974 – The Commission on the Law of Adoption, 1980 – The Waruhiu Commission, 1984 – The Miller Commission, 1990 – The Gicheru Commission, 1994 – The Commission of Inquiry into the Cult of Devil Worship in Kenya, 1994 – The Mtongwe Ferry Disaster Commission, 1998 – The Akiwumi Commission, 1998 – The Davy Koech Commission, 1999 – Commission of Inquiry into the Land Law Systems of Kenya, 2003 – The Bosire Commission, 2003 – The Commission of Inquiry into the Illegal and Irregular Allocation of Public Land, 2003 – The Ndung'u Commission, 2003 – The Muthoga Commission, 2006 – The Kiruki Commission.

19 AfriCOG (2008).

20 The Annotated Agenda and Timetable for the National Dialogue and Reconciliation, signed on 1 February 2008, recognised that poverty, the inequitable distribution of resources and perceptions of historical injustices and exclusion on the part of segments of Kenyan society constituted the underlying causes of the prevailing social tensions, instability and cycle of violence.

21 The KNDR was negotiated under four agenda items: (1) immediate action to stop violence and restore fundamental rights and liberties; (2) immediate measures to address the humanitarian crisis, promote reconciliation and healing; (3) how to overcome the political crisis; (4) long-term issues and solutions (including constitutional, legal and institutional reform; tackling poverty, inequity and regional development imbalances; tackling unemployment, particularly among the youth; consolidating national cohesion and unity; undertaking land reform; and addressing transparency, accountability and impunity).

22 George Wachira and Prisca Kamungi (2010) *Noble Intentions, Nagging*

Dilemmas: In the Context – Responsive Truth Commissions in Africa, Nairobi, Nairobi Peace Initiative (NPI-Africa), International Development Research Centre (IDRC) and West African Network for Peace Building (WANEP): 2–3; Amnesty International (2007); OHCHR (2006).

23 Ibid: 2–3.

24 These are the six individuals being investigated by the ICC (popularly referred to as the 'Ocampo Six', the name of the ICC prosecutor being Louis Moreno Ocampo) over their possible role during post-election violence. They are Hon Henry Kosgei, Ambassador Francis Muthaura, Major General Hussein Ali, Hon Uhuru Kenyatta, Hon William Ruto and Joshua Arap Sang (a journalist). For details see: International Criminal Court, Pre-Trial Chamber II, 'Decision(s) on the Prosecutor's Application for Summons to Appear for William Samoei Ruto, Henry Kiprono Kosgei and Joshua Arap Sang; and Francis Kirimi Muthaura, Uhuru Muigai Kenyatta and Mohammed Hussein Ali, Nos, ICC-01/09-01/11 and ICC-01/09-02/11-March 8, 2011'. While the PNU side of the government supports a deferral of the case and a local tribunal, the ODM is for referral to the ICC.

25 OHCHR (2006): 8–9 (see note 7).

26 Amnesty International (2007): 15 (see note 3).

27 Government of Kenya (2008) The Truth, Justice and Reconciliation Commission Act: 6–16.

28 The NFD, currently North Eastern province and the adjacent districts which include Lamu, Isiolo, Tana River and Marsabit, wanted to break away and join Somalia, for the residents felt their interests were not addressed by the post-independence government. Many violations were committed by the military against the local people who wanted to secede. Since then, the region has experienced other violations in the form of systemic exclusions and massacres.

29 Truth, Justice and Reconciliation Commission (2011) 'Re: KTJN statement on TJRC of 31 January 2011': 4. See also Kenya Transitional Justice Network (KTJN) (2011) 'Civil society calls for re-engineering of the truth seeking process in Kenya', 31 January: 1–2.

30 Stephen Makabila (2011) 'TJRC: Besieged commission struggles to beat its deadline', *The Standard*, 8 February.

31 Kenya Transitional Justice Network (KTJN) (2010) 'Communiqué from the 3rd National Dialogue Forum on the Truth, Justice and Reconciliation at the Kenyatta International Conference Centre, 2–3 September'. It is important to underscore the fact that some civil society organisations have been working with the TJRC. This dichotomy occasioned a parallel press conference at the dialogue forum.

32 OHCHR (2006): 13 (see note 7).

33 The national commissioners are Bethwel Kiplagat (chair), Betty Murungi (former vice-chair, since resigned), Tecla Namachanja (vice-chair and acting chair), Margaret Wambui Shava, Major General (rtd) Ahmed Sheikh Farah and Tom Ojienda. The international commissioners are Gertrude Chawatama (Zambia), Berhanu Dinka (Ethiopia) and Ronald Slye (US).

34 Dr Robert Ouko was a minister of foreign affairs who was murdered in February 1990. At the time of his death, Kiplagat was his permanent secretary. A parliamentary select committee established to investigate the murder in 2003 recommended that Kiplagat be investigated. The Wagalla massacre took place at Wajir airstrip in February 1984 and Kiplagat is alleged to have attended the meeting which approved the murder. The events in which the chair is alleged to have been involved form part of the mandate of the TJRC. Civil society organisations and victims have petitioned the government a number of times to establish a tribunal in order to investigate the alleged conduct of the chair. The TJRC presented its petition to the Chief Justice asking for the said tribunal.

35 Kenya National Commission on Human Rights (KNCHR) (2012) 'Legal Opinion to Advice Removal of Kiplagat from the TJRC Process', March: 1.

36 TJRC (2010) 'Briefing Note from Truth, Justice and Reconciliation Commission to the Kenya National Dialogue and Reconciliation (KNDR), Two Years on: Where are we?', 2–3 December at the Crown Plaza Hotel, Nairobi: 2.

37 TJRC (2010): 4.

38 *Daily Nation* (2011) 'Engendering the Truth, Justice and Reconciliation Commission of Kenya – keeping the promise', 23 December: 38.

39 KTJN (2011): 1 (see note 29).

40 Section 27 of the TJRC provides for the establishment of special units.

41 'Basic Principles and Guidelines on the Right to a Remedy and Reparation for Victims of Gross Violations of International Human Rights Law and Serious Violations of International Humanitarian Law', adopted and proclaimed by UN General Assembly resolution 60/147 of 16 December 2005.

42 The commission argues in its 3 March 2011 rejoinder to civil society that it has focused on the victims who qualify for support; it has a code of code of conduct concerning confidentiality, bias, professionalism and integrity; and has adopted a policy where any person who is uncomfortable speaking to a particular commission official (whether that commission official is a victim or not) may ask to speak to another person.

43 Wachira and Kamungi (2010) (see note 22).

44 Wachira and Kamungi (2010): 4 (see note 22).

45 OHCHR (2006). Section 25 of the TJRC Act also provides for protection of victims, witnesses and perpetrators especially during the hearings of the commission, for instance through in-camera hearings. The Witness Protection Act provides for the Witness Protection Programme through the Office of the Attorney General.

46 Colleen Duggan (2010) 'Editorial note', *The International Journal of Transitional Justice*, 4(3): 315.

47 Tricia D. Olsen, Leigh A. Payne, Andrew G. Reiter and Eric Wiebelhaus-Brahm (2010) 'When truth commissions improve human rights', *The International Journal of Transitional Justice*, 4(3): 469.

6

Transitional justice and human rights in Africa

Christine Alai

Defining human rights and transitional justice

Human rights are entitlements that every human being possesses by virtue of being human; they are derived from the inherent dignity of being human and apply regardless of sex, national or ethnic origin, race, colour, religion, language or any other status.[1]

The International Centre for Transitional Justice defines transitional justice[2] as a response to systematic or widespread violations of human rights which often occur in the context of authoritarian regimes and/or civil strife. Transitional justice seeks recognition for victims of violations and to promote possibilities for peace, reconciliation and democracy. Transitional justice is not a special form of justice but rather justice adapted to societies transforming themselves after a period of pervasive human rights abuse. In some cases, these transformations happen suddenly; in others, they may take place over many decades. Looked at from a holistic perspective, transitional justice is both backward and forward looking; it seeks to ensure accountability for past abuses while guaranteeing their non-recurrence.

Some of the transitional justice approaches that have been adopted by governments include criminal prosecutions, truth seeking, reparation programmes, and the reform of key institutions including the security sector and the judiciary.

Linkage between transitional justice and human rights

Transitional justice's core concern is to seek accountability and redress for systemic or widespread human rights abuses. It is one of the tools that could be used to advance the protection and realisation of human rights, albeit within a political transitional context.

Transitional justice can be characterised as a right in itself. Today, the concept of transitional justice has gained significant recognition in international law. Noteworthy is the 1988 decision of the Inter-American Court of Human Rights in the case of *Velasquez Rodriguez vs Honduras*[3] in which the court found that all states have four fundamental obligations in the area of human rights:

- To take reasonable steps to prevent human rights violations
- To conduct a serious investigation of violations when they occur
- To impose suitable sanctions on those responsible for the violations
- To ensure reparation for the victims of the violations.

These principles have been explicitly affirmed by later decisions of the Inter-American Court of Human Rights and endorsed in decisions by the European Court of Human Rights, and United Nations treaty body decisions such as the Human Rights Committee (under the International Covenant on Civil and Political Rights). The Rome Statute, which established the International Criminal Court, also enshrines state obligations of vital importance to the fight against impunity and respect for victims' rights.

Transitional justice has at its heart the recognition of victims' right to a remedy. This right is espoused in the *United Nations Basic Principles and Guidelines on the Right to a Remedy and Reparation for Gross Violations of International Human Rights Law and Serious Violations of International Humanitarian Law*.[4] The guidelines entrench victims' right to:

- Equal and effective access to justice
- Adequate, effective and prompt reparation for harm suffered
- Access to relevant information concerning violations and reparation mechanisms.

The Universal Declaration of Human Rights (Article 8) provides for victims' right to an effective remedy by competent national tribunals for acts violating the fundamental rights granted by the constitution or by law. This right is echoed and further entrenched in various core regional and international human rights instruments including:

- The International Covenant on Civil and Political Rights – Article 2(3)
- The African Charter on Human and Peoples' Rights – Article 7(a)
- The Rome Statute
- The Protocol to the African Charter on Human and Peoples' Rights on the Rights of Women in Africa (Maputo Protocol) – Articles 4 and 25
- Nairobi Declaration on Women's and Girls' Right to a Remedy and Reparation
- African Commission on Human and Peoples' Rights Resolution on the Right to a Remedy and Reparation for Women and Girl Victims of Sexual Violence

Transitional justice aims to promote opportunities for peace, reconciliation and democracy which provide an enabling environment for the protection and realisation of human rights. The interrelationship between democracy and human rights was aptly articulated by Thomas Jefferson at the declaration of America's independence in 1776 when he stated that:

> [W]e hold these truths to be self evident, that all Men are created equal, that they are endowed by their Creator with certain unalienable Rights, that among these are life, liberty and the pursuit of happiness – That *to secure these Rights, Governments are instituted among Men, deriving their just powers from the consent of the governed* [i.e. through democracy – my emphasis].

Dictatorships or states experiencing retrogression in democratisation neither adhere to the democratic principles of popular control and political equity, thereby violating fundamental freedoms, nor do they create democratic institutions to guard against corruption, malfeasance, mismanagement and waste of public resources, all of which grossly hinder the realisation of socio-economic rights.

The protection of human rights can only be guaranteed within a state that possesses some level of democratic governance which creates room for transparency, accountability, inclusiveness and respect for the rule of law – all tenets of good governance and democracy which transitional justice aims to achieve.[5]

Moreover, accountability for past abuses and injustices in the context of transitional justice contributes to the consolidation of democracy by restoring confidence in its institutions.

Key challenges and considerations in Africa

The concept of transitional justice has its genesis in the political changes experienced in Latin America and Eastern Europe in the late 1980s and early 1990s. At the time, human rights activists sought to address the systematic human rights abuses by former regimes without endangering the political transformations that were underway. However, this concept seems to be evolving somewhat as we witness instances of transition – from authoritarian regimes and civil war to more peaceful societies – but with few political make-overs, thus limiting the potential of transitional justice measures and in effect, the comprehensive protection of human rights (drawing on the earlier discussion of the correlation between transitional justice and human rights).

One critical question that emerges from such a context is how to address past abuses when perpetrators still wield considerable political power, as has often been the case in many transitioning states in Africa. It is imperative for transitional governments to appreciate that they not only have obligations to desist from perpetuating abuses or to stop ongoing conflict but to also undertake measures to improve the state of human rights protection by ensuring accountability and institutional reforms.

Paige Arthur in discussing various transitional contexts asserts that states encounter a similar challenge as they attempt to move from dictatorial to democratic systems of governance – 'in essence, the question of what to do with the former torturers in their midst'.[6] She cites the Argentine case, noting that there the questions raised:

> were not only of justice: Whom to punish, by what authority, and on what grounds? What to do for victims and their loved ones? Rather, they were questions about justice and prudence; balancing competing moral imperatives; reconciling legitimate claims for justice with equally legitimate claims for stability and social peace; and the relationship between fostering justice for crimes of the past and fostering a more just political order in the present.[7]

One of the common measures adopted to address this dilemma has been the provision of amnesties for rebel or military groups in order to maintain peace. Amnesty has been the brokering factor in the cessation of civil conflicts in Burundi,[8] Côte d'Ivoire,[9] Sierra Leone,[10] and northern Uganda[11] and was also applied in post-apartheid South African to facilitate disclosure. While in some cases international crimes, and human rights and humanitarian law violations have been excluded from the ambit of the amnesties, the provision of protection for past perpetrators has in several instances violated victims' right to remedy and negated accountability for past abuses.

The use of traditional justice measures can raise the thorny issue of universality versus cultural relativism.[12] All transitional justice approaches are based on a fundamental belief in the universality of human rights, so every society must take its own transitional path. However, this should not occasion further injustices or perpetuate violations.

In charting context-specific measures, some communities have opted to adopt traditional justice measures such as the Timor-Leste Commission for Reception, Truth and Reconciliation (CAVR), the Rwanda *gacaca* courts and traditional cleansing ceremonies such as the *mat oput* in northern Uganda. While these measures ease the strain on the formal justice system, particularly in the case of petty offences, in some cases they have perpetuated violations against women and further entrenched impunity: for instance in cases where women are considered as inferior within a cultural context and therefore receive lower reparation for violations.[13] Furthermore, traditional approaches have not previously been applied in the context of mass atrocities and therefore lack the capacity to fuse traditional approaches from varied cultures and/or to address gross violations such as sexual slavery.

It is often the case that in many transitions, emphasis is laid on criminal accountability for past violations with little regard for the underlying causes or impact of the violations.

Furthermore, transitional justice has tended to focus on civil and political rights as well as individual victims and perpetrators, thus failing to interrogate the systems that enable violations to occur. In South Africa, for example, the Truth and Reconciliation Commission failed to interrogate apartheid as a system of governance and its contribution to human rights violations so treating perpetrators as violators within a normal system whereas apartheid had been declared a crime against humanity several years earlier.[14]

This is of great concern in Africa where most conflicts have been triggered by despotic regimes and underlying grievances that remain unaddressed for decades. Systemic discrimination and social inequalities, disregard for the rule of law, blatant abuse of rights, access to justice only for the highest bidder, use of political office as a repressive tool, and flawed elections are some of the underlying factors that have triggered and exacerbated social tension in virtually every conflict-afflicted country in the continent.

Louise Arbour, the former UN high commissioner for human rights, underscores the imperative of addressing the underlying causes of violence and states that 'given transitional justice's additional objective of bringing about social transformation that will prevent resurgence of conflict, it is not only important to build dispute-resolution institutions, but even more effective to attack sources of legitimate grievances, that if unaddressed, are likely to fuel the next conflagration'.[15]

Moreover, there needs to be greater focus on the impact of violations, especially given the limited reach of formal reparation mechanisms. In South Africa, for instance, the definition of victims who were entitled to reparations excluded dependants and recognised family members only of deceased individuals, paying no attention to the impact of, for example, detention on the family members of detained victims. In Sierra Leone, the truth commission recommended reparation programmes for sexually violated victims but overlooked the plight of children conceived out of sexual violence. In countries emerging from conflict, such as in Sierra Leone, perpetrators seem to receive preferential consideration over victims as they benefit from demobilisation packages while victims have to wait for years before the initiation of reparation programmes.

Notes

1 Civil, political, economic, social and cultural rights are protected in various core human rights instruments including the 1948 Universal Declaration of Human Rights, and the International Covenants of Civil and Political Rights, and Economic, Social and Cultural Rights, both adopted in 1966.
2 See the ICTJ website: www.ictj.org.
3 IACtHR *Velasquez vs Rodriguez* (Compensatory Damages), 21 July 1989 (Ser. C, No. 7, case No. 7920).
4 Adopted through the UN General Assembly Resolution 60/147, on 16 December 2005.
5 Crises occasioned and/or exacerbated by a lack of accountability for or impunity from past abuses, for instance in Darfur, Somalia, Northern Uganda and Kenya's 2007 election-related violence, among several other instances around the African continent, all attest to this fact.
6 Arthur, P. (2009) 'How "transitions" reshaped human rights: a conceptual history of transitional justice', *Human Rights Quarterly*, 31(2): 321–67.
7 Ibid: 323.
8 Burundi Arusha Accord on Peace and Reconciliation (2000).
9 Côte d'Ivoire Linas-Marcoussis Agreement (2003).
10 Sierra Leone Lome Peace Agreement (1999).
11 Uganda Amnesty Act (2000).
12 Cultural relativism is the view that all beliefs, customs and norms are relative to individuals within their own social context; what is considered moral in one society may be considered immoral in another. It is distinct from a universal acceptance of norms regardless of social, religious or cultural context.
13 For instance among the Somalis, a person who kills a man is obliged to pay his family 100 head of camel while a woman's death attracts 50 camels.
14 As early as 1966, the United Nations General Assembly had passed a resolution (2202 AXXI of 16 December 1966) considering apartheid as a crime against humanity. The General Assembly later adopted the International Convention on the Suppression and Punishment of the Crime of Apartheid on 30 November 1973, which came into force on 18 July 1976.
15 Statement made at the 2nd Annual Transitional Justice Lecture hosted by the New York University School of Law Centre for Human Rights & Global Justice and the International Centre for Transitional Justice, 25 October 2006.

7

The nexus between forced displacement and transitional justice

Lucy Hovil

This chapter explores the relationship between forced displacement and transitional justice – two distinct yet closely connected areas of study. Given the huge scope of such an exploration, it focuses primarily on the Great Lakes region, where civil and international conflicts have uprooted millions from their homes and forced them into exile for years or even decades.

To date, the two 'fields' of forced migration and transitional justice have remained largely disconnected from each other[1] – certainly in practice if not in theory. This disconnect is concerning given that both focus on the fall-out from conflict, war or other human rights abuses and both are concerned with addressing the political implications of conflict, at least at a theoretical level. Displacement is a consequence of the violence that transitional justice processes seek to address, and it can also become a cause of future violence if not dealt with properly. Indeed, a significant indicator of a successful transition is one in which displaced persons can not only safely return home, but in which future displacement is prevented. In any context of widespread displacement, therefore, transition needs to actively incorporate mechanisms by which a community, a country or a region moves from a period of instability and conflict to a sustainable level of peace and stability such that people are able to return to their homes.

While good in theory, however, in practice relatively little thought – or certainly little action – has been given to how, in reality, the two interact: displaced populations rarely participate in the negotiation of transitional justice mechanisms and are often on the margins of the process. This is partly due to logistical con-straints – their physical absence is a factor if not an excuse – and partly a reflection of a broader lack of engagement of the general conflict-affected population regardless of whether they have been displaced. In particular, it reflects the way in which refugees and internally displaced people (IDPs) are perceived as primarily a humanitarian problem that can be fixed with adequate aid money rather than a political issue that deserves political resolution.

As a result of this failure to place issues of justice and the broader political implications of displacement within the param-eters of so-called protection – both during displacement and in the implementation of durable solutions – displaced populations rarely participate in the negotiation of transitional justice mecha-nisms. Instead, rebel factions and political parties, who may or may not represent the views of these communities, are often the ones whose voices are heard in any negotiations.

Consequently, transitional justice mechanisms can easily move forward without adequate buy-in from displaced communities – or, worse, can inadvertently harm displaced groups. This, in turn, jeopardises the wider success of any process of transitional justice, which, after all, can be judged at least in part by the extent to which it has the support of those who are its supposed benefi-ciaries and the degree of inclusiveness of a process that seeks to break cycles of marginalisation.

Of course, there are exceptions to this. In Kenya, IDP-related issues have been placed firmly on the transitional justice agenda: the Truth and Justice Reconciliation Commission (TJRC) developed procedures and recruited people to specifically target IDPs to record statements, and took statements from refugees living in camps in neighbouring Uganda. Likewise, the Liberian truth commission also had statement takers in the diaspora, and there has been consider-able discussion about the need to engage with the thousands of IDPs displaced by conflict in Darfur. It could also be argued that repatria-tion that includes the recovery of land and other property in and of itself is an enactment of transitional justice being realised. However, the issue here is not so much a recognition of the need to incorporate displaced groups in discussions on transitional justice as much as the fact that this engagement remains fairly rhetorical. All too often, therefore, a divide remains between theory or ideals, and practice.

The nature of the relationship

So what are the main factors that drive the relationship? At its most elemental, the reason why transitional justice is relevant to resolving displacement is that displacement represents a violation of the rights of those who have been displaced. The chaos of flight and the turmoil of violence that uproots someone from their home; the experience of exile that is often characterised by continued insecurity and a lack of protection; the continuing lack of justice that is often an obstacle to return; and the fraught process of return (as the most favoured of the three so-called durable solutions) all represent a litany of abuses of human rights that need to be acknowledged and addressed. And transitional justice, with its imperative to right wrongs, is a significant tool that can be used to address the massive deficit in justice in the aftermath of conflict and to work towards breaking the vicious cycle of conflict and displacement.

For instance, the successful reintegration or rehabilitation of former combatants; prosecutions that deal with perpetrators of violence that were the cause of flight; restoration of, or at least reparation for, land and other property lost through flight; and truth-telling processes that acknowledge the impact, scale and implications of displacement are all key components to creating the conditions for the meaningful and enduring return of displaced populations.

And at the root of this lies the key issue of restoring the bond of citizenship, a bond that transitional justice mechanisms deliberately seek to restore or strengthen. Displacement, by definition, represents a fundamental rupture between the individual and his or her homeland; it is the ultimate demonstration of a government's failure to protect – or, worse still, of its role as the perpetrator of abuse against its citizens. Whether it results in refugees who have fled over their border or IDPs who have remained within the geographical borders of their state, all displacement represents a chronic failure on the part of the government to ensure the safety of its citizens. If displacement and conflict are representative of a major rupture in the bond between citizens and the state, appropriate and meaningful forms of justice in the aftermath of conflict represent the potential restoration of that bond, on the foundations of which the future stability of the country lies. While those who have been displaced are not the only ones who have had this bond broken, their ability to return home and re-activate their citizenship is a crucial indicator that peace has been restored.

The restoration of this bond lies at the heart of the relationship between transitional justice and displacement. Adversely, the failure to address the specific injustices that generated and were created by displacement threatens to derail, or certainly undermine, the integrity of the objectives of transitional justice processes.

Therefore, at its most fundamental level, the need to deal with the fall-out from displacement is critical to the future reconstruction of the state in the aftermath of conflict and to the rebuilding of the crucial bond of citizenship. It highlights the need to address the key goals of transitional justice as recently outlined by de Greiff: to provide recognition to victims; to foster civic trust; to contribute to reconciliation; and to contribute to democratisation.[2] In fact, transitional justice mechanisms cannot afford to overlook this critical area of injustice.

The state of the relationship

Having established the link between the two, which few would dispute, the crucial question is what the current state of the relationship is in practice. At a legal level, and despite the fact that displacement is a trademark of many of today's wars and their aftermath, legislation and mechanisms that deal with the legacies of displacement lag far behind the need for action. This deficit is nowhere more apparent than in the Great Lakes where Uganda, Sudan, Rwanda, Burundi, Kenya[3] and Democratic Republic of Congo (DRC) have all experienced massive levels of war-induced displacement. Although the region is now host to a proliferation of ongoing and proposed experiments with the legal tools of transitional justice – from truth and reconciliation commissions, to *gacaca*, to international and hybrid tribunals, special courts and five International Criminal Court (ICC) situation investigations – the issue of identifying individual criminal responsibilities for forced displacement and its consequences is only just beginning to be explored.[4]

At the same time, however, there are a number of encouraging signs of change in the region – at least at a normative level

– augmented by international developments. First, the International Conference on the Great Lakes Region process (involving 11 states in the region) and its groundbreaking pact have explicitly recognised that redressing the wrongs of displacement is core to the achievement of peace, security and development in the region.[5] Two new regional protocols are devoted exclusively to rights issues in displacement, dealing not only with the rights of displaced persons in exile, but also with justice at the point of return, in particular, property rights.[6] Other protocols of the pact put ensuring accountability for serious crimes committed during conflict and displacement at the heart of reconstructing a stable region, emphasising collective transnational obligations to combat impunity.[7]

Second, the recently adopted African Union Convention on the Protection and Assistance to Internally Displaced Persons in Africa requires states to respect, and ensure respect for, international humanitarian law regarding the protection of internally displaced persons, including ensuring individual responsibility for acts of arbitrary displacement in accordance with applicable domestic and international criminal law. Critically, in the light of the nature of the region's conflicts and the mass exploitation of economic and natural resources which leads to displacement, the accountability of non-state actors, including by implication actors such as multinational companies and private military or security companies, for acts of arbitrary displacement or complicity in such acts, is also a focus.

For better or worse, at the time of writing in 2012, the ICC was engaged in seven investigations in Africa, and five of these situations are in the Great Lakes region in countries with significant displaced populations. The entry of the ICC onto the stage in the region has the potential to significantly impact the experience of justice for the displaced – although, once again there may be a gap between the theory and the reality. Three brief reflections are offered. First, there is a real opportunity now for the act of displacement itself to come under the scrutiny of the court and to act as a specific deterrent. Although to date charges directly dealing with displacement as a war crime have not been brought, 'acts of forcible transfer' of population have been alleged in the charge of crimes against humanity against President Bashir of

Sudan, which is a start. In addition, the court has addressed crimes against those attempting to protect the displaced: there are currently two accused before the court in the Darfur situation, who are charged, inter alia, with 'intentionally directing attacks against personnel, installations, material, units or vehicles involved in a peacekeeping mission'.[8] In addition, all six individuals charged by the ICC in Kenya have been accused of forced displacement and persecution.

Second, displaced populations from the target countries have been a focus of various organs of the court both in terms of gathering evidence for its investigations and in ensuring victim participation in the cases. The ICC's victim-participation process presents a huge opportunity for victims of displacement to have their story told and to help direct the court's focus on the causes and consequences of displacement, albeit that the process is still evolving and complex. Finally, the question regarding the extent to which the threat of justice in The Hague acts as a deterrent to the commission of crimes that cause displacement, or which exacerbate the sufferings of exile, is also now being tested. The unanimous 2011 referral by the UN Security Council of the situation in Libya to the court as part of a package of measures specifically tailored to deter further mass atrocity and displacement indicates that the court is being viewed as a tool of prevention. The next few years will be critical for the court and international justice as a preventative tool and a tool of transitional justice.

However, such measures remain largely untested in their impact, and the relationship between transitional justice and displacement continues to be largely tangential. Two case studies (although not intended to lead to generalisations) illustrate some of the dynamics – both positive and negative – that surround this relationship as it is experienced on the ground. The first example is from Burundi[9] and the second from Rwanda.[10] Both draw on research carried out as part of a broader project on the linkages between displacement and citizenship in the Great Lakes region and incorporate the views of those who are caught in the midst of conflicts or are living through a transition from conflict to stability, and who have either returned home or are unable to do so.

Burundi

After almost 15 years of intense war, Burundi is now in a fragile period of transition to stability. Following the signing of the Arusha Peace and Reconciliation Agreement in August 2000, a painstaking peace process led to the approval of a power-sharing constitution, and a new parliament was elected in 2005. Since then, approximately half a million people have returned home, some after more than three decades in exile. Nowhere is the need for coordination between transitional justice and displacement more applicable. In practice, the main area of progress in post-conflict reconstruction is the reform of the army, which can be considered as a form of guarantee of non-repetition. The possibility of other mechanisms of accountability, such as truth telling, vetting or prosecutions, seem more distant. Although the Arusha agreement contains the mechanism for the formation of a truth and reconciliation process, it has not yet been implemented.

However, while such mechanisms have not been formally instituted, recognition of the need for reconstruction efforts to take place within a broader framework of reconciliation and accountability is at least part of the political discourse. Specifically, the findings showed that the government is using language associated with transitional justice in its handling of the key and potentially volatile issue of land ownership and the redistribution of land in the context of widespread return. It recognises – if only for pragmatic reasons – that addressing current demands on land in a way that is simultaneously equitable and feasible is critical to the long-term stability of the country.

What this means in practice is that many of those returning are being asked to share their land with current land occupiers in the name of 'reconciliation'. In many ways, this is a realistic and sensible way forward: neither has a unproblematic legal claim to the land (land law states that those who have been off their land for more than 30 years are no longer entitled to claim possession of it, while those who are currently on the land were often illegally allocated it in the aftermath of a genocide intended to free up land for that purpose). It also allows for those who are returning to get relatively quick access to some land and for those already on the land to be able to have continued access to livelihoods, albeit at a reduced level.

However, pursuing sharing as a means to 'reconciliation' without addressing problems connected with livelihoods, identity and perceptions of justice are likely to ultimately undermine its achievement. Without additional measures such as compensation for loss of original land, therefore, it is proving to be hugely problematic. At a practical level, it is compromising peoples' livelihoods as plots of land have been significantly reduced and family sizes have increased – a problem that existed regardless of the wide-scale return. However, the problem goes deeper than that: land is much more than an economic commodity, and the redistribution of land is not just an economic and pragmatic exercise. The equitable distribution of land relates to issues of justice, good governance and sustainable peace, and has enormous consequences for reintegration and notions of belonging and inclusion.

Returnees saw their access to ancestral land as being critical to the reinstatement of the legitimacy to belong. It represents continuity with the past and a reinstatement of the access to political rights that were disrupted by their exile. Regaining their land is equated with the restoration of their Burundian citizenship in a context where notions of identity are, literally, rooted in the soil. While the research showed that this imperative is counterbalanced by a certain amount of realism, current acceptance of the status quo, whereby people are being asked to either share their land with the current occupier or move elsewhere to so-called 'peace villages' should not be equated with reconciliation per se. What is acceptable in the short term might not be adequate to ensure sustainable peace in the long term.

Key to the concerns raised by those returning was the fact that they had not been consulted in the political dialogues that produced the different arrangements in the Arusha agreement. While this was also true for the Burundian population more generally, refugees suffered an additional layer of marginalisation not least in a context in which they are now often suffering the harshest consequences of having to share their land. This enforced sharing, over which they have not been given a choice, does not take into account the factors that caused them to flee (for many a calculated genocide that forced them off their land); nor the experience of displacement that has inevitably shaped their views on issues such as land; nor the fact that access to their ancestral land was seen as a key factor in restoring the bond between citizen and state, which had been so brutally ruptured by the conflict.

The incorporation of their ideas on return and the land redistribution process would have ensured considerably more buy-in into the process. But instead, returnees feel they have had this choice forced onto them. As a result, the emphasis on sharing land, based on the principles of mediation and reconciliation but without other supporting mechanisms, presents considerable challenges for the reintegration of returnees. While it has appeal in as much as it attempts to mediate the interests of both parties resolving a complex problem, it offends fundamental traditional values attached to land and the potential alienation when separated from that land – which, in turn, has serious implications for bringing about genuine reconciliation.

In this context, paying lip-service to justice without fully delivering upon it could prove to be extremely dangerous: asking people to 'reconcile' without providing a fair basis on which that can happen is putting unreasonable demands on the population. The government recognises this and, to a certain extent, its limited resources and the multiple challenges it is facing lie at the heart of its actions. After all, the country is feeling its way through a fragile transition towards sustainable peace after decades of conflict: its economy is in tatters, it is demobilising thousands of former rebels and mopping up the excesses of war, and it is trying to reconstruct governance and judicial institutions that are critical to the running of the country. In these circumstances, and with expectations running high, it is important to ask how the demands for a just and workable system for resolving land disputes can, in practice, be met.

However, at the very least there needs to be recognition of the limitations of what is taking place and for there to be an acknowledgment of the acute need for transitional justice mechanisms to deal substantially and meaningfully with the legacy of displacement and its many ramifications. The real question, therefore, is this: can the country afford not to address these demands, not least in a context in which population growth is already putting extraordinary pressure on land? In dealing with the country's legacy of violence by past governments and politicians, which has effectively broken the bond of citizenship between the government and its people, the ability for those who have been living in exile to genuinely reintegrate into Burundian society is an indicator of the potential to restore this broken bond or social contract. And it is precisely the restoration of such broken bonds that is the heartbeat of the goal of transitional justice.

Rwanda

While Burundi remains at a relatively early stage of post-conflict recovery, as emphasised by the somewhat precarious situation surrounding its elections in 2010, Rwanda provides an example of a country that has implemented a number of mechanisms of justice to deal with the legacy of the 1994 genocide, including a war crimes tribunal, the re-activation of local community courts and the setting up of memorials. But have these transitional justice mechanisms created justice, and what specifically have been the implications for displaced populations?

For those who have been displaced from Rwanda – either in the aftermath of the genocide or in subsequent years – the linkages between displacement and transitional justice are particularly important. For many, it is these very mechanisms of justice that are preventing them from returning home. Many of the problems relate to the failure to implement justice mechanisms in the immediate aftermath of the post-genocide mass exodus in 1994 when asylum seekers were not adequately screened, if at all, a failure that was in part due to the fact that the those fleeing Rwanda were seen only in terms of humanitarian assistance. The absence of justice at that point has meant that the implication of guilt continues to haunt many Rwandans, especially those who are in exile: with no determination of the few who were guilty, guilt was attributed to all those who had fled.

Specifically, as recent research suggests, it created the context in which mechanisms of justice in the aftermath of the genocide have metamorphosed into a tool for ongoing repression against some of the population. Many of those in exile claim that they have been accused of being involved in the genocide – either by virtue of their ethnicity, or as evidenced by the fact that they were in exile – or both. In particular, refugees fear the *gacaca* courts, a traditional community-level mechanism of justice that was transformed into a tool for dealing with perpetrators of genocide. While the courts represent a pragmatic and creative response to the overwhelming need for justice, and have achieved this goal in some respects, in practice, according to those interviewed, they are increasingly vulnerable to manipulation by those seeking to settle personal grudges or as an instrument of government repression.

A number of other mechanisms for invoking guilt for the genocide as a means of repression were also cited, including the operation of the Ibuka victims group,[11] genocide remembrance events and the promotion of anti-Hutu stereotypes. Ascription of collective guilt was also seen as a cover for enforcing the expropriation of Hutu property: the majority of those interviewed who had tried to reclaim land or other property after their initial return had failed. Instead, their land had been taken over by refugees who had fled Rwanda decades earlier and had returned in the aftermath of the genocide. Attempts to access justice had led to intimidation and exile. Not surprisingly, these refugees are not only reluctant to return home, they are also scared.

What these findings point to is the fact that the absence of open conflict is not an adequate benchmark against which to promote return. Return must be considered in terms of political openness and factors such as good governance (however that might be defined) and effective systems of justice, mechanisms that are increasingly being promoted within the ambit of transitional justice. These are more reliable indicators that it is not only safe to return home, but that return will be a genuinely durable solution. As with the Burundi situation, successful repatriation is not about stepping over a border: it is a long-term process of negotiated access to human rights protection and is strengthened by addressing threats to post-conflict recovery and reconstruction. And ensuring the buy-in of those in exile into post-conflict justice processes – and certainly not prolonging their exile as a result of them – is a key component in this.

Conclusion

This paper has focused, albeit briefly, on two countries in transition from violence to peace. It has shown that, in theory, the link between transitional justice and displacement not only makes sense but is also an imperative in any situation of post-conflict reconstruction where people have been displaced. As a result, it is clear that any resolution to the ramifications associated with forced migration needs (or will need) to connect with transitional justice paradigms and mechanisms, particularly in as much as they connect with the process of return and repatriation; and any transitional justice mechanisms need to be mindful of the implications of displacement in order to ensure the cohesion and legitimacy of the broader goals of transitional justice. Few people would dispute this.

Moving from theory to practice, however, remains a huge challenge as we have seen with these two examples. In particular, the lack of buy-in to processes of justice – or worse, the marginalisation of displaced people as a result of justice mechanisms – shows how critical it is to engage displaced populations in a meaningful way. In contexts of low resources and undemocratic governmental control of justice processes, somehow this gap between ideals and their realisation needs to be reduced. Recognition of the linkages is an important first step. But proper and inclusive implementation must follow or the very essence of transitional justice risks being yet another good idea that has failed those who most deserve its benefits.

Notes

1   The application of the word 'field' to transitional justice is much debated – less so with forced migration, which is more established as a 'field'. Christine Bell, for instance, talks of the fact that transitional justice is not a 'field' but a 'label or cloak that aims to rationalise the diverse set of bargains in relation to the past in an integrated endeavour, so as to obscure the quite different normative, moral and political implications of the bargains' (C. Bell (2009) 'Transitional justice, interdisciplinarity and the state of the "field" or "non-field"', *International Journal of Transitional Justice*, 3: 5-27). The term is used here in its loosest sense.

2   Pablo de Greiff, 'Theorising transitional justice' (forthcoming in Melissa Williams, Rosemary Nagy and Jon Elster (eds) (2012) *Transitional Justice, Nomos*, LI).

3 The National Dialogue and Reconciliation Process (4 Agendas) placed displacement squarely on the transitional justice agenda for both immediate short-term responses, and long-term issues, including land and justice (prosecutions, compensation, building houses for the displaced).

4 Article 8 (2) (e) (viii) of the Rome Statute defines a war crime in non-international armed conflict as, inter alia, '[o]rdering the displacement of the civilian population for reasons related to the conflict, unless the security of the civilians involved or imperative military reasons so demand'. Interestingly, the African Commission on Human and Peoples' Rights has made findings relating to state responsibility for forced displacement and exile.

5 See in particular, International Refugee Rights Initiative and the Internal Displacement Monitoring Centre (2008) 'The Great Lakes Pact and the rights of displaced people: a guide for civil society'.

6 See the Great Lakes Pact's Protocol on the Protection and Assistance of Internally Displaced Persons and the Protocol on the Property Rights of Returning Persons, http://www.lse.ac.uk/collections/law/projects/greatlakes/ihl-greatlakes-summary-new-docmt.htm, accessed 12 April 2012.

7 The Protocol on the Prevention and Suppression of Sexual Violence against Women and Children, and the Protocol on the Prevention and Punishment of the Crimes of Genocide, War Crimes and Crimes against Humanity, for example, particularly aim at ensuring that accountability for these crimes is not avoided by flight across borders. For more information on the pact see www.icglr.int.

8 See the *Prosecutor vs Nourain* and *Prosecutor vs Jerbo Jamus*.

9 International Refugee Rights Initiative and REMA Ministries (2009) 'Two people can't share the same pair of shoes: citizenship, land and the return of refugees to Burundi', Citizenship and Displacement in the Great Lakes region, Working Paper 2, November.

10 International Refugee Rights Initiative and Refugee Law Project (2010) 'A dangerous impasse: Rwandan refugees in Uganda', Citizenship and Displacement in the Great Lakes region, Working Paper 4, June.

11 Ibuka, which means 'we should always remember' in Kinyarwanda, was officially formed in 1995 as an umbrella organisation for 'survivor' organisations in Rwanda to address issues of justice, memory, and social and economic problems faced by survivors.

8

The Peace, Recovery and Development Plan for Northern Uganda

Robert Senath Esuruku

Introduction

Development theory and practice to date has not engaged extensively with transitional justice, a field of human rights that has received growing attention over the past decade (Lenzen 2009, de Greiff and Duthie 2009). Transitional justice, which is a process through which a society seeks to come to terms with a past of massive human rights violations, can be of instrumental value to larger development goals in post-authoritarian and post-conflict societies (de Greiff 2009). However, the inadequate research in the area is one of the stumbling blocks in advancing much-needed post-conflict development programming. This chapter is an attempt to initiate a debate about the link between transitional justice and development from the perspective of Uganda. This debate is driven by the implementation of the Peace, Recovery and Development Plan for northern Uganda (PRDP) (GoU 2000), which sits uncomfortably between reparation measures and development services.

The PRDP is a stabilisation plan which has separated out northern Uganda from national sector plans, and it is the framework for post-conflict recovery and development intervention. The targets of the PRDP include the consolidation of state authority, strengthening the rule of law and access to justice, rebuilding and empowering communities, peace building and reconciliation, and revitalising local communities (GoU 2007). Within the framework of the PRDP, development partners are invited to implement specific development programmes in the region. The PRDP is based on the premise that effective peace building, recovery and development strategies in the northern region of Uganda require an in-depth understanding of the different armed conflicts which have severely affected women, men and their children. The plan also has a monitoring framework to track the progress of development investments to ensure that the targets set by the government are met. The PRDP strategy is to address the unique challenges in each of the sub-regions based on their conflict status and the extent of their vulnerability (GoU 2007).

The first part of this chapter provides the background to the conflict in northern Uganda. The post-conflict socio-economic background in the region provides a basis for understanding the transition from war to peace. The second section centres on the PRDP and sets the conceptual framework for understanding the links between peace, justice and development. Lastly, the chapter concludes that peace, justice and development in northern Uganda can be achieved if it is an inclusive process for all stakeholders. Although the transitional justice processes included in the government's peace-building strategies point to a comprehensive justice framework, the implementation of the mechanisms appears to lack the genuine political and financial support that would enable it to meet the grievances of its people and address the root causes of the conflict.

Background to the conflict in northern Uganda

The over two decades of rebellion by the Lord's Resistance Army (LRA) in Acholi and Lango, which also affected parts of Teso and West Nile, has been the most virulent of the conflicts Uganda has seen in recent times (Brett 1995, Dolan 2005, Latigo 2008). The other rebel groups that have operated previously in different parts of northern Uganda include the West Nile Bank Front (WNBF), Uganda National Rescue Front II (UNRF II) and the Uganda People's Army (UPA) in Teso. Aside from the 'political' conflict in the other areas of the north, inter-clan and inter-tribal armed cattle raids in Karamoja have also resulted in insecurity, death and low development, much as in the war areas. The Karamoja situation not only affects communities inside Karamoja, but also neighbouring districts in Acholi, Lango and Teso sub-regions.

The origin of the conflict in northern Uganda can be traced to the deeply rooted ethnic mistrust perpetrated by the colonialists (Kasozi 1994, Mutibwa 1992, Latigo 2008, Tripp 2010). The British colonial administration recruited people from the northern region into the armed forces while people from the other regions of the country were mainly employed to work as civil servants. This scenario created a division between the northern and other regions of the country, with the latter becoming more developed while the northern region remained poorer with its population relying on cattle keeping as its main source of livelihood (Dolan 2005, Gersony 1997, Kasozi 1994, Mamdani 1999). The successive undemocratic governments since independence in 1962 have stoked the war in northern Uganda.

The more than two decades of war in northern Uganda began in 1986 in the Acholi sub-region. The Ugandan People's Democratic Army (UPDA), led by Brigadier Odong Latek, was a group who fled from Kampala when the National Resistance Army/ Movement (NRA/M) took power in 1986 after a five-year guerrilla war (Dolan 2005, Mutibwa 1992). By April 1986, the Acholi had largely come to terms with the NRA/M victory and the majority of former Uganda National Liberation Army (UNLA) soldiers also heeded the appeal made by the government to hand over their arms and demobilise (Otunnu 2002). However, after months of relative calm, anxieties escalated when the NRA began to commit human rights abuses in the name of crushing a nascent rebellion (Gersony 1997, Otunnu 2002). Over time NRA/M soldiers plundered the area and committed atrocities, including rape, abductions, confiscating livestock and killing unarmed civilians; the destruction of granaries, schools, hospitals and bore holes escalated. These atrocities in Acholiland were justified by some as revenge for the 'skulls of Luwero' (Gersony 1997, Otunnu 2002).

The NRA/M also allowed Karamojong cattle raiders to loot with impunity as far west as Gulu town, sometimes participating in the looting themselves, and this destruction of one of the bases of Acholi livelihood became additional proof of the NRA/M's plans (Bradbury 1999, Gersony 1997, RLP 2004). Powerful and heartbreaking allegations and testimonies by a number of human rights activists and ordinary people from northern Uganda also suggest that NRA/M soldiers gang-raped Acholi men soon after they captured power in 1986. The NRA/M's revenge rape against Acholi men was widespread enough that the Acholi invented a new vocabulary to describe this new tactic as *tek gungu*, which literally means 'the way which is hard to bend' (Human Rights Watch 1997, Van Acker 2004).

Against this background of mistrust and violence, in May 1986 the government ordered all former UNLA soldiers to report to barracks. The order was met with deep suspicion, in part because it was reminiscent of Amin's edict that led to the 1971 massacre of Acholi soldiers. Some ex-UNLA soldiers went into hiding, others fled to Sudan and some decided to take up arms (Otunnu 2002). The rebellion gradually transformed itself into a highly structured rebel group with cult-like qualities (Otim and Wierda 2010). The Holy Spirit Movement started by prophetess Alice Auma Lakwena garnered enormous support against Museveni's NRA/M, now known as the Uganda People's Defence Force (UPDF). Lakwena, a spirit-medium, was fighting to purify the aggrieved northern Acholi people. She promised her fighters that the use of her 'holy oil' would protect them from bullets, turning them to water. The followers believed that magic potions protected them in battle against the government forces (Behrend 1999).

After the defeat of Alice Lakwena, Joseph Kony quickly took charge of the remnants of Lakwena's army and Severino Lukoya's Lord's Army, renamed his army the Lord's Resistance Army (LRA) and continued to fight against the government and the people of northern Uganda. With financial and military support from the Sudanese government in Khartoum and using South Sudan as a launch pad for its operations, the LRA proved difficult to defeat (Ehrenreich 1997, Latigo 2008). The brutal campaigns by the LRA mostly targeted civilians accused of collaborating with the Ugandan government (Otim and Wierda 2010, Otunnu 2002).

The horrendous atrocities inflicted by the LRA and UPDF held back, and caused total destruction in, the northern Uganda region and, more specifically, the Acholi sub-region and the districts of Apac, Lira, Katakwi and Soroti. More than 38,000 children were abducted and forcefully recruited into the rebel army (Pham et al 2007). More than 1.8 million people were forced into internally displaced persons' (IDPs) camps throughout northern Uganda and parts of West Nile and eastern Uganda for more than two decades (Huber 2009). Women and young girls were abducted and taken as wives and sex slaves for the LRA commanders. Some widely documented serious crimes include murder, abduction, forced marriage, sexual assault and horrific mutilation including amputating limbs and cutting off ears, noses and lips (Dolan 2005, Pham et al 2007, ICG 2004). These atrocities by the LRA constituted deliberate attempts to instil terror, to violate local values and power structures, and to swell rebel ranks (ICG 2004, Otim and Wierda 2010).

Social services, including agriculture, education and healthcare systems, were severely undermined or wrecked and many professional employees deserted the region. The earlier attempts by the government to rebuild the region through development programmes such as the Northern Uganda Social Action Fund (NUSAF) were driven by elite socio-economic and political interests and succumbed to massive corruption (Hickey 2003). Although the social fund approach has the advantage of devolving responsibility to the community and protecting those responsible for project implementation from undue political influence, the availability of substantial resources for development purposes was an attractive source of political patronage in a region that had suffered a long deprivation of resources. The political imperative of ensuring a balanced spread of project benefits undermined the equity objective of NUSAF in prioritising the most vulnerable groups and areas. Politicians keen to re-establish their legitimacy in the region often used the programme as a foothold for gaining political advantage and advancing their political ambitions.

The destruction of the region's economic base and the breakdown in social cohesion have been strongly felt by communities. At the root of this conflict lie issues of inequality and exclusion from important state appointments and development opportunities, which have marginalised a large proportion of vulnerable groups in the northern region. Explanations for the conflict are complex and intertwined and include Uganda's colonial history, a tradition of political mobilisation along ethnic and regional lines since independence and the LRA's religious and identity-driven agenda (Allen 2006, Dolan 2005, Doom and Vlassenroot 1999, Van

Acker 2004). Insecurity in the Karamoja sub-region, partly rooted in the proliferation of small arms and problematic disarmament programmes, has hampered the administration and expansion of central government services, resulting in a chronic breakdown of law and order and underdevelopment of the region (UNDP 2008).

The post-conflict socio-economic profile of northern Uganda

The impact of the conflicts across the north has been phenomenal. While the national average of Ugandans living in absolute poverty declined from 38.8 per cent in 2002/03 to 31.1 per cent in 2005/6 and to 24.5 per cent in 2009/10, poverty levels in northern Uganda increased from 2.9 million in 2002/03 to 3.3 million in 2005/06 and decreased to 2.9 million in 2009/10 (UBOS 2010). Despite the overall significant reduction in poverty, the northern Uganda region has remained poorer than the other regions, as illustrated in Table 1. Furthermore, while northern Uganda performed poorly by most human development indicators, Teso sub-region performed better than Acholi and Lango, while Karamoja performed worst (UBOS 2006). This means that nearly one-third of chronically poor

Table 1 Poor people (in millions) 2002–10

	2002/03	2005/06	2009/10
Uganda national	9.81	8.44	7.51
Residence			
Rural	9.31	7.87	7.10
Urban	0.50	0.57	0.42
Regions in Uganda			
Central	1.67	1.30	0.87
Eastern	3.19	2.45	2.20
Northern	2.90	3.25	2.84
Western	2.06	1.44	1.60

Source: UBOS 2003, UBOS 2006, UBOS 2010

people in Uganda come from the northern region alone. Northern Uganda to date has a large number of national and international actors providing humanitarian, recovery and development support to war-affected communities.

The human development indices (HDIs) and human poverty indices (HPIs) demonstrate that northern Uganda is lagging behind the rest of the country in regional and district-specific breakdowns (UNDP 2007). While the national HDI had improved from 0.488 in 2003 to 0.581 in 2006, there were regional imbalances that were skewed against the northern region. The central region, for instance, scored the highest HDI of 0.650, followed by the eastern region with an index of 0.586. The western region registered 0.564 while the northern region brought up the rear with 0.478 (UNDP 2007).

Furthermore, while the national income per capita is estimated at Uganda shillings (UGX) 570,000, the figure for the northern region stands at a paltry UGX 153,000, which is about 27 per cent of the national average. Although at national level income poverty fell from 56 per cent in 1992 to 31.1 per cent in 2006 and 24.5 in 2009/10, 46.2 per cent of the residents in the northern region have remained poor, as seen in Table 2. Although the mean

Table 2 Poverty estimates by region 2009/10

Location	Population share %	Mean CPAE	Poverty estimate		
			P0	P1	P2
Uganda national	100.0	62,545	24.5	6.8	2.8
Rural	85.0	52,467	27.2	7.6	3.1
Urban	15.0	119,552	9.1	1.8	0.6
Regions in Uganda					
Central	26.5	100,441	10.7	2.4	0.8
Eastern	29.6	49,697	24.3	5.8	2.1
Northern	20.0	38,988	46.2	15.5	7.3
Western	24.0	56,232	21.8	5.4	2.0

Source: UBOS 2010

consumption expenditure per adult equivalent has increased from UGX 55,092 in 2006 to UGX 62,545 in 2009/10, the expenditure in the north has remained at UGX 38,988 (UBOS 2010). Similarly, while Uganda's national infant mortality rate stands at 76 per 1,000 live births, the average rate for the north is a hefty 106 per 1000 live births (UBOS 2003). Similarly, as of 2005, the north had the highest HPI of 30.7 per cent as compared with the central region, which had 20.19 per cent, the western 20.56 per cent and the eastern 27.11 per cent (UNDP 2007).

In Acholi, Lango, parts of Teso and West Nile, the immediate effect of the armed conflicts was loss of life, massive destruction of property and breakdown of the social, economic and other infrastructures, and also massive population displacement into IDP camps. By September 2006, there were 1.3 million IDPs in Acholi sub-region alone (Amuru, Gulu, Kitgum and Pader), which was estimated to be equivalent to over 98 per cent of the sub-region's population. By the end of 2006, there were 202 IDP camps in northern Uganda, some with a population of over 60,000 IDPs, producing a population density as high as 1,700 persons per hectare. By January 2007, the number of IDPs in northern Uganda numbered more than 1.7 million people (UNHCR 2010).

In Karamoja and neighbouring districts, the armed conflicts associated with cattle raids have increasingly undermined the ability of households to cope with the harsh physical conditions, which increased their vulnerability to food insecurity. Many people in IDP camps in Teso and some parts of Lango and Acholi were displaced by the cattle rustling. These conditions have prevailed in these areas for nearly 20 years (UNDP 2008). While there is some confidence that security in the region will improve, due in part to increased military and police deployments, the environment remains highly volatile, with the persistence of ambushes and killings by illegally armed elements. Continuing cattle raids have on occasion prompted extreme responses from the UPDF, including aerial bombardments of kraals in Kotido during January 2010 (Onyango 2010, UN 2010).

Background to the post-conflict development programmes

Since the early 1990s the government of Uganda with donor support has implemented a number of programmes to improve local infrastructure and the livelihoods of the war-ravaged communities in northern Uganda, to enhance the protection of the civilian population and to try and return the region to normalcy. As part of its response to pillar 5 of the Poverty Eradication Action Plan (PEAP), security and conflict resolution, the government developed a comprehensive IDP policy and programmes including the Emergency Humanitarian Action Plan (EHAP), Northern Uganda Reconstruction Programme (NURP) and the Northern Uganda Social Action Fund (NUSAF).

The earliest development programme implemented in the region was the NURP-I, with support from the International Development Association (IDA). It was designed to upgrade the infrastructure in the region through the construction of roads, provision of water supplies, health facilities and schools. In the West Nile sub-region, a demand-driven programme called Community Action Plan (CAP), funded by the Netherlands government, was implemented. Initially, CAP was part of the NURP-I before it became an independent development programme.

In 2002, the Ugandan government designed the five-year NUSAF development programme, which was funded by the World Bank. The goal of NUSAF was to help local communities in, by then, 18 districts of northern Uganda that had been ravaged by conflict. This money was given directly to members of the community so they could invest in infrastructure and training for long-term development. NUSAF was a community-driven development programme in which local communities identify, plan and implement sub-projects geared to improvement of local infrastructure, promotion of livelihood opportunities and resolve conflict.

Other development programmes implemented in the northern region before the PRDP were the Northern Uganda Rehabilitation Programme (NUREP) and the Karamoja Integrated Disarmament and Development Plan (KIDDP). These two development programmes were later incorporated into the PRDP. NUREP, which is a European Union funded programme, is geared to strengthening the self-reliance and protection of the local population in northern Uganda, rehabilitating social infrastructure and improving the capacity of Ugandan stakeholders to respond to conflicts and disasters. The KIDDP, on the other hand, has the overall goal of contributing to human security and promoting conditions for recovery and development in Karamoja by dealing with the problem of small arms and light weapons.

Transition from war to relative peace

The negotiations between the Government of Uganda and the LRA, which began on 14 July 2006 in the Southern Sudan capital of Juba, have resulted in relative calm in northern Uganda. The signing of a Cessation of Hostilities Agreement on 26 August 2006 led to the 29 June 2007 Principles of Accountability and Reconciliation and the final disposal of all items on the negotiation agenda. The Comprehensive Peace Agreement (CPA) has not been signed. This has in part been attributed to the impasse around the International Criminal Court (ICC) indictments of some of the LRA leaders. Nonetheless, the relative calm in the region has resulted in large numbers of IDPs moving back to their homes. The IDPs were first placed in transit camps to prepare them to return to their original homes. For example, by March 2007, Pader district had 160 transit camps created out of the original 31 IDP camps. According to the UN Interagency Standing Committee (IASC), by June 2007, there were 367 transit camps in northern Uganda, nearly four times the number of IDP camps in June 2006.

In Teso and Lango, particularly in areas not neighbouring Karamoja, the IASC report in June 2007 indicated a close-to-total return of displaced persons to their former villages, having started returning as early as January 2006. By July 2007, more than 90 per cent of the IDPs in Teso had returned to their homes. A close-to-total return had been registered in Kaberamaido district by June 2007, from an estimated 98,500 IDPs in December 2003 when the LRA made incursions into Teso. However, in Acholi, by June 2007, only 1 per cent had returned to their home sites, while 24 per cent were in transit camps. About 75 per cent of the IDPs in Acholi were still in 'mother' IDP camps.

Despite these challenges, the peace talks have given the communities some level of the hope and optimism needed to embark on the long process of recovery. Since 2007, large numbers of IDPs have moved to either their original homes or transit sites located in the parishes nearest to their homes. The figures vary across the region from those in the less affected Lango region to the highly affected areas such as Amuru and parts of Kitgum. The December 2010 report by the UNHCR indicates that nearly all the IDPs have returned to their homes, as seen in Table 3.

In Gulu only one camp is operational, four camps in Pader and Agago, three in Kitgum, four in Lamwo and one in Amuria district. The reasons for the slow return in these camps are complex and related to long-term displacement, insufficient sensitisation of the displaced population to the options available to them, lack of basic services and infrastructure in areas of return, and continued security concerns about Karamojong incursions and the presence of unexploded ordinance (UNDP 2008).

Table 3 Camp update in Acholi, Lango, Teso and Madi sub-regions

Districts	Gulu	Amuru	Pader	Kitgum	Lamwo	Katakwi	Amuria	Lira
Govt-recognised IDP camps	31	34	31	11	14	44	17	41
Camps decommissioned 2006/08	0	0	0	0	0	37	4	41
Camps decommissioned 2009	16	0	4	5	1	5	8	0
Camps decommissioned 2010	14	34	23	3	8	2	4	0
Residual active IDP camps	1	0	4	3	5	0	1	0
Total camps decommissioned	30	34	27	8	9	44	16	41

Source: UNHCR 2010

The return and settlement of the former IDPs are affected by several factors, including security, the availability of tools for bush clearing, opening up of land for cultivation, planting materials and inaccessible roads due to non-maintenance. While there is less congestion in the return areas than in the IDP camps, basic social services such as primary healthcare, safe water, education, nutrition, protection and shelter are seriously lacking. The over 21 years of exposure to armed conflicts and life in encampment have changed not only lifestyles but more significantly social values with increased instances of domestic violence. Most of the families returning to pre-displacement sites are broken families headed by divorcees, widows or widowers, single parents and many child-headed households. The returnees are facing significant problems accessing land in areas of return. While living in the camps, most men, due to frustration and redundancy, became accustomed to consuming a lot of alcohol and doing very little work (Pham et al 2005). The burden of looking after the homes fell on the women. There are also problems over resettling the elderly and disabled people.

After the LRA guns fell silent, armed thugs who operated under their shadow emerged as the leading cause of terror for IDPs returning to their homes. Different criminal gangs continue to terrorise communities in Amuru, Gulu, Kitgum and Pader districts. The need for an effective police force cannot be over-emphasised. Although the strength of the police force has grown from 27,000 in 2006/07 to 48,000 by July 2007, there is still a manpower deficit in all of northern Uganda (UNDP 2008). The performance of the justice, law and order sector is also affected by the extremely slow trial processes for suspects, which undermines confidence in the justice system. By June 2007, 4,000 of the 32,000 inmates countrywide were in war-torn northern Uganda. The judiciary and public prosecution departments are still weak, despite nationwide efforts to improve the performance of these institutions. There are also challenges related to explosive ordnance disposal. Recent assessments, however, show that the threat from mines within the war-affected districts is very low (UNDP 2008).

The Peace, Recovery and Development Plan

The overall goal of the PRDP is stabilisation in order to regain and consolidate peace and lay the foundations for recovery and development in northern Uganda. The PRDP was initially conceived as a 'master plan' for northern Uganda. Its general target is to promote development of the districts so that northern Uganda achieves national averages in its main social and economic indicators (Claussen et al 2008). The PRDP is managed and coordinated under the Office of the Prime Minister (OPM). It is under the political supervision of the minister of state for northern Uganda and technical management of the permanent secretary in the OPM.

Ongoing programmes in the north such as NUSAF, NUREP, KIDDP, the Transition to Recovery Programme, the Mine Action Programme, the Northern Uganda Youth Rehabilitation Programme, the Northern Uganda Youth Centre, the North-West Smallholder Agricultural Programme and the Northern Uganda Data Centre (NUDC) have all been realigned with the PRDP objectives. The strategy is not only a response to immediate, specific post-conflict issues, it also aims to eliminate the great discrepancies in development between the northern and southern parts of the country. Through the adoption of a set of coherent programmes, the government of Uganda, together with all the stakeholders in the PRDP's implementation process, seeks to achieve four strategic objectives: consolidating state authority; rebuilding and empowering communities; revitalising the economy; and peace building and reconciliation.

The Department for Pacification and Development in the OPM is in charge of the coordination of the PRDP, which is spearheaded by the undersecretary for pacification and development. The government's efforts to realise the strategic objectives provide testimony to its great commitment to stabilise and recover northern Uganda. In the framework of the PRDP, sector technical planning and coordination will continue to be done by the sector ministries and levels of local government (GoU 2007). Hence, execution remains to a large extent with the regular system and procedures for implementing sector programmes and district development plans. The chief administrative officer (CAO) is responsible for the general management and coordination of the

PRDP at the local government level. In each PRDP district the CAO appoints a PRDP liaison officer whose task is to follow up the implementation of the PRDP in close collaboration with all the stakeholders that are operating in a given district.

The conceptual link between transitional justice and development

To begin with, transitional governments are often characterised by a rush for resources under the guise of economic rehabilitation, to the disadvantage of the politically voiceless and to the advantage of those with power (Harwell and Le Billon 2009). Such corrupt tendencies do not advance economic growth over the long term and instead drain government revenues and encourage inefficient resource management. Additionally, persistent impunity for widespread economic crimes frequently sends the message that there is still no rule of law. A lack of political will to pursue cases by those in power undermines genuine justice, accountability, peace and development. These are issues of great concern for both development and transitional justice.

At a policy level, development is also concerned with the capacities and conditions for peace because without peace, development gains are eroded and it is impossible to achieve equity. Similarly, the development community has come to terms with the fact that its interventions can do harm and fuel violent conflict if it remains ignorant of the conflict dynamics present in every society (Lenzen 2009). At a practical level, some development actors have adapted conflict-sensitive approaches as a way of fostering conditions for sustainable peace and development. Transitional justice, on the other hand, involves peace building and development particularly by addressing, through the mechanisms of relationships and governance, the legacies of mass atrocities, death, human anguish, the destruction of property and social dislocation or exclusion. In the same vein, development also addresses the structural conditions of inequality and poverty which are often intricately linked to the histories of violence that peace building tries to overcome. These are also issues transitional justice tries to deal with as a way of providing the necessary conditions and processes for sustainable peace building and development.

In recent years, development practice has also sought to integrate human rights elements through political conditionality, positive support and the human rights-based approach to development. Consequently, poor people are perceived as rights-bearers and claimants rather than just recipients of development aid and programmes. A link exists between development and human security when a holistic view of the needs of the poor are taken into account by increasing the efficacy of development initiatives. Similarly, the notion of rights-bearers also informs transitional justice measures, particularly development programmes. The rights-based approaches to development are therefore important in shaping development programmes in a way that takes account of the beneficiaries rather than seeing them as passive victims. Also, the concept of vulnerability can be used to articulate the relationship between material deprivation and the effects of armed violence and oppression. In this respect we may note that: (1) vulnerability has several planes – economic, social, political and physical; (2) these planes reinforce one another to produce both poverty and violence; (3) both transitional justice and development have often failed to adequately grasp the interaction of different forms of vulnerability; and (4) this misapprehension has often compromised the effectiveness of the interventions (Harwell and Le Billon 2009). A focus on the role of natural resources in different forms of vulnerability can improve the effectiveness and coherence of development and transitional interventions.

Conflict sensitivity in development programmes can serve not only to decrease levels of violent conflict but also increase the effectiveness of development programmes. Violent conflicts lead to poverty, particularly where such violence is protracted and it is associated with the collapse of state institutions (Iversen 2009). Direct consequences of conflict have long-term political, economic, environmental and social costs. These include erosion of political institutions, reduction of the state's capacity to provide basic social services, destruction of the production base, capital flight, loss of food production, depletion of natural resources and the destruction of social networks. In these cases, truth seeking and legal accountability may undercut impunity and help generate public discussion and raise awareness, which may help to build civic trust, facilitate democratisation and contribute to genuine reconciliation and development (Harwell and Le Billon 2009).

Participation through community engagement places emphasis on the local community, especially vulnerable community members who are often excluded from the process of identifying their own needs. The participatory approach to development also works for post-conflict programming because it promotes individual and collective voices rooted in truthfulness. This approach can bring benefits to communities if such a community is empowered to claim their needs and hold their leaders accountable. However, the process of empowerment and building the capacities of communities takes time. There is also need to guard against further conflicts; community elites may reorganise themselves because they fear losing their stranglehold on power and their access to resources, which in turn may instigate new conflicts.

The PRDP and transitional justice

In the preamble to the Agreement on Comprehensive Solutions, the Uganda government and the LRA recognised the existence of regional disparities and imbalances in the country's socio-economic development as a result of the conflict. As a result, article 10 of the agreement recognised the vital need to adopt an overarching framework for delivering sound and comprehensive programmes for the recovery of conflict-affected areas in north and north-east Uganda. The agreement provided for the development, adoption and quick implementation of the PRDP, the primary tool for addressing the socio-economic inequalities of northern Uganda. The PRDP was designed to initiate the process of community reconciliation and mitigate sources of conflicts to provide a basis for sustainable development in the region. It was hoped that communities would identify conflict mitigation measures to address and overcome the legacy of violence and its underlying causes. The development interventions would flow out of conflict management processes by providing former combatants, abductees and victims of violence with livelihood opportunities and secure sources of income from labour and contracts for community infrastructure projects.

During the Juba talks, the Uganda government and the LRA delegations also drew up agreements that sought to address the political and economic grievances that lie at the root of the conflict and to heal the social wounds of northern Uganda by bringing justice to victims and reconciling former fighters with their communities. Here I will briefly discuss the challenges of addressing the socio-economic and political marginalisation identified by delegations as the key causes of the conflict and their ramification for development and transitional justice.

Socio-economic recovery and employment

Economic inequality between northern and southern Uganda and the sense of disenfranchisement that accompanied it has been identified as one of the key factors that fuelled the war in northern Uganda. The loss of cattle and economic assets and being moved into encampments for over two decades has robbed communities of meaningful livelihood opportunities. The region's shattered infrastructure undermined the capacity of local and central governments to deliver the necessary social services. The reintegration of large numbers of ex-combatants and the securing of meaningful and sustainable economic livelihoods for them has remained a largely unfulfilled objective. Massive unemployment in the region is a time bomb waiting to go off particularly for young women and men. Moreover, the communities are struggling to cope with a host of socio-economic problems left behind by the war as well as rising land disputes and conflicts as returnees try to sell communal land to an influx of business interests (ICG 2010, International Alert 2010). Furthermore, dependency on handouts and exposure to Western influences in the IDP camps has contributed to the erosion of traditional values and a rise in alcoholism and domestic abuse. The International Crisis Group (ICG) warns that if these issues are left unaddressed, such problems risk feeding perceptions of neglect among the communities in the northern region and antagonising the north–south relationship. All these are issues that development and transitional justice attempts to deal with.

While objectives 2 and 3 of the PRDP centres on rebuilding and empowering communities and revitalising the economy in the region, the plan has been criticised by many as a tool for satisfying the government's political agenda rather than fostering peace and development. For example, the government has been criticised for using the PRDP to create a patronage system in northern Uganda, thereby buying political support in a region which is an opposition stronghold (Iversen 2009, Tripp 2010). ICG argues that the primary beneficiaries of the PRDP are government-connected contractors, the political elite and employees of government agencies. In most districts where PRDP is currently being implemented, there is no evidence to demonstrate that the priorities selected are conflict sensitive and considered in a participatory manner. The priorities have not included the voices and the needs of the victims and have largely remained gender insensitive (Isis-WICCE 2010). There are cases where the implementation of the PRDP has created conflicts when its purpose was to mitigate these. For instance, the repair of the Anamido-Adero landing site road in Amolator district led to destruction of property and crops, prompting protest from the community. The contractor abandoned the procurement requirements and opened up a new road instead of rehabilitating the existing road, without consulting the local community. The case has put at risk intended governance outcomes such as conflict mitigation, strengthening local government capacity and the empowerment of local communities. As a result, land and crop destruction have now become the new source of conflicts in the district.

Governance and the rule of law

Government structures in most parts of the region were destroyed and replaced by camp commandants. With the influx of humanitarian assistance, the north became a relief-dominated economy, while the district authorities have very few resources at their disposal. Staff attrition is extremely high and on average between only 35 and 55 per cent of posts are filled (GoU 2006). Many critical positions in both the administrative and technical cadre remain unfilled. The situation is even worse at lower local government levels where many sub-county and parish chief positions are occupied by people in an acting capacity. Among the technical departments, the health sector is the worst affected given the acute shortage of health workers in the region. An assessment conducted by the ministry of local government in December 2006 indicated that the Acholi region had a 63.2 per cent staffing gap;

West Nile sub-region 56.1 per cent; Lango 51.1 per cent; Teso 44.6 per cent; and Karamoja 50 per cent gap.

In addition to low staff numbers, many local councils in the conflict-affected districts also lack basic office facilities, equipment and logistics to support their operations. Because of the security threats, poor living conditions, lack of social infrastructure, poor office amenities and low local revenue the districts continue to experience difficulties in attracting and retaining qualified personnel. Staffing gaps in some districts have also been attributed to the creation of new districts, which have further depleted the older districts of their staff complement. Low staffing levels and the inability to retain qualified staff due to the lack of basic facilities and amenities has had an adverse impact on key functions like internal audit and control. Low management capacity, lack of compliance with government regulations and weak internal control systems have resulted in significant amounts of unauthorised expenditure in many districts. Mitigating these requires the close monitoring of compliance with government public financial management regulations and the following up of audit qualifications.

The PRDP appears preoccupied with the technical aspect of rebuilding central and local government institutions, improving service delivery and revitalising the economy, presumably so as to improve the popularity of the government. It seems less concerned with providing comprehensive political solutions to peace building and national reconciliation, which are probably better pursued by the implementation of the Agreement on Comprehensive Solutions. Although the PRDP is the overarching framework, as provided for in the agreement, to deal with the economic and social development of northern Uganda, the political agenda surrounding the plan makes it look as if it is a separate tool. Also, the PRDP geographically covers 55 districts in eight regions rather than focusing on the initial 18 LRA-affected districts, which raises questions as to how adequate it is in addressing the specific needs and grievances of the people of northern Uganda. Nevertheless, the PRDP's potential to contribute to achieving peace and strategic objective 1, which further consolidates cessation of armed hostilities and the rule of law, remains good. Strategic objectives 2 and 3 address the safe return of IDPs to their home areas while seeking to revitalise the economy in northern Uganda to diminish the gap between the north and south. All these are crucial steps in achieving national justice, reconciliation, peace and development. Failing to adequately address the grievances of the people in northern Uganda is likely to result in the continued presence of 'negative peace', understood as merely the absence of violence, or it may result in recurrent conflicts.

Conclusion

Northern Uganda is just emerging from protracted civil conflict into relative peace, which has enabled the majority of the IDPs to return to their home areas and begin to revive their lives. The region is beset by poverty, inequality, weak institutions and insecurity. Massive human rights violations, social torture and dislocation have left the region severely marginalised. Uganda's comprehensive transitional justice strategy, which includes international and national criminal justice, traditional justice, truth telling, reparations, and political and economic reforms, provides a promising framework which has the potential of contributing to national reconciliation, peace and development. At first glance the Agreement on Comprehensive Solutions of 2007 appears a promising tool for addressing the root causes of the more than two decades of conflict which has led to socio-economic inequality and political disempowerment.

The PRDP is a positive step towards addressing the marginalisation of northern Uganda from the rest of the country, which is necessary if northern Uganda is to achieve long-term reconciliation. However, inadequate funding, implementation problems and the risk of corruption severely jeopardise the achievement of the PRDP. The lack of livelihood support for the IDPs returning to their home areas as well as disputes over land demonstrate the government's failure to meet the needs of its people. The administrative impunity caused by the absence of adequate vetting mechanisms and a partial judicial system significantly compromise the population's trust in state institutions. If the government does not address the root causes of the conflict, it is unlikely that Uganda will move from a situation of relative stability towards lasting peace and development.

References

Allen, Tim (2006) *Trial justice: The International Criminal Court and the Lord's Resistance Army*, London, Zed Books

Behrend, Heike (1999) *Alice Lakwena and the Holy Spirits: War in Northern Uganda, 1985–97*, Oxford, James Currey

Bradbury, Mark (1999) *An Overview of Initiatives for Peace in Acholi, Northern Uganda*, Cambridge, Reflecting on Peace Practice Project

Brett, E.A. (1995) 'Neutralising the use of force in Uganda: the role of the military in politics', *Journal of Modern African Studies*, 33: 129–52

Claussen, J., Lotsberg, R., Nkutu, A. and Erlend, N. (2008) *Appraisal of the Peace, Recovery and Development Plan for Northern Uganda*, Oslo, Norwegian Agency for Development Cooperation

de Greiff, Pablo (2009) 'Articulating the links between transitional justice and development: justice and social integration', in de Greiff, Pablo and Duthie, Roger (ed) *Transitional Justice and Development: Making Connections*, New York, Social Science Research Council

de Greiff, Pablo and Duthie, Roger (eds) *(2009) Transitional Justice and Development: Making Connections*, New York, Social Science Research Council

Dolan, G.C. (2005) 'Understanding war and its continuation: the case of northern Uganda', PhD thesis, London School of Economics and Political Science

Doom, Ruddy and Vlassenroot, Koen (1999) 'Kony's message: a new Koine? The Lord's Resistance Army in Northern Uganda', *African Affairs*, 98: 5–36.

Ehrenreich, Rosa (1997) *The Scars of Death: Children Abducted by the Lord's Resistance Army in Uganda*, New York, Human Rights Watch

Gersony, R. (1997) *The Anguish of Northern Uganda: Results of a Field Based Assessment of the Civil Conflict in Northern Uganda*, Kampala, USAID.

Government of Uganda (GoU) (2000) *Peace, Recovery and Development Plan for Northern Uganda (PRDP)*, Kampala, Ministry of Finance Planning and Economic Development.

Government of Uganda (GoU) (2006) *A Rapid Assessment Study for Support to Local Governments in Northern Uganda*, Kampala, Ministry of Local Government

Government of Uganda (GoU) (2007) *Peace, Recovery and Development Plan for Northern Uganda 2007–2010*, Kampala, Ministry of Finance, Planning and Economic Development (MoFPED)

Harwell, Emily E. and Le Billon, Philippe (2009) *Natural Connections: Linking Transitional Justice and Development through a Focus on Natural Resources*, New York, The International Centre for Transitional Justice (ICTJ) Research Brief

Hickey, Sam (2003) 'The politics of staying poor in Uganda', Manchester, *CPRC Working Paper*, 37.

Huber, Jessica (2009) 'Stability peace and reconciliation in northern Uganda', Kampala, *Conflict and Recovery Briefing Report*, 6

Human Rights Watch (1997) *The Scars of Death: Children Abducted by the LRA in Uganda*, New York/ Washington/ London/ Brussels, Human Rights Watch

International Alert (2010) 'Changing fortunes: women's economic opportunities in post-war northern Uganda', *Investing in Peace*, 3

International Crisis Group (ICG) (2004) 'Northern Uganda: understanding and solving the conflict', *International Crisis Group Africa Report*, 77, 14 April

International Crisis Group (ICG) (2010), 'LRA: a regional strategy beyond killing Kony', *Crisis Group Africa Report*, 157, 28 April

Isis-WICCE (2010) 'After a decade: whom has UNSCR 1325 benefitted?' *Newsletter of Isis-WICCE*, 2(2)

Iversen, Ann Kristine (2009) *Transitional Justice in Northern Uganda: A Report on the Pursuit of Justice in Ongoing Conflict*, Roskilde, Roskilde University

Kasozi, A.B.K. (1994) *The Social Origins of Violence in Uganda*, Kampala, Fountain Publishers

Latigo, James Ojera (2008) 'Northern Uganda: tradition-based practices in the Acholi region', in Huyse, Luc and Salter, Mark (eds) *Traditional Justice and Reconciliation after Violent Conflict: Learning from African Experiences*, Stockholm, International Institute for Democracy and Electoral Assistance.

Lenzen, Marcus (2009) 'Roads less traveled? Conceptual pathways (and stumbling blocks) for development and transitional justice', in de Greiff, Pablo and Duthie, Roger (eds) *Transitional Justice and Development: Making Connections*, New York, Social Science Research Council

Mamdani, Mahmood (1999) *Politics and Class Formation in Uganda*, Kampala, Fountain Publishers

Mutibwa, Phares Mukasa (1992) *Uganda Since Independence: A Story of Unfulfilled Hopes*, Trenton, NJ, Africa World Press

Onyango, Eria Olowo (2010) 'Pastoralists in violent defiance of the state: the case of the Karimojong in northeastern Uganda', PhD thesis submitted to university of Bergen

Otim, Michael and Wierda, Marieke (2010) *Uganda: Impact of the Rome Statute and the International Criminal Court*, New York, The International Centre for Transitional Justice

Otunnu, Ogenga (2002) 'Causes and consequences of the war in Acholiland', in Lucima, Okello (ed) *Protracted Conflict, Elusive Peace Initiatives to End the Violence in Northern Uganda*, London, Conciliation Resources

Pham, P., Vinck, P. and Stover, E. (2007) 'Abducted: the Lord's Resistance Army and forced conscription in northern Uganda', Berkeley-Tulane Initiative on Vulnerable Populations, http://www.law.berkeley.edu/HRCweb/reports.html, accessed 12 January 2012

Pham, P., Vinck, P., Wierda, M., Stover, E. and di Giovanni, A. (2005) *Forgotten Voices: A Population Based Survey of Attitudes about Peace and Justice in Northern Uganda*, Berkeley, CA, The International Centre for Transitional Justice and the Human Rights Centre

Refugee Law Project (RLP) (2004) 'Behind the violence: causes, consequences and the search for solutions to the war in northern Uganda', Kampala, *Refugee Law Project Working Paper*, 11

Tripp, Aili Mari (2010) *Museveni's Uganda: Paradoxes of Power in a Hybrid Regime*, Boulder, CO and London, Lynne Reinner

Uganda Bureau of Statistics (UBOS) (2003) *Uganda National Household Survey 2002/03 Report on the Socio-economic Module*, Kampala, UBOS

Uganda Bureau of Statistics (UBOS) (2006) *Uganda National Household Survey 2005/2006: Report on the Socio-economic Module*, Kampala, UBOS

Uganda Bureau of Statistics (UBOS) (2010) *The Uganda National Household Survey 2009/10: The Socio-economic Module*, Kampala, UBOS

United Nations Development Programme (UNDP) (2007) *Uganda Human Development Report 2007: Rediscovering Agriculture for Human Development*, Kampala, UNDP

United Nations Development Programme (UNDP) (2008) *Committed to Northern Uganda's Recovery*, Special Edition: Crisis Prevention and Recovery Programme, Kampala, UNDP

United Nations High Commissioner for Refugees (UNHCR) (2010) *Camp Phase-out Update for Acholi, Lango, Teso and Madi Sub-regions*, Kampala, UNHCR

United Nations (UN) (2010) *Uganda: Mid-Year Consolidated Appeal*, http://ochadms.unog.ch/ quickplace/cap/main.nsf/h_Index/MYR_2010_Uganda/$FILE/MYR_2010_Uganda_SCREEN.pdf?OpenElement, accessed 17 February 2011

Van Acker, Frank (2004) 'Uganda and the Lord's Resistance Army: the new order no one ordered', *African Affairs*, 103(412): 335–57

9

Deconstruction and demonisation: the role of language in transitional justice

Pius Ojara

A perspective on transitional justice

The first problem transitional justice faces is that it has to work with the untold legacies of conflicts. As a result transitional justice deals with sick and divided social contexts with a negative legacy of misrepresentation, dehumanisation, mass violence and torturous conflicts affecting the common well-being. This legacy needs to be addressed through multi-layered inclusion processes and institutional reform mechanisms. In summary, transitional justice involves righting human relations in contexts where there has been gross harm and the abuse of people and their dignity.

Transitional justice includes efforts directed towards understanding and initiating the processes of justice, issues of accountability and the roles of traditional institutions and governance mechanisms. In one sense, transitional justice audits and seeks to find how existing structures of society and capacities of communities can again make possible harmonious coexistence after a narrative of violence, unstable social conditions and disruptions, and a history of struggles and pain. This is also to say that the recognitional and restorative functions of transitional justice comprise a series of processes and mechanisms within a society that seeks to restore civic trust by resourcefully and effectively dealing with the legacy of a painful past, ensure accountability for abuse, serve the course of justice and achieve reconciliation. Indeed, reconciliation and healing lie at the core of the efforts that drive and encourage the *why*, *what* and *how* of transitional justice processes and mechanisms, measures and procedures that may include prosecutions, truth seeking, vetting and dismissals, institutional reforms, reparations, remembrance and memorialisation, and amnesty.

The very notion of transitional justice presupposes the struggle of human communities with the question of meaning and fair relations after much harm has been inflicted. And the kind of issues that we deal with in transitional justice concern a painful past that is best handled, in some important respects, through narratives or story telling.

The logic of transitional justice cannot be separated meaningfully from the logic of social reconciliation, which may include forgiveness. Transitional justice refers to how best to respond to the experiences of mass violence and atrocities. It attempts to let words replace violence and fairness replace terror. The restoration of the humanity of both victim and wrongdoer lie at the heart of the ethics of transitional justice. Socially, the workings of transitional justice involve the provision of structures and processes by means of which a fractured society can be reconstructed truthfully and justly. This further implies coming to terms with a painful past, which includes some measure of reparation to the victims. Creating a social atmosphere of trust therefore becomes important for the processes of transitional justice. It is not enough to denounce abuses and violations; these need to be redeemed through structural protection. Transitional justice discourse and mechanisms seek to initiate and establish a more just and safe society in which the violence and abuses of past wrongs will be prevented from occurring again. But a successful process of transitional justice requires the leadership of reconciled individuals.[1] The inspiring conviction is that that there should not be any recourse to the old and destructive ways of living and doing things.[2]

And one pivotal tool that we human beings have in matters of transitional justice is language.

Basic dimensions and functions of language

In logic – the study of human reasoning and the art of crafting arguments – language is critical. Language stands out as one of the distinguishing features in understanding how human beings communicate and construct action-oriented systems of meanings, or what may precisely be termed their world.

The study of language looks at two dimensions of language, elements that scholars in philosophy like David Braine designate as *qualia* and *parole*, which basically refer respectively to the experience and expression of language. In other words, the experiential and psychological aspects of language always mark human beings and human relationships.

From the perspective of logic, the two dimensions of language enable us to immediately appreciate the four functions of language. First, language performs a declarative function. In this function, language makes a claim about something in the world. This is the propositional character of language that makes assertions about concrete data of experience.

Language also serves the interrogative as when people ask questions of why, when, how, where and what? In this function language serves to unravel or unveil what may not be clear.

Further, language has the imperative function, by means of which people issue injunctions, commands and obligations. This function of language directs purposes and activities in particular contexts.

In addition, language serves the expressive function as when a person declares, 'Wow', 'Ah', 'My God' to indicate emotional responses to particular experiences.

Human experience demands language that frames it since it supplies the currency for conveying information and sentiments. By means of language, people can conceal and reveal, uplift and injure, protect and hide, expand and recover realities of personal and common experiences in vivid ways. It is in expressing their experience in language forms that people may awaken to what meaning or significance underlies some particular experience. In this way, language enables people to penetrate their experiences by delimiting and illuminating, gathering and uniting aspects of their lives. The power of language to encode thought and reality is one reason why meaning is frequently contested.

Frequently, when people capture their joyful and difficult, uplifting and dismal experiences through the four functions of language, they do so by means of stories or narratives that they then tell themselves and others. In one sense people do inhabit the stories or narratives that they tell themselves, what others tell them and what they tell others. In short, story telling marks human relationships and interactions in a deep way. Accordingly, before we can even start talking about transitional justice we must understand that there are always narratives that precede atrocities and acts of mass violence.

The narrative origins of mass violence

First, at the origins of mass violence or atrocity lies a certain successive struggle for a narrowly based power which, to a very large extent, consists of the ability to make others inhabit one's stories of their reality. This ability may also imply killing the other to make that happen. The power that leads to mass violence and atrocities is frequently a narrowly based power that eschews inclusive political settlement, which establishes a lasting elite bargain and serves the interests of the powerful political players; a broadly based power requires a truer story at its core and protects its subjects from abuses.[3] Such a power is sensitive to the glue that holds society together. How people inhabit their stories is important for their sense of identity. In this respect, people are often functions of how they imagine themselves and how others imagine them. This often involves claims that relate to privileges, arrogance, greed, indifference, ignorance and fear. The ideas that others have of us define us sharply. Paradoxically, as others make our lives their business, they make us vividly aware and alive. In consequence, the only times when persons are truly free to imagine themselves are their private times when they are inviolably on their own.[4]

The stories people tell themselves frequently raise questions about the humanity of others, who may be perceived as rivals or menaces and whose presence creates a unifying spectre of a common enemy. And when others are seen as absolute menaces, rivals and enemies, an absolute means of eradication is then devised through suggestive messages and direct commands to kill or be killed.[5] Tellingly, then, the stories people tell about others and themselves shape relational expectations, attitudes and habits. And the kinds of stories that lie behind mass violence and atrocity tend to place others at the periphery of humanity. A typical tactic consists in addressing others by means of abstract and offensive categories of enemy, rival or menace.

This is where labelling comes in. Labelling is the stuff born of the mass-man or mass-woman, the public self, which nullifies love. In fact, labelling cannot be separated from a certain lack of love, that is, the inability to treat a human being as a human being and using an abstract designation for a human being. In this way, labelling makes it possible to deny the personal existence of individuals and groups of persons and reduces them to objects so that the worth of a human subject is deprived of its intrinsic justification. This is what calling into question the dignity and personal existence of another is about. In other words:

> In order to transform him into a mere impersonal target, it is absolutely necessary to convert him into an abstraction: the communist [the terrorist, the black, the white, the Jew, the Tutsi, an Acholi, a Shona, a Ndebele, a Muganda, a Munyakole, a Kikuyu, a Kalenjin] ... and so on ... I am not, of course, in any sense making the claim that this is a method which any human mind sets out coldly and consciously to apply. The truth lies much deeper.[6]

In order to be violent a person must depersonalise the other, that is, interpretatively deny him or her individual share in intrinsic preciousness and desirability. Here we may observe that:

> as soon as people (people, that is to say, the State or a political party or a faction or a religious sect, or what it may be) claim of me that I commit myself to a warlike action against other human beings whom I must, as a consequence of my commitment, be ready to destroy, it is very necessary from the point of view of those who are influencing me that I lose all awareness of the individual reality of the being whom I may be led to destroy.[7]

In labelling a person in terms of, say, their tribe, race, gender, creed, sexual orientation, financial status, political affiliation or background, the human subject is reduced to an impersonal target of a danger, a threat, a thief, or an enemy. A denial of the sacred character of persons hermeneutically constitutes the perceptual and existential desacralisation of life which constitutes its dehumanisation.[8] This fact commonly neutralises the sense of respect due to the humanity of others. A process of dehumanisation takes place that then makes it easy to humiliate, injure and annihilate others. Often labelling works by making appeals to a sense of collective weakness and blame. This explains why in order to move a huge number of people to do wrong, it is necessary to appeal to their passion for strength. And as people surrender to hatred they also aspire to controlling power.[9]

The significance of narrative language in transitional justice

Handling of space and time frequently involves the use of narrative in the working out and construction of personal identity and history. An intimate alliance exists between lived experience and narrative. When people tell their stories they weave together into narratives events of special significance and in so doing shape their own self-understanding and sense of identity. The way people tell their stories to themselves, friends, colleagues, families, or communities gains them insights into who they are, how they believe in themselves, and where they come from. The ways people tell their stories gain them new perspectives which, frequently enough, enable them to recognise, modify, and appreciate their present situations.

In telling a story a person discloses, unifies and orders the presence and absence of lived tensions and surprises, startling triumphs and reversals, unexpected turns and events, hopes and anticipations, possibilities and realities. Stories make ideas and memories, realities and absences accessible, noteworthy and, perhaps, testable if they ring true to lived experience. The full range and the multiple dimensions of life, which can be ravaging and provocative, questioning and confronting, freeing and healing, reconciling and exalting, find fitting and accessible re-expression in narrative itself. Remarkably then:

My life presents itself to reflection as something whose essential nature is that it can be related as a story ('If I told you the story of my life, then you really would be astonished!') ... and this is so very true that one may be permitted to wonder whether the words 'my life' retain any precise meaning at all, if we abstract from the meaning we attach to them any reference whatsoever to the act of narration.[10]

What is more, in narrative we do not only express who we are; we profoundly express the beliefs that inform our shared sense of meaning and purpose. In narrative we express the ongoing shared sense of meaning and purpose of the culture in which we participate.

In addition, a person always transcends what he or she understands about himself or herself. 'In telling our life stories we only allude to something which, of its very nature, will not let itself be fully expressed in words, and which is something I have lived through.'[11] At the same time, 'we have to acknowledge that my life, as it has really been lived, falls outside my thinking's present grasp. The past cannot be recaptured except by a lightning flash, a sudden glare, of memory, for which the fragments are present and not past.'[12] 'I am the more my past the less I treat my past as a collection of events jotted in a notebook as possible answers to eventual questions. I am the less I look on myself as a tabulation or "repertory".'[13] Or again, 'it is not true to say that the past is immutable; for we cannot legitimately distinguish between material events which are fixed, and an illumination which varies according to its source, a source which is the experienced present itself.'[14] Furthermore, 'To narrate can only be to summarise and yet the summarising of the parts of a tale is in a certain sense obviously an opposite kind of operation from the unfolding of the tale as a whole.'[15] So, 'it would be an illusion to claim that my life, as I turn it into a story, corresponds at all completely with my life as I have actually lived it'.[16] The past cannot be separated from its consideration. 'My history is not transparent to me. It is only my history in so far as it is not transparent to me. In this sense, it cannot become part of my system and perhaps it even breaks up my system.'[17] My life as a whole cannot be recounted. In this regard a person's life cannot be put on a filing card; this is what is meant by the assertion that a person's life cannot be recounted or totalised. There is in a life that is lived something which resists being reduced to entries placed one after another.[18] My life is not a simple given. 'There is a sense in which it is true to say that every life can be recounted. And there is another sense more profound by which we should affirm, on the contrary, that a life cannot be retold.'[19] 'My life infinitely transcends my possible conscious grasp of my life at any given moment; fundamentally and essentially it refuses to tally with itself.'[20]

In dealing with pain that typifies contexts of transitional justice, contexts in which persons suffer greatly, perhaps because they are violated, betrayed or have experienced injustice, it is important to understand the issues and alternatives, and to grasp the data and principles, the backgrounds and experiences, the rugged and the beautiful elements that play out in the experience. And through narrative language, people can shift from a prelinguistic state within which they are overwhelmed by the extent of suffering to the point where they take control of suffering, at least to the point of being able to speak about it. In any event, a memory captured in words can no longer haunt, push people around, or bewilder them because they can begin to wrestle with the possibility of moving it.[21]

The sensibilities and risks connected with narrative language

There exists a common tendency in the way people tell stories about the past and their position or role in the past. Individuals and organisations, minorities and majorities, communities and movements, groups and nations tend to give a one-sided picture of their stories, especially in contexts that generate the need for transitional justice. Frequently, it is the narratives from the perspectives of victimhood or the victorious that tend to carry the day. All the same, any suppression of a dimension of experience in living memory is a sad and ugly truncation. It is important to appreciate and take note of this tendency because when we speak about our past we assume only certain perspectives governed by our 'lived' experiences.[22] We cling recognisably to our past in a very uneven way; we are our past in a very uneven way. And it must be added that this unevenness is related to a similar unevenness in our present condition.[23] Yet when we say 'our past' we imply that everything that happened to us constitutes a whole which is capable of being augmented as long as we live.[24] The unity we attribute to 'our past' frequently belongs only to thought. For what are given to us are shreds, certain qualities or indefinable signs or markers.[25]

It is incorrect, then, to give only a festive interpretation or celebratory account of our roles in the past. History is often not only about what has come to prevail or succeed. Shortcomings and weaknesses typify genuine historical narratives. The defeated, destroyed and shameful are part and parcel of our history as well. One side of the human story, the 'bad', should not be ignored or repressed. In other words, the 'good' should not be over-stressed at the expense of the 'bad'. Heritages are complex and messy in that they involve varying and differing elements in combinations or mosaic forms that also remain preliminary, fragmentary and changeable. To concede ambivalence in historical narrative is to grant a sense of wholeness, which consists of the beauty and ugliness that characterise every human history or narrative associated with it. Stories that concede wholeness help in the interior reformation of persons and communities, which also renews the human spirit and human relations. The ugly in the past needs not be suppressed; rather, it needs to be owned and honoured. Experience will frequently disclose its attractive and disturbing dimensions.

The meaning of history, personal and organisational, social and political, depends on those who survived and became successful as well as on those who failed, that is, the vanquished, the oppressed and suppressed, the forgotten and neglected, the buried traces of shame and struggles, revenge and darkness. When we acknowledge the ambivalent and disjointed elements in our histories, we truly begin to define behaviours and aspirations in a more realistic and holistic way. History is a mesh that is messier than is frequently conceded. Honouring and/or telling the truth, in all its dimensions, is decisive in the construction of a liberating narrative that transforms the process of transitional justice.

Nobody possesses the fiat to let a difficult past merely pass by; to do so would be to partially dishonour living history. In any case, an unacknowledged past holds people hostage to captive living. After all, in all contexts of transitional justice, all elements of the past (including estrangement and chasms as well as the marginalised and anonymous dimensions) have contributed to a surviving and shared identity that remains tied up with memory. Any hermeneutical and practical denial of an ugly past dehumanises people by impugning their lived experience. It also silences and distorts wholesomeness In spite of everything, elemental identifiers in a history repeatedly try to stake out their claims on the turf of narratives.

In fact, while the possibility of creating a sense of wholesome history will remain incomplete, every narrative legitimises history's key and identifying elements. The very act of remembering is not equal to truth. The risk remains that a narrative that postulates someone as a victim may also easily authorise them to do harm to others. The telling of stories is as important as the story itself.

So, a healing re-creation of the past takes place at the great price of authentic acknowledgment and as a process of integrating the imbalances in lived narrative. This process of embrace and acknowledgement, however, needs to be sensitive and wise, imaginative and concrete while also being symbolic. It is prejudicial to only commemorate or sideline the discomforting features of histories that always remain complex and, perhaps, wicked. All this is important to note because while there is an awful depth of depravity to which people can sink in giving narrative accounts, they also have an extraordinary capacity for magnanimity and excellence.

In other words, there is nobody who is not in a position to encourage, within and beyond themselves, the spirit of truth.[26] Through the illuminations of the spirit of truth, the human self reaches an identity that makes possible a narrative which acknowledges partiality and honours the greater truth of ambivalent wholeness. Individual and shared history is constructed through elements of life that frequently remain unstructured and dynamic, and which comprise victories and defeats, joys and sufferings. Attempts to silence, obscure and marginalise certain dimensions of lived experience in a narrative do not easily work. It is also the silent episodes and muted events that promote, punctuate and sustain the storylines of narratives about the past. Insofar as they are embedded in narrative threads or supply follow-up notations, obscured dimensions in a narrative contribute to the scuffling of the story world. The living consciousness of the past never fully disappears. It is not completely replaced.

In short, in transitional justice, remembering the past is costly but it is costlier not to remember and not to acknowledge it in its complexity of deep hurts and anger. The ugly past may still repeat itself in a new and more vicious variety. What and how we tell stories shape the way we construct, project and anticipate the riddles of reconciliation processes. Narratives influence people's lives. Narratives about the past have the capacity to enlighten us as to what is possible and practical in life. Practical consequences do arise from narrative practices. How we tell stories matters; it redefines and privileges or abuses and denigrates people and relationships for the sake of some interests, aims or goals. Only in fostering sensitivity to the apparently marginal yet real experiences within these narratives about the past are we able to make a particular contribution towards some fuller existence. The past always lives in the present.

The pivotal role of truthfulness in transitional justice

The preceding considerations make one thing clear: new life and new existence spring from truthfulness, which involves a genuine candour with the self and others. Truthfulness challenges us to renewed and bold honesty. At the heart of truthfulness lies the quest for truth and we can rely upon the truth because the truth is dependable and liberating.

It is important to note that we live in times when there exists a passion for truthfulness but that this can be corrupted by sensationalism and exhibitionism. Interestingly enough, too, we live in a time when there is a new feeling for constructive self-criticism, sincerity, straightforwardness and truthfulness in life. A truthful person lives in harmony with himself or herself inwardly; he or she affirms their innermost self and morality. In other words, truthfulness refers to the way we place ourselves in relation to ourselves. It relates to the inward relationship of frankness and genuineness that we have towards ourselves. It constitutes the basic personal attitude and transparency that we have in regard to ourselves. It also forms the basis of authentic identity, authentic selfhood and inner personal substance.

At the same time, we must recognise that untruthfulness contrasts with truthfulness. Untruthfulness is hypocrisy; what an untruthful person says does not correspond with what they believe or think. Personal and interior discordance belongs to the character of untruthfulness. Irrespective of social standing or religious profession, an untruthful person tends to be deeply dishonest. In this way, conscience does not disturb an untruthful person. An untruthful person is not honest and their lack of harmony with themselves does not disturb or bother them. When people become untruthful, it means that they cease to be genuine and transparent in regard to themselves and others. They then soften and break down in their innermost and basic morality and lose all sense of genuineness in their interactions and relationships with others. They do not have to admit responsibility for their lack of truthfulness. Consequently, they also lose moral constraint on considerations of compliance, expedience and interior incongruence – and this is dangerous for the exercising of justice, the discharging of authority and common life and the professional discharging of responsibilities.

Habitually untamed greed and the unbridled quest for power mark the personal ambition, behaviour and interactions of a deeply dishonest man or woman. The resultant ways of dealing with others perceived as obstructing or threatening their pathways or strangleholds on positions of power can become malicious, vicious and heartless.

We must also not forget that the risk that remains closely associated with truthfulness is fanaticism for truthfulness. Fanaticism for truth often implies abandoning our responsibility to and for others. Fanaticism rejects, indicts, annihilates, pummels, and renders contemptible other people's perspectives. The fanatic belittles others with whom they disagree; they judge out of hatred and without due consideration for the limits that concrete reality imposes. In this way, a fanatic does not allow for human weakness; the fanatic desecrates the mystery of persons, breaks confidence in common life and, in the end, serves the fragmentation of human relations. A fanatic believes that they possess the truth and so easily believe that they have the right to hurt and wrong others in the name of honesty and sincerity. The zeal associated with fanaticism intrudes stubbornly into the lives of others. The fanatic seeks to realise truth at the expense of communication and conversations in the community and so sacrifices the common good and common welfare. This means that we need to learn to tell the truth in the right way and hold lightly what we believe to be the truth.

Subsequently, when people tell the stories of their suffering truthfully, they unburden and transform our lives and relationships. Truth anchors the values that count in our lives and to which we can willingly commit ourselves. Within this perspective, renewing regard for truth implies that we also become increasingly aware that truth remains deeply relational, historical and contextual in its character. Besides, at the human level concern for truth grounds our quest for justice as a species of truth. Frequently, to promote justice touches on our willingness to reveal and face the truth of injustices and exhibit solidarity with victims of injustices. In a sense, love of truth and love of justice hang together.

In fact, truth telling in the right way and in the right forum breeds trust among people. It gives direction and meaning to astonishing human life. When we fail to be true to ourselves, our communication becomes insincere and our dealings dishonest. At the same time, the complexity of human reality and the fragmentary nature of human knowing calls forth our humility in the face of truth. This humility entails sensitivity to our historicity and contingency. We need to continually strive for more objective and manifest truth. Certainly, our grasp of truth always remains ambiguous, uncertain, temporary and dialogical. Yet at the same time, the steady and diligent drive for truth or the search for truth must continue no matter how strenuous the process may be. In a sense, truth does not exist outside a man's or woman's interactions with the social and physical world.

The delivery of transitional justice, which cannot be separated from a certain grounding in truthfulness, initiates the beginning of sympathy, of a sense of togetherness, and of the building up of the human community through some form of reconciliation and of renewing of trust among people. The trajectory of transitional justice can stimulate a transformation which offers the promise of a new creation of humanity in peace.

The grammar of human rights and transitional justice

The telling and retelling of stories can also take place through the language of human rights, which can make known the circumstances, antecedents, factors and contexts of violations and the needed process of reconciliation and reconstruction. The rhetoric of human rights, as a response to unjustified suffering, provides people with the grammar to speak about their stories of suffering. The human rights language, it may be noted, springs out of the concrete sufferings of individuals in particular histories and cultures. Of course, in all this is also the affirmation of fundamental human dignity, as an individual and collective reality, which endows abuses and violations with moral significance. Embedded in the human rights language is the sense of mutual and relational obligations that people owe to one another for harmonious coexistence. The language of human rights grounds itself in the conviction of the sovereign and relational self so that the language of human rights touches on people's legitimate interests. As a moral vocabulary the language of human rights offers ways of talking about the experiences of people; the language offers a way of perceiving, imagining and interpreting suffering. In effect, as a narrative grammar the language of human rights allows people to name the prejudices and violations that affected their persons and relationships. It also makes possible the imagination of new ways of describing behaviours and conduct appropriate to social reconstruction.

The grammar of human rights helps further in disclosing the historical progression in the violations of persons and human relations and in establishing accountability. Conditions that precede mass violence and atrocity are often nurtured over a long time. They often follow long-standing toleration of violence and systemic distortions that threaten people's rights to subsistence, security and liberty of participation in social and political life and processes. Through abuses of rights a gradual withdrawal takes place of some people's sense of humanity. Erosion of human agency through the creation of conditions that make it difficult for some people to realise a fuller sense of their dignity is a common yet critical marker in the degradation of life, which culminates in mass violence and atrocity.

In the light of the common good, the grammar of human rights makes possible certain narratives of people in the light of shared living, heritages, aspirations, and common humanity. In implicating people in the moral community, dignity implies that people are responsible not only for themselves as individuals but also for others and shared heritages, memories and hopes. The language of human rights enhances the experience and expression of human historical agency in justice that affirms and recognises the humanity of all peoples and cultures.

Reconciliation and memorials in transitional justice

We could say that one of the key goals of transitional justice is the attainment of reconciled communities and individuals within the context of an ambivalent past. The enterprise of reconciliation seeks to restore the humanity of both the victim and the wrongdoer. Yet the restoration of the humanity of the victim must include the painful experiences of violence which now mark the victim's memories and identity.[27]

We may note that reconciliation begins with the victim whose humanity the wrongdoer tried to call into question, wrest away or destroy. It is through the victim that the wrongdoer is called to repentance and forgiveness. Restoring the humanity of the victim expresses itself in practices and attitudes which create space for truth and justice, healing and new possibilities. Such practices and attitudes lead further to the creating of communities of shared memories and hope that generate safe places for exploring and untangling the complexity of a painful past and for cultivating a culture of truth telling in order to overcome the lies of injustice and wrongdoing.[28]

It is further important to recognise that the victims' memories of death tend to focus attention on experiences of loss and absence and the abyss that the victims of violence or atrocity faced. The sense of an abyss reveals the enormity and complexity of a painful past. Through the absence victims of mass violence and atrocities acknowledge who they have become because of the past and the need to transcend the past so that it no longer controls their current directions of existence.

Mass violence and atrocity leave human wreckage in their wake. The yawning abyss of absence which confronts the victims of violence and atrocity provides them with the loci for recognising the sense of loss and the skein of emotions that surround their painful experiences. Out of the loci of absences tend to flow memories through which new relationships can be worked out. Yet the strength to deal with absences positively and creatively requires a steadfastness of faith, trust and hope.[29] Establishing a focus for grief is, then, important. Within this perspective, memorials become important for effecting the reconciliation of individuals and communities. They provide people with a space for grieving. When people grieve they proclaim that they cannot allow acts of violence or atrocities to engulf their world. It is in this regard that burial places and monuments offer places where people can engage in the rituals that allow them to re-establish a foothold in an otherwise shaking and unstable world. One cannot hold onto the dead; a new kind of relationship has to be worked out, shaped and established.[30] Memorials provide people with a feeling that their grievances and pain are being recognised and heard by others. In this way, there also comes a re-awakening of some sense of justice and catharsis.

The significance of the dead is concretely mediated through aspects of the exigencies that acts of mass violence and atrocities assault, injure and exterminate.

Human exigencies and the dignity of life

The proper use of language in transitional justice cannot afford to avoid reference to human exigencies. An exigency[31] is a need and aspiration to living a fuller human life that a person has a responsibility to meet and a right to satisfy. An exigency is not only a need but also something that is demanded.[32] Exigencies define people and their lives.[33]

There are four distinguishable exigencies that are identifiable as people participate in this world. These are the psychic, psychological, social and productive exigencies. The exigencies signify that the human subject always remains active within the world in the sense that a person cannot really stand aside from the universe, even in thought. Only by a meaningless pretence can a person place themselves at some vague point outside of the world. In other words, I cannot place myself outside myself (a revealing parallel).[34] And the exigencies interpenetrate and interconnect; each exigency requires the vitality and the impulses of the others.

The psychic exigency means that I am an 'I', a centre of freedom and a self-present being. It means a human being experiences, attends and intends some goal, evaluation or decision as well being a locus of inherence or self. A human being is aware of being a conscious subject, however fragmentary or incoherent this may be. The personal life of a human being is marked by self-governance and impulses for transformation that come with continually clarifying one's position in the world. Significantly, the human subject always remains individually and relationally available.

The psychological exigency refers to the responsiveness that is habitually pre-reflective yet expressive of the human motivations which shape interactive and functional behaviours. The psychological exigency arises from the fact that we are interpretatively conscious beings. This is partly because the very nature of consciousness is such that it cannot detach itself from itself, or behold itself while in the very act of contemplation; consciousness is above all consciousness of something which is other than itself.[35] So, we have the responsive demand to be recognised by others and to recognise others within an existential space. We experience our need and aspiration to be acknowledged and responded to in the very process of being in the world. Consciousness of existing is linked up with the urge to make ourselves recognised by some other person, some witness, helper, rival or adversary who is needed to integrate the self.[36] The psychological sphere is a milieu of responsive living with others.

The social exigency refers to the public exchange of interacting and interpretative relationships within broadly pre-existing and structured patterns and possibilities of human relations. This exigency grounds healthy give-and-take in our broader social relationship with other persons, without which connectedness our lives would be different. In this regard, as thinking beings we are involved in a vast communion, a vast *co-esse*, of which I can only have a fragmentary awareness through key experiences.[37] In other words:

> I find myself in strictly determined circumstances regarding my birth, the milieu in which I live, the people I have met, and

> so on ... It would be altogether inadequate to maintain that these conditions are due to pure chance and for that reason, insignificant. It is in relation to them that I have to assert my freedom, and in the course of doing so I am let to appreciate my circumstances as having been – in the strongest sense of the word – given. In this way I come to think of a will which is giving and at the same time free.[38]

Social exigency undergirds and informs the human experience of being a subject of a certain thrust of connectedness and vast relations with others that make a person into who and what they are: 'to exist is to co-exist'.[39] Coexistence with others informs the sense of being relevant in life. Indeed:

> A secret voice which I cannot silence assures me in fact that if others are not there, I am not there either. I cannot grant to myself an existence of which I suppose the others are deprived; and here 'I cannot' does not mean 'I have not the right' but rather 'It is impossible for me'. If others vanish from me, I vanish from myself.[40]

Concretely, as we grow up and live in a given historical cultural context, we make and unmake and remake ourselves. As we live with others we affect social life by our own views as that life is also affected by the views and judgments of others. Our relations with others create 'a primordial bond, a kind of umbilical cord, which unites the human being to a particular, determined, and concrete [physical and social] environment.'[41] We commonly call this culture. In the social world we also develop our own thinking and feelings, likes and dislikes, aspirations and set of possibilities through which we define ourselves through living with others so that *to be among others* evidently belongs to what I am.[42]

Productive exigency embraces a personal sense of giftedness as well as accomplishment and achievements. It refers to the productivity and creativity of human spirit and labour derived from an understanding of this life as a gift and a task, a challenge and a responsibility. At the same time, production needs to be distinguished from creation: any production depends on a technique and creation is a response to a call received.[43] Creation is never a production; it implies an active receptivity.[44]

To some extent there is freedom wherever and whenever there is creation, even at the humblest levels.[45] Moreover, creation is not necessarily the creation of something outside the person who creates. To create is not, essentially, to produce. There can be production without creation, and there can be creation without any identifiable object remaining to bear witness to the creation. In the course of our lives we probably already know some persons who are essentially creators. The radiance of charity and love shining from their being simply add a positive contribution to the invisible work which gives the human adventure the only meaning which justifies it.[46] Wherever there is creativity, that is to say, liberative affirmation, there is to some degree participation in being, that is, sharing in the experience and expression of life's intrinsic significance.[47]

Accordingly, the exigencies mean that who I am depends on my relation to myself, to the world, to fellow men and women, and to activities that engage my loyalty and attention. It also includes being in this or that way of life, this or that field of values. The exigencies require a certain minimum of realisation for a man or woman to survive, live and flourish. They signify that a human subject has original and specific abilities and duties to discover and establish how their life as an individual and as a member of the community can flourish. 'The existent being which I am is defined by the multiplicity of possibilities or of possible actions which are in me; they constitute a network or gridiron which confers a meaning upon things or places them in a certain totality which we call the world'[48] Personal destiny is by no means a solitary affair; it involves participating in the vicissitudes of life that involves others. The assurance of our individual and collective existence only takes place in relation to the world.[49]

The exigencies further mean that people experience deep within themselves the need for being, that is, the demand for dignity. This demand requires that not everything be reduced to a game of successive and inconsistent appearances, which are of no intrinsic significance, or to 'a tale told by an idiot'.[50] People experience and embody the deep demand for something of permanent value and significance. The exigencies are grounded in the intrinsic value and significance of persons, they entitle you and me as human subjects to rights and responsibilities which interpenetrate and reinforce one another. In other words, because humans are gifted with the intrinsic value of dignity, they have the rights and responsibilities to care for and protect, sustain and promote their worth as persons. In part, the task of transitional justice belongs to the awakening of this consciousness and lifting up the precious-ness of human life as well as the kinship links that tie all people together. This is what the deep human desire to live in peace with one another is about.

Conclusion

Language remains a distinguishing feature of human beings. The experience and expression of language mark people with their influences, with the way people commonly appreciate experi-ences and with the power to construct and define relationships. Through language people do lift up and sideline, praise and problematise others. In other words, the effective use of language affects concepts of identity, of relationships and a sense of com-mon purpose. The adversarial use of language also mobilises people in ways that can lead them to do great harm and commit great atrocities. In the context of transitional justice, therefore, language performs a double function. Yet, paradoxically, it is the same language that enables people to name their painful experi-ences through the grammar of human rights, the grammar of basic human exigencies (needs and demands), through truth tell-ing, and the memorialisation of a painful past. All these vehicles of language enable it to play the apparently contradictory roles of demonisation and deconstruction that mark the process and trajectories of transitional justice. Indeed, it cannot be emphasised strongly enough that changing the structures and attitudes of violence, injustice and gross violations of human rights that tran-sitional justice sets itself to do – in order to achieve sustainable peace, unity and reconciliation – always remains a demanding endeavour, challenge and opportunity.

Notes

1 Philip Gourevitch (1993) *We Wish to Inform You that Tomorrow We Will Be Killed With Our Families: Stories from Rwanda,* New York, Picador, St Martin Press: 65.
2 Robert J. Schreiter (2004) *The Ministry of Reconciliation: Spirituality and Strategies,* Maryknoll, New York, Orbis Books: 8.

3 Gourevitch (1993): 48, 181.
4 Gourevitch (1993): 71.
5 Gourevitch (1993): 95.
6 Gabriel Marcel (1971) *Man Against Mass Society,* Chicago, Henry Regnery: 157–8.
7 Marcel (1971): 157.
8 Gabriel Marcel (1973) *Tragic Wisdom and Beyond,* Evanston, IL, Northwestern University Press: 109.
9 Gourevitch (1993): 128–9.
10 Gabriel Marcel (1984a) *The Mystery of Being Vol.1: Reflection and Mystery,* Lanham, MD, University Press of America: 154.
11 Marcel (1984a).
12 Marcel (1984a): 155–6.
13 Gabriel Marcel (1952) *Metaphysical Journal,* Chicago, Henry Regnery: 249.
14 Gabriel Marcel (1982) *Creative Fidelity,* New York: The Crossroad Publishing Company: 52.
15 Marcel (1984a): 155.
16 Marcel (1984a).
17 Gabriel Marcel (1965) *Being and Having: An Existential Diary,* New York, Harper and Row: 129.
18 Gabriel Marcel (2003) *Awakenings,* Milwaukee, WI, Marquette University Press, 34.
19 Marcel (2003).
20 Marcel (1984a): 167.
21 Charles Villa-Vicencio (2004) *The Art of Reconciliation,* Uppsala, Life and Peace Institute: 18.
22 Gabriel Marcel (1967a) *Presence and Immortality,* Pittsburgh, Duquesne University Press: 56.
23 Marcel (1984a): 184.
24 Marcel (1967a): 52.
25 Marcel (1967a): 51.
26 Marcel (1967a): 269.
27 Schreiter (2004): 17–18.
28 Schreiter (2004): 15.
29 Schreiter (2004): 37–9.
30 Schreiter (2004): 35.
31 In his writings, Marcel frequently uses the word *exigence* instead of exigency.
32 Gabriel Marcel (1984b) *The Mystery of Being Vol. 2: Faith and Reality* Lanham, MD, University Press of America: 37.
33 Marcel (1973): 34.
34 Marcel (1965): 19.
35 Marcel (1984a): 51–2.
36 Gabriel Marcel (1965a) *Homo Viator: Introduction to a Metaphysics of Hope,* New York, Harper and Row Publishers: 15.
37 Gabriel Marcel (1991) 'Reply to Gene Reeves', in Paul Arthur Schilpp and

Lewis Edwin Hahn (eds) *The Library of Living Philosopher Vol. XXVII: The Philosophy of Gabriel Marcel*, La Salle, IL, Open Court: 274.

38 Gabriel Marcel (1963) *The Existential Background of Human Dignity,* Cambridge, MA, Harvard University Press: 30.

39 Marcel (1967a): 205.

40 Marcel (1965a): 138.

41 Marcel (1973): 38.

42 Gabriel Marcel (1967b) *Searchings,* New York, Newman Press: 62.

43 Marcel (1963): 126.

44 Marcel (1984b): 139.

45 Marcel (1963): 160.

46 Marcel (1984b): 45.

47 Gabriel Marcel (1965b) *Philosophical Fragments 1909–1914 and the Philosopher Fragments,* Notre Dame, IN, Notre Dame University Press: 84.

48 Gabriel Marcel (1967c) *Problematic Man,* New York, Herder and Herder: 111.

49   Marcel (1967c): 112.

50   Marcel (1967c): 139.

10

Reflections from practice: on learning, monitoring and evaluation in transitional justice programmes

Undine Whande

> What makes any social-living-system work is not how cleverly it is conceived and mapped, but how wisely and mutually it is understood and valued, enabling those who have and take leadership to see and work with what is there and what is possible, and with each other. (Reeler 2010)

In the past ten years, the development sector has seen a widening polarity in the evolution of monitoring and evaluation (M&E) methodologies. On one side of the polarity is an increasing awareness that monitoring and evaluation practices need to be context, actor and organisation specific, tailor-made and rooted in human relationships. There is a realisation that if M&E is to be experienced as useful and meaningful, it requires regular quality time for reflection and conversation, in organisations, among peers and between grant makers and grantees. This has led to the honing of emergent, conversational approaches, now known broadly under the heading 'developmental' or 'emergent' evaluation practices. On the other side of the polarity, however, the still more established, linear log frame-based approaches, whose origins date back to the Second World War, remain the norm and base of many a development programme.

The log frame became prominent in the late 1970s and was further developed by aid agencies, in particular by USAID and later by German Technical Cooperation (GTZ), as a participatory planning tool. It was evolved into a widely applied methodology known in English as GOPP – goal-oriented project planning. This method often resulted in vast amounts of little note cards with many ideas. It presented a useful brainstorming tool. However, a sense of success in generating a participatory mode was often dampened when the emerging complexity, the many issues and strands that local development actors would raise and then want to discuss, were in the end once more condensed into the confines of cause–consequence thinking. In the attempt to reduce complexity in order to make the social processes observed 'manageable', the GOPP process often flattened the experiential realities of local actors back into linear outcomes that could be 'managed'. The 'problem tree' for instance, was one such tool, often used to fixate a cause–consequential chain of envisioned results. Rather than generate conversation about the different layers and levels of interdependency between the phenomena observed in a given situation, I witnessed people spending a lot of time debating whether poverty was a root cause or a symptom of violence. The value of the tool, however, rested not in deciding on a unidirectional cause–consequential link but in lifting out interdependencies and generating reflection on what could be observed.

An increasing emphasis has since been placed by development aid funders on refining results-based monitoring through the use of such technical tools, in particular the now popular 'results chains', arguably at the expense of the initial participatory intent. For the majority of grantees this has meant working with tight templates to gather statistical data. There is an emphasis on an M&E orientation that espouses notions of 'evidence', 'proof of effect' and 'efficiency'. In particular, the terminology of effectiveness and efficiency govern proposal language. The hunt for visible effects and cost-benefit analyses are seen to be markers of both the quantitative and qualitative success of an intervention, but the terms are rarely defined or their meaning explored further. However, social transformation efforts resist being reduced to economical equations that could be measured through an input–output paradigm.

Monitoring and evaluation in transitional justice interventions

In many of the scenarios described by transitional justice organisations in the African Transitional Justice Research Network (ATJRN), funders currently appear to practitioners to overemphasise accountability in the technical sense: reporting against preconceived plans and templates, often in terms of numbers of workshops conducted, brochures produced, products and trainings delivered, etc. A major shift was the move from this merely output-driven dimension (what was done or produced) to an outcomes orientation (what beneficiaries did with the experiences, products and learning). The outcomes orientation, however, often remains tied to preconceived indicators that are rarely revised in the process of project/programme emergence. Rather, in response to current M&E frameworks, actors tailor their thoughts on what has actually transpired during the activities to fit the indicators. The loss is not only valuable information that is not deemed relevant, not asked for and, hence, not reported, but also the potential for learning from what has actually emerged during the process of implementation. In response, transitional justice practice becomes activity driven, so as to produce countable results.

This means that the supposed 'second leg' of M&E – if accountability is one and learning the other – is not fostered in the current grant-making and related M&E practices. Transitional justice practice becomes activity driven, so as to produce countable results. The critical dimension of monitoring as learning, monitoring as a constant reflective reading of the situation, is not evolved as a conscious practice. There is not yet an M&E approach that is specifically tailored to the needs of practitioners working in the sensitive arena of dealing with the past after – and often within the continuities of – violent conflict.

Transitional justice practitioners engaging with the learning, monitoring and evaluation in transitional justice work commented at the Institute for African Transitional Justice (IATJ) on a lack of learning spaces inside their organisations, where practice is often driven by activity and the context response and characterised by a near-furious busy-ness, particularly in activist-minded organisations and coalitions. M&E is thus often dreaded as an 'external eye', with many of the experiences sketched representing the parachute-in-a-consultant-at-the-end-of-the-project approach. Summative evaluations are favoured over formative approaches that accompany a project process over time. External consultants then conduct arm's-length, often rushed appraisals according to the indicators and needs of the funder. Terms of reference are neither jointly defined nor discussed in depth with the practitioners as the process of implementation unfolds. Rarer are reports of evaluations where terms of reference are negotiated, where time is taken for pre-conversations, where reflective practice – engaged in with some insiders and some outsiders to the project process – generates an evaluative exchange dimension that is experienced as meaningful and productive by all. The later examples left practitioners with a sense of satisfaction, based on the feeling of respect, being taken seriously and able to share processes, results, learning and expertise with the review teams. In particular, the peer reviews that were conducted by the ATJRN were experienced as productive. The ATJRN developed a peer review methodology and has run peer reviews between transitional justice organisations in Uganda and Sierra Leone, South Africa and Kenya, and Kenya and Zimbabwe.

The least developed (or perhaps conscious) aspect of M&E practice in transitional justice organisations, however, seems to be the ongoing monitoring. This is an area where M&E, in-house knowledge management and an organisation's development practices meet, at best, in an organisational culture that encourages reflective practice, learning, the revealing of mistakes and learning from failures. Monitoring is much more than the technical exercise of 'counting' deliverables that it is sometimes made out to be. It is intimately linked with questions of organisational management and culture as sources for innovation and development. Many organisations struggle with developing systems that make sense for their specific organisational context, their staff, the origin and orientation of the organisation and its work because they feel they have to adhere to M&E conventions and standards, even if they do not suit them. The impulse to institutionalise an M&E system often comes from the outside. It is not driven by an internal intent to learn and improve one's work. Hence, M&E is seen as a 'necessary evil', a donor requirement to release funds rather than a means to generate learning and further excel in one's work. This reflects pragmatism in that donors might indeed refuse funding if their requirements for a stringent M&E are not met. Yet often, a conversation about a transitional justice organisation's needs and finding more constructive ways of doing M&E is not even attempted though it could serve both sides and enhance the learning dimension of the work. Instead, M&E processes are resented. Reports are written grudgingly, producing flat, boring narratives that are then not read and result in little response beyond 'received with thanks'. The end result is an emptying of energy and meaning in the exchange between grant makers and grantees.

At the same time the current drive to develop detailed 'frames' for M&E is also recognised as having the potential to evolve more ongoing reflective practices in transitional justice-oriented organisations. Since there is funding available for M&E systems development, these could also be used to develop and institutionalise learning from experience in ways that suit practitioners and further the evolution of organisations and contexts. Practitioners in transitional justice work thus face several critical challenges with regard to M&E work and the trends sketched above.

Showing impact – key challenges

Attempting to make sense of these challenges in monitoring and evaluation, there emerged three key polarities that transitional justice actors move between:

1 *Linear–nonlinear*: linear images of envisioned outcomes are confronted by the non-linear nature of unfolding social transformation processes
2 *Visibility–invisibility*: the attempt to create visibility (of victims' concerns, of truths about the past, of perpetrators and their crimes) and needing to operate in the invisible, at times even facilitating concealment
3 *Ownership–letting others claim results*: the tension between claiming ownership of a result and holding silent joy in knowing one had an impact but allowed others to claim the limelight and credit for it (i.e. policy-influence, advisors of political entities, etc).

Moving between high visibility and operating in the invisible

Due to the sensitivities of dealing with the past, some of the transitional justice organisations' practice takes place behind the scenes or in the realm of the invisible. Advocacy strategies for transitional justice processes are usually two (or more) pronged: partly geared at taking a confrontational, public 'naming and shaming' approach, and partly focused on more associative, dialogue-oriented, winning-over key actors approaches that take place away from the public eye. While the former can be documented, traced and 'exposed', with the latter strategy it is more difficult to 'prove impact', for in revealing that impact, it is lost. An example here is the process of advising policymakers, who cannot be seen as 'unknowing' in public but who appreciate quality information, reflection and engagement, and smaller-scale learning processes in trusted environments. These can be offered by civil society actors who manage to build trusting relationships and keep the engagement completely confidential.

Thus, the work of effective transitional justice depends on a dance between revelation and concealment. This limits the possibility of publicly claiming certain 'successes', even in a donor report, while sensitive processes are still ongoing. Some of these success stories might be told only years later and have to be kept confidential at the time so as to not jeopardise their impact in the moment. As for the failures, which usually yield the richest learning experience if explored, there seems little scope for people to openly admit their sense of having failed in a particular transitional justice-related intervention. Still, in trusted conversations among peers, such failures are explored, pondered and learned from. The results of such, often informal, conversations are mostly what evolves into future strategies for handling similar challenges or inspires a change of course in an intervention. It is reported that the best ideas are born in the informal sphere of peer exchange (see also Mncwabe 2010).

Taking ownership – letting others claim results

The sensitive nature of the engagement in transitional justice work described above, between civil society actors, policymakers and implementers of transitional justice, means that if advice is given or any critical input is taken on board by decision makers, this cannot be claimed directly by the practitioners. Then ownership would no longer rest (publicly at least) with those who were quietly advised and who might feel their trust betrayed. Concealment and strategic revelation are then both strategy and source of success in the transitional justice field, as is the case in many conflict-related interventions. In addition, seeing an immediate effect does not reveal the impact of an intervention over time. Most of the time, the impact reported was achieved by the collaborative effort of a range of actors and through the interactions of several projects, individuals, groups and institutions over time. Money, flowing from various sources, enabled the interaction of varied activities and actors in an interconnected manner that cannot easily be traced back to a single intervention or organisation in a transitional justice process.

Hence, it is at times difficult to prove later which process in this entangled and interconnected web of actions and interdependencies has produced a particular, visible effect that can then be claimed as a result. On occasion, positive results and stories are claimed, told and 'sold' as a success by several actors. There are as yet few efforts to read projects, programmes and interdependent results in a context together in a systemic way (see Körppen et al 2008). Instead, effort is often spent looking at individual strands that fit a project proposal and a set of indicators that by then are often more than two years old. It is then a struggle to squeeze out an appropriate report against these criteria.

Frequently, the report is not engaged with beyond the 'accountability' dimension of the work (was it done, did it have an effect, was it visible?). The learning dimension, which could possibly be part of ongoing reflections prior to report writing, or even ongoing writing out of practice, is usually not followed up because of a perceived lack of time and the pervasive sense among practitioners in implementing organisations and desk officers in donor agencies that they are overwhelmed. This general feeling of being

overloaded results from the sheer number of activities implemented and an inherent assumption that 'more is better', which
is often not questioned. In addition, the mass of information dealt
with on a daily basis leads to a sense of being saturated and 'over-
full' most of the time with meetings, engagements, interactions
and data consumption. Small corridor and lunchtime conversations begin to happen, a relief from the bustle. This is where much
of the 'real' learning seems to be taking place – in those snippets
of debriefing while standing in the doorway of a colleague's
office, in the aftermath of an intense workshop where those pack-
ing up at the venue get talking, driving back in the car after a
policy meeting, in the conversations at the office in the afterglow
of an inspiring event, when spontaneously reflecting on a news
headline or a significant contextual happening that requires new
strategic thinking. These in-between spaces are where practitioners are momentarily not driven by the pressures of performance,
formality and hierarchy in their organisations. Such spaces produce moments of freedom from anxiety and expectation of what
'must be done' and an inner movement to explore what could be
brought to life in the future. Such moments were described by
most practitioners as a source of inspiration that drives them and
keeps them going with their work. They describe a sudden energy
rush and connection to self in such moments, when they can say
to themselves: 'I know why I am doing what I do. It suddenly
makes sense again and I know we are having an impact. I can see
it even if others can't or if I cannot talk about it.'

Non-linearity as a gift

Another character trait that transitional justice work shares more
broadly with peace and development work is the unpredictable,
non-linear nature of how processes unfold, often characterised by
advances and setbacks, detours and surprises. Often, practitioners
reflect, the best ideas come out of crises and setbacks as supposed
failures are processed and reflected upon. What seemed like an
unnecessary and burdensome obstacle, when a process does not
go 'to plan' turns out to alert practitioners to an important dimension that had been overlooked or a group of actors that needs
inclusion. How do transitional justice practitioners deal with the

nonlinearity of the work of social transformation? How do they engage with social change processes which require stepping out of the binaries of thinking: right or wrong, success or failure?

One valued insight that emerged from conversations with transitional justice practitioners about M&E was that, consciously or unconsciously, all are monitoring and evaluating their work all the time. Every practitioner is constantly pondering what she does, wondering if it makes sense, if it is having an impact, if there is a need to shift course, to do something differently. This is almost like an internal navigation system, an impact navigator that traces and 'reads' the situation, one's own intervention, the responses of others, one's own internal reactions to their response; this happens all the time without a break. There is an individual, intuitive and natural sense-making process that takes place. This covers all eventualities and situations and is particularly alert when things unfold unexpectedly (which is usually the case in social transformation work).

This internal navigator serves an inherent M&E function; it evaluates continuously how we impact on the world and how it impacts back on us. One could regard this as an internal observational eye that takes a multi-fold reading of the situation, absorbs detail meticulously (a particular policymaker's reaction in a meeting, the response of a group participant in a workshop, the vibe in the crowd at a village gathering), yet which is also able to see larger 'wholes' emerging. Among groups of peers and colleagues, such observations and readings are then put to the test – how does what I saw resonate with another colleague's observations? How do we make sense of what happened collectively? As the informal conversations described above ensue, such joint interpretation processes prove invaluable, not only to read a situation in the moment but to make meaning of it and arrive at a shared understanding of the situation. It is this sense of a shared understanding emerging that confirms to the internal navigator a sense of having 'read' the moment, process or situation accurately and comprehensively.

Such an ongoing internal assessment skill serves practitioners well in the transitional justice field, who are often facing fast-paced and unpredictable changes in how their work, their contexts and even their own lives as activists unfold. M&E, seen in this way, is therefore an already existing skill and faculty that reads emergence in a social situation and that can be built upon. This means that an essential asset to a strategic and successful practitioner is usually already well developed; it is just not consciously seen as a strategic capacity for M&E. This links directly to the often underdeveloped capacity in organisations for reflective writing as an ongoing practice of documentation that can serve good M&E, knowledge management, organisational development and the personal and professional evolution of practitioners. Tim Murithi suggested at the IATJ 2010 that one of the critical strategies for developing the transitional justice field in Africa is for young and coming practitioners to 'witness and write'. My experience in building M&E practices that serve African transitional justice practitioners and that enhance impact resonates strongly with this (re)quest for witnessing and writing.

An interesting set of questions about practice emanates from this strand of reflection at the IATJ 2010, which asks for further inquiry:

- Rather than transferring technical skills to implement a preconceived template-based M&E, how could practitioners make their continuous informal reflective practices conscious and visible?
- How can practitioners use these inherent observation skills to reflect and make meaning of their doing as interventions develop? How can they actively sharpen their perception skills and in that sense evolve their intuition further as a monitoring tool?
- How could the learning dimension (L) of M&E be strengthened so as to build reflective practice more consciously as a set of LM&E skills?
- What enables practitioners to build their writing practice so that the inherent stream-of-consciousness M&E becomes a conscious reflection process on the page?
- In the moment, practitioners know when they are having an impact, desired or undesired. How can confidence and skill be built further to use this inherent knowing for learning and improving their work?

The current realities of transitional justice practitioners are characterised by being frantically busy, a mode of working that seems to be high-performance at face value, but that is described as draining and distracting from achieving meaning and substance through the work. How can practitioners observe more consciously? When do their best ideas emerge? What feeds their energy and sense of purpose? How can they strengthen resourcefulness rather than just look for gaps and weaknesses in the work?

References

Körppen, Daniela, Schmelzle, Beatrix and Wils, Oliver (eds) (2008) *A Systemic Approach to Conflict Transformation*, Berghof Dialogue Series, 6, http://www.berghof-handbook.net/dialogue-series/no.-6-a-systemic-approach-to-conflict-transformation, accessed 12 February 2011

Mncwabe, Nokukhanya (2010) 'African Transitional Justice Research Network: critical reflections on a peer learning process', *The International Journal of Transitional Justice*, 4(3)

Reeler, Doug (2010) Quoted with permission from a personal reflection shared via e-mail on the Outcomes Mapping Listserver on 6 August

11

Towards African models of transitional justice

Tim Murithi

Introduction

Transitional justice is now acknowledged as a central feature of efforts to restore peace and stability to societies that were previously suppressed by authoritarian regimes, impacted by regime change, or affected by conflict. Transitional justice in this context is understood as endeavouring to promote a deeper, richer and broader vision of justice which seeks to confront perpetrators, address the needs of victims, and start a process of reconciliation and transformation towards a more just and humane society. The field of transitional justice, however, has become inundated with concepts and frameworks developed outside Africa. Consequently, the dominant discourses in transitional justice demonstrate this external bias. There is a need to draw upon Africa's knowledge systems, its traditions and culture of jurisprudence to articulate and document indigenous models of transitional justice. However, such an activity has to be informed by the fact that Africa is not a homogenous entity and within its societies there is a vast array of different approaches to dealing with the issues of peace and justice. This chapter will discuss where we can begin to draw upon indigenous sources to develop African models of transitional justice.

Culture gives distinctiveness to a particular society's way of doing things. This chapter will discuss how there have always been customary rules, social sanctions and ethical precepts to regulate African societies. While each society has its own specific approach to dealing with social problems, some common themes emerge across societies. In the majority of African communities studies have shown that the individual is not considered a separate, autonomous entity but always part of a larger collective of human beings.[1] Family groupings give way to the formation of clan communities and then ethnic nations. These groupings have a responsibility to maintain social harmony. Due to the importance of maintaining harmony, peaceful approaches to resolving disputes are preferable to more confrontational and belligerent strategies (which are also occasionally utilised). This chapter will therefore discuss how most African societies have developed rich cultural traditions of transitional and restorative justice as well as reconciliation for preserving harmony, making and building peace and maintaining this peace by cultivating group solidarity and avoiding aggression and violence.[2]

Understanding the role of justice in African culture

Some African conceptions of the individual, and their role and place in society, can provide an alternative framework for establishing more harmonious political and economic relations at local, national, continental and even global levels.[3] Through the (African?) emphasis on the value of social harmony and non-adversarial dispute resolution, there are lessons that can be learned and applied to contemporary conflict situations. It is necessary to question the notion of a universal conception of justice that can be advanced by a 'world court'. This universalising tendency is often driven by a 'civilising' and 'modernising' imperative, which self-evidently marginalises the 'other's' conception of justice. It regrettably assumes that there is one way of conceptualising justice, which is erroneous at best and coercive and alienating at worst. Instead, we need to embrace the idea that notions of justice can be locally specific and culturally defined. As highlighted at the beginning of this chapter the purpose of justice is to achieve redress and ensure accountability for harm done. If cultural forms of justice can achieve this in a way that does not rely exclusively on a prosecutorial imperative, then it is vital to draw lessons from such approaches. As discussed above, African conceptions of justice emphasise communal harmony over the general tendency within Western notions of justice to prioritise individual culpability.

As with most human societies African communities also tended to be patriarchal in nature, which often led to discrimination on the basis of gender. Patriarchal cultures have influenced legal systems, with the result that governance structures have tended to uphold the unequal status of women. As we proceed into the second decade of the 21st century it is clear that gender-sensitive strategies for restoring the human dignity of all members of society need to be adopted. This means challenging the social norms that try to enforce the subservience of women to men. The fact that there are these inequalities does not, however, mean that indigenous approaches to peace building have nothing to teach us. Many of these approaches offer progressive value systems for maintaining social relationships and promoting harmonious coexistence which can provide insights that can contribute toward building peace in Africa. We shall now assess some examples of these traditional approaches.

Ubuntu and reconciliation

This section outlines the five stages of the peace and reconciliation processes found among ubuntu societies, including: acknowledgement of guilt, showing remorse and repenting, asking for and giving forgiveness, and paying compensation or reparation as a prelude to reconciliation. Potential lessons for peace and reconciliation efforts are highlighted with the premise that the ubuntu approach to the building of human relationships, while rooted in local tradition, can also offer an example to the world.

Desmond Tutu reflects in his book *No Future Without Forgiveness* that he drew upon both his Christian and cultural values when carrying out his duties as the chairman of the South African Truth and Reconciliation Commission.[4] In particular, he highlights that he constantly referred to the notion of ubuntu when he was guiding and advising witnesses, victims and perpetrators during the commission hearings.

Ubuntu is found in diverse forms in many societies in various parts of Africa. More specifically among the Bantu languages of

East, Central and Southern Africa the concept of ubuntu is a cultural world view that tries to capture the essence of what it means to be human. In southern Africa we find its clearest articulation among the Nguni group of languages. In terms of its definition, Tutu observes that:

> ubuntu is very difficult to render into a Western language. It speaks to the very essence of being human. When you want to give high praise to someone we say, '*Yu, u nobuntu*'; he or she has ubuntu. This means that they are generous, hospitable, friendly, caring and compassionate. They share what they have. It also means that my humanity is caught up, is inextricably bound up, in theirs. We belong in a bundle of life. We say, 'a person is a person through other people' (in Xhosa *Umntu ngumntu ngabanye abantu* and in Zulu *Umuntu ngumuntu ngabanye abantu*…). I am human because I belong, I participate, I share. A person with ubuntu is open and available to others, affirming of others, does not feel threatened that others are able and good; for he or she has a proper self-assurance that comes with knowing that he or she belongs in a greater whole and is diminished when others are humiliated, or diminished when others are tortured or oppressed, or treated as if they were less than who they are.[5]

As a 'human being through other human beings', it follows that what we do to others feeds through the interwoven fabric of social, economic and political relationships to eventually impact upon us as well. Even the supporters of apartheid were in a sense victims of the brutalising system from which they benefited economically and politically: it distorted their view of their relationship with other human beings, which then impacted upon their own sense of security and freedom from fear. As Tutu observes: 'in the process of dehumanising another, in inflicting untold harm and suffering, the perpetrator was inexorably being dehumanised as well'.[6]

This notion of ubuntu sheds light on the importance of peace-making through the principles of reciprocity, inclusivity and a sense of shared destiny between peoples. It provides a value system for giving and receiving forgiveness. It provides a rationale for sacrificing or letting go of the desire to take revenge for past wrongs. It provides an inspiration and suggests guidelines for societies and their governments on how to establish laws which will promote reconciliation. In short, it can culturally re-inform our practical efforts to build peace and heal our traumatised communities. It is to be noted that the principles found in ubuntu are not unique; as indicated earlier, they can be found in diverse forms in other cultures and traditions. Nevertheless, an ongoing reflection and reappraisal of this notion of ubuntu can serve to re-emphasise the essential unity of humanity and gradually promote attitudes and values based on the sharing of resources and on cooperation and collaboration in the resolution of our common problems.[7]

How, then, were the principles of ubuntu traditionally articulated and translated into practical peacemaking processes? Ubuntu societies maintained conflict resolution and reconciliation mechanisms which also served as institutions for maintaining law and order within society. These mechanisms pre-dated colonialism and continue to exist and function today.[8] Ubuntu societies place a high value on communal life; maintaining positive relations within the society is a collective task in which everyone is involved. A dispute between fellow members of a society is perceived not merely as a matter of curiosity over the affairs of one's neighbour; in a very real sense an emerging conflict belongs to the whole community. According to the notion of ubuntu, each member of the community is linked to each of the disputants, be they victims or perpetrators. If everybody is willing to acknowledge this (that is, to accept the principles of ubuntu), then people may either feel a sense of having been wronged, or a sense of responsibility for the wrong that has been committed. Due to this linkage, a law-breaking individual transforms their group into a law-breaking group. In the same way a disputing individual transforms their group into a disputing group. It therefore follows that if an individual is wronged, they may depend on the group to remedy the wrong, because in a sense the group has also been wronged. We can witness these dynamics of group identity and their impact on conflict situations across the world.

Ubuntu societies developed mechanisms for resolving disputes and promoting reconciliation with a view to healing past wrongs and maintaining social cohesion and harmony. Consensus building was embraced as a cultural pillar in regulating and managing relationships between members of the community.[9] Depending on the nature of the disagreement or dispute, the conflict resolution process could take place at the level of the family, at the village level, between members of an ethnic group, or even between different ethnic nations situated in the same region.

In the ubuntu societies found in southern Africa, particularly among the Xhosa and the Sotho, disputes would be resolved through an institution known as the *inkundla/lekgotla,* which served as a group mediation and reconciliation forum.[10] This *inkundla/lekgotla* forum was communal in character in the sense that the entire society was involved at various levels in trying to find a solution to a problem which was viewed as threatening the social cohesion of the community. In principle the proceedings would be led by a council of elders and the chief or, if the disputes were larger, by the king himself. The process of ascertaining wrongdoing and finding a resolution included family members related to the victims and perpetrators, as well as women and the young. The mechanism therefore allowed members of the public to share their views and to generally make their opinions known. The larger community could thus be involved in the process of conflict resolution. In particular, members of the society had the right to put questions to the victims, perpetrators and witnesses as well as to put suggestions to the council of elders on possible ways forward. The council of elders in its capacity as an intermediary had an investigative function and it also played an advisory role to the chief. By listening to the views of the members of the society, the council of elders could advise on solutions which would promote reconciliation between the aggrieved parties and thus maintain the overall objective of sustaining the unity and cohesion of the community.

The process involved five key stages:

1 After a fact-finding process where the views of victims, perpetrators and witnesses were heard, the perpetrators – if considered to have done wrong – would be encouraged, both by the council and other community members in the *inkundla/ lekgotla* forum, to acknowledge responsibility or guilt.
2 Perpetrators would be encouraged to demonstrate genuine remorse or to repent.
3 Perpetrators would be encouraged to ask for forgiveness and victims in their turn would be encouraged to show mercy.

4   Where possible and at the suggestion of the council of
    elders, perpetrators would be required to pay appropriate
    compensation or make reparations for the wrong done. (This
    was often more symbolic rather than any repayment in kind,
    with the primary function being to reinforce the remorse of
    the perpetrators.) Amnesty could thus be granted, but not
    with impunity.

5   The final stage would seek to consolidate the whole process
    by encouraging the parties to commit themselves to
    reconciliation. This process of reconciliation tended to include
    the victim and their family members and friends as well as
    the perpetrator and their family members and friends. Both
    groups would be encouraged to embrace coexistence and to
    work towards healing the relationship between them and thus
    contribute towards restoring harmony within the community,
    which was vital to ensure the integrity and viability of the
    society. The act of reconciliation was essential in that it
    symbolised the willingness of the parties to move beyond the
    psychological bitterness that had prevailed during the conflict.

This process was not always straightforward, and there would
naturally be instances of resistance at various stages of the peacemaking process. This was particularly so with respect to the perpetrators, who tended to prefer that past events were not re-lived
and brought out into the open. In the same way, victims would
not always find it easy to forgive. In some instances forgiveness
could be withheld, in which case the process could reach an
impasse, with consequences for the relations between members
of the community. However, forgiveness, when granted, would
generate such a degree of goodwill that the people involved, and
the society as a whole, could then move forward even from the
most difficult situations. The wisdom of this process lies in the
recognition that it is not possible to build a healthy community
at peace with itself unless past wrongs are acknowledged and
brought out into the open so that the truth of what happened
can be determined and social trust renewed through a process of
forgiveness and reconciliation. A community in which there is no
trust is ultimately not viable and gradually begins to tear itself
apart. This process draws upon the ubuntu values and notions of

'I am because we are' and 'a person being a person through other people' when faced with the difficult challenge of acknowledging responsibility and showing remorse, or of granting forgiveness.

As mentioned earlier, this traditional peacemaking process covered offences across the board from family and marriage disputes, theft, damage to property, murder and wars. In the more difficult cases involving murder, ubuntu societies sought to avoid the death penalty because, based on the society's view of itself – as people through other people – the death penalty would only serve to cause injury to society as a whole. Though it would be more difficult to move beyond such cases, the emphasis would still be on restoring the broken relationships between the victim and the perpetrator caused by the death of a member of the community.

The guiding principle of ubuntu was based on the notion that parties need to be reconciled in order to rebuild and maintain social trust and social cohesion, with a view to preventing a culture of vendetta or retribution from developing and escalating between individuals, families and the society as a whole. We continue to observe how individuals and sections of society in South Africa, epitomised by Mandela and Tutu, have drawn upon some aspects of their cultural values and attitudes to enable the country to move beyond its violent past. The South African Truth and Reconciliation Commission, which has as many critics as it has supporters, also relied on the willingness of victims to recognise the humanity of the perpetrators, and there are documented cases of victims forgiving particular perpetrators. Tutu himself would always advise victims – if they felt themselves able to do so – to forgive. His guiding principle was that without forgiveness there could be no future for the new republic.

Justice and reconciliation among the Acholi of northern Uganda

In northern Uganda the government is in conflict with a resistance movement calling itself the Lord's Resistance Army (LRA), which continues to make incursions from neighbouring countries.[11] In this conflict the social provisions, such as security and the protection of internally displaced persons, notably children, which normally would have been provided for by the state are also lacking.

The majority of the peoples from these region are from the Acholi ethnic group. Many Acholi have found themselves divided by their different loyalties: many support the rebellion due to grievances that they hold against regimes which have ruled over them, while others remain neutral and yet others support the government due to the rebel incursions and the LRA's practice of abducting children to join the ranks of its soldiers. Social cohesion is fragmented and the persistence of violence and abductions has thoroughly undermined levels of social trust.[12] From this complex matrix of factors brought about by violent conflict there has been an urgent need to identify mechanisms and institutions for conflict resolution which could achieve the medium- to long-term goal of rebuilding social trust and reconciliation.

An examination of some of the features of the reconciliation mechanism found among the Acholi may be informative.[13] The Acholi have a conflict resolution and reconciliation mechanism called the *mato oput*, which also served as an institution for maintaining justice, law and order within the society. This mechanism pre-dated the colonial period and is still functioning in some areas. The Acholi place a high value on communal life. Maintaining positive relations within society is a collective task in which everyone is involved. A dispute between fellow members of the community is not perceived as only the concern of one's neighbours, but in a very real sense an emerging conflict belongs to the community itself. Each member of the Acholi community is in varying degrees related to each of the disputants. To the extent that somebody is willing to acknowledge this fundamental unity, then people can either feel some sense of having been wronged or some sense of responsibility for the wrong that has been done. Due to this linkage, a law-breaking individual thus transforms their group into a law-breaking group. In the same way a disputing individual transforms their group into a disputing group. It therefore follows that if an individual is wronged they may depend upon their group when seeking a remedy to what has transpired, for in a sense the group has been wronged. The Acholi society therefore developed *mato oput* to resolve disputes and promote reconciliation based on the principle of consensus building. Consensus building is embraced by the Acholi as a cultural pillar of their efforts to regulate relationships between members of a community.

The Acholi leadership structures are based on models designed to build consensus. There are councils of elders or community leadership councils made up of both men and women. All members of the society have a say in matters affecting the community. With the passage of time, however, colonialism and the onset of post-colonial regimes have undermined the adherence to this value-system among most of the population. Today there are ongoing efforts to revive this way of thinking as a means to promoting more sustainable peace by using consensus to determine wrongdoing as well as to suggest remedial action.

The peace process in the Acholi context, therefore, involves a high degree of public participation. As noted earlier, under the timeless Acholi world view a conflict between two members of a community is regarded as a problem which afflicts the entire community. In order to restore harmony and rebuild social trust there must be general satisfaction among the public, in particular the disputants, with both the procedure and the outcome of the dispute resolution effort. The *mato oput* process therefore allows members of the public to make their opinions known. Through a public assembly known as the *kacoke madit*, those supervising the reconciliation process (normally the council of elders, who have an advisory function with respect to the chiefs) listen to the views of the members of the public, who have a right to put questions to the victims, perpetrators and witnesses as well as make suggestions to the council.[14]

Due to the emphasis on inclusion and participation, the peace process can at times be a lengthy affair. The victims, perpetrators or disputants have to make certain commitments. The process generally proceeds through the following five stages:

1 The council of elders convenes a process in a communal and public setting. Witnesses present evidence alleging the transgressions by perpetrators. If perpetrators are prepared to do so, they acknowledge the harm done and accept their liability for what happened.
2 The council of elders guides the perpetrators to engage openly with the process and convey remorse for the transgressions against their victims.
3 The council of elders guides the victims to accept the show of remorse by the perpetrators, after which the perpetrators

are encouraged to request a pardon and forgiveness from the victims. Similarly, victims are encouraged to show mercy and accept the appeal by the perpetrators.

4 If the previous stages are successfully carried out the council of elders can then suggest that the perpetrator pay compensation to the victim if it is possible. In most instances this might be a symbolic gesture of reparation or restitution, which is supposed to symbolise the perpetrator's sense of remorse.

5 The process concludes with an act of reconciliation between the representatives of the victims and the representatives of the perpetrators. This act of reconciliation is conducted through the ceremony of *mato oput,* which is the drinking of a bitter tasting herb derived from the *oput* tree. The bitter drink *oput* symbolises the psychological bitterness that prevailed in the minds of the parties during the conflict. The act of drinking it is an indication that an effort will be made to transcend this bitterness in order to restore harmony and rebuild trust.

In Acholi society the *mato oput* process covers offences across the board, from minor injustices such as theft to more serious issues involving violence between members of a society, the taking of a life, even accidentally, and conflict situations. The Acholis strive to avoid recourse to retributive justice and in particular the death penalty because of how the society views itself and the value that it attaches to each of its members. While the sense of and demand for vengeance may be great among some victims, the perception in the community is largely that permitting the death penalty for murder would only serve to further multiply the effects of suffering in other parts of society and ultimately undermine any possibility of re-establishing harmonious coexistence.

Depending on the level of the offence the *mato oput* reconciliation act is followed by two other ceremonies. In all dispute situations the community leaders or council of elders of both genders – the male leaders are referred to as *rwodi moo* and the female leaders are known as the *rwodi mon* – give a final verbal blessing to mark the end of the conflict. In the case of a murder or warring situation, a ceremony called the 'bending of the spears' is conducted by the two parties to the conflict in order to symbolise an end to hostilities and the disposal of the instruments of its execution.

It is evident, then, that the guiding principle and values of this approach are based on the notion that the parties must be reconciled in order to rebuild social trust and maintain social cohesion and thus prevent a culture of vendetta or feud from developing and escalating between individuals, families and other members of the society. This is one reason why the *mato oput* act of reconciliation always includes the disputants, victims, perpetrators and their representatives. Public consensus also plays a significant role in the post-conflict situation, particularly when social pressure is utilised to monitor and encourage the various parties to implement peace agreements. Any breach of the act of reconciliation by either side would represent a far worse offence than the original offence because it would set a precedent that could eventually lead to the fragmentation of communal life.

In sum, the Acholi method for resolving disputes provides us with some practical insights into how we can refer to culture in our efforts to establish mechanisms for promoting reconciliation and rebuilding social trust, across Africa as well as other parts of the world. Civil society groups, religious leaders, parliamentarians in the Acholi community of northern Uganda together with Acholis in the diaspora have been advocating the revitalisation and integration of the *mato oput* into current peace initiatives. The process is being utilised in various local efforts within the region with significant results in the termination of violent conflict and the healing of communities. Many believe that the *mato oput* mechanism has the potential to contribute significantly towards repairing the relationship and healing tensions between the Lord's Resistance Army and the government of Uganda. There are also efforts through a government amnesty bill to bring aspects of the *mato oput* mechanism into the reconciliation and pardon initiatives to reintegrate perpetrators, some of whom are still minors, back into society.

Efforts to resolve the LRA standoff using traditional approaches were derailed by the International Criminal Court's (ICC) indictment of LRA leaders, including the militia group's commander, Joseph Kony. The ICC's action triggered a debate in Uganda about the merits and demerits of pursuing international criminal prosecutions as opposed to a traditional reconciliation process. The Ugandan government has been criticised for manipulating both the ICC and Acholi traditional leaders in order to pursue its own political ends. In particular, the Ugandan government is viewed as having opted for ICC prosecutions for LRA leaders in order to advance its own political agenda of suppressing and ultimately eliminating the armed militia group, which was a potential political adversary. As a result, the neutrality of the ICC has been called into question. Further, it is held that Acholi traditional leaders have been pressured by the Ugandan government to silence dissent in their communities and to distance their communities from the objectives of the LRA. As with any political process there are, of course, still obstacles to policy implementation, which undermine the potential to use these mechanisms in current peace efforts. The fact that politicians can instrumentalise the ICC or co-opt traditional leaders does not in and of itself negate the important insights and practices that can be gleaned from cultural practices. Continued leadership and vision on all sides is required to ensure that judicial and quasi-judicial processes do not in effect become politicised.

The recent inroads made by the Acholi system of reconciliation as far as its impact on government policy is concerned, suggest that there is an opportunity for this model to promote the legal acceptance of alternative forms of restorative justice within national constitutions. The interplay or cross-fertilisation of law, politics, morality and social values is indeed possible; beyond that, however, it is also necessary and desirable in the interests of building sustainable peace and democratisation through reconciliation. One key inference that we can draw from the Acholi system of reconciliation and the cultural wisdom handed down by generations of these people is that punitive action within the context of retributive justice may effectively decrease social trust and undermine reconciliation in the medium to long term and that such action is therefore ineffective as a strategy for promoting social cohesion.

The utility and limitations of African models

A key utility of African models of transitional justice is that they emphasise that peace is not just the absence of violence but the presence of communal harmony and a commitment to coexistence. In this regard, bringing about healing and reconciliation through the promotion of non-violence and consensus building becomes the organising principle of society.[15] African institutions for justice and reconciliation[16] can contribute towards enhancing political participation and decision making since they:

- are more accessible to all members of a given society
- cost less to manage than mechanisms for the administration of justice inherited from the colonial era
- are already embedded in the social norms and political structures of a given society and therefore the rules and procedures are more readily accepted and internalised
- enable all members of a society to be aware of their responsibilities and rights with regard to the community as a whole.

The two case studies above have illustrated some of these points.

However, efforts to revitalise and adopt indigenous structures and institutions for justice and reconciliation are constrained by the structures and frameworks of governance which are prescribed by the international system of states. There needs to be a shift in attitude over the way sub-state actors are accorded recognition in the international arena. Innovations at an international level could create institutionalised mechanisms that respond to local and traditional mechanisms of justice and reconciliation. Ultimately, a degree of complementarity between institutions at local, national and global levels is vital in order to promote public participation in the administration of justice and promotion of reconciliation. In Africa, the constitutional integration and recognition of sub-national or indigenous mechanisms for promoting transitional justice and reconciliation with those of the state is an important first step towards addressing the scourge of conflict which afflicts most of the continent.

Choosing modern or African models?

There is an artificial dichotomy between so-called modern and African models of transitional justice and reconciliation. In most instances these processes function in parallel. Externally driven modern efforts to resolve conflict situations are often faced with the limitation that the local parties are unwilling, or unable, to relate to these initiatives. In such circumstances the traditional processes are deployed by the communities themselves, sometimes independently of modern processes. These cultural approaches are not used sufficiently and they tend to be used at the periphery of reconciliation efforts whereas they should be informing mainstream peace-building initiatives. A healthy balance between tradition and modernity when it comes to the strategies deployed to promote justice and reconciliation is necessary for achieving the objectives of peace in Africa.[17] Ultimately, modern approaches need to develop a greater synergy with traditional approaches in order to foster integrated peace-building processes.

How, then, can we begin to revitalise African approaches to justice and reconciliation? The most important starting point is to understand that Africa is not a homogenous entity. With 57 countries, and at least 3,500 different ethnic groups and a total population of about one billion (not counting the African societies in the diaspora), Africa does not lend itself to a monolithic framework of analysis or generalised prescriptions. Approaches to promoting justice and reconciliation in Africa can only be defined by first understanding some of the world views that are commonplace in Africa. As we saw earlier, some African societies affirm the existence of a universal bond between people that transcends the usual family ties. They then use this existing normative framework to establish traditions and mechanisms for managing disputes between members of society and for administering justice and promoting reconciliation in a way that reduces tendencies which would otherwise foster suspicion and fear and lead to harm and destruction. It is important to note that African approaches to justice and reconciliation can only be understood in their specific and local context. However, these approaches can provide insights into how peace building can be enhanced across the continent. The need to educate for peace has become urgent.

214

Conclusion

Based on the discussion above we can consider how modern approaches can benefit from complementary African models of transitional justice and reconciliation. In particular, the training of peace practitioners, government officials and civil society actors, using the principles drawn from African models, can provide an advocacy and lobbying framework to promote the practical use of these approaches in ongoing dispute resolution efforts on the continent. It is also necessary to identify ways in which peace-making insights drawn from the heritage of African models of restorative justice and reconciliation need to be integrated and mainstreamed into educational curricula at secondary and tertiary levels. This will provide learners with a unique perspective and world view, which can only contribute towards fostering a global culture of peace. Peacebuilding needs to be context specific, in the sense that it is relates to the local communities' concepts of peace and is sensitive to social and cultural traditions. In Africa, the colonial methods of dispute management were retained in the post-colonial state and superimposed on African systems of peacemaking, justice and reconciliation.[18] This chapter has discussed how African models of justice and reconciliation address a given situation. If an individual or a group has perpetrated a crime or acted violently, the leadership of a community asks the relatives of the individual or the group to pay reparations to the victims and the entire society participates in redeeming that individual. The perpetrator is exposed to the shame of their family and pressure is put on the individual to behave in a manner that is acceptable to society in the future. The whole exercise is aimed at bringing people back into the embrace of their families and societies once again, which lays the foundation for increasing the levels of peace, tolerance, solidarity and social harmony.

African approaches to transitional justice and reconciliation can offer other important lessons as we continue to work towards global peace. Four key lessons include: (1) the importance of public participation in administering justice and promoting reconciliation; (2) the utility of supporting victims and encouraging perpetrators as they go through the difficult process of making restorative justice; (3) the value of acknowledging guilt and remorse and the granting of forgiveness as a way to achieve reconciliation; (4) the importance of referring constantly to the essential unity and interdependence of humanity and living out the principles which this unity suggests, namely empathy for others, the sharing of our common resources, and working with a spirit of cooperation in our efforts to resolve our common problems. Reconciliation understood from this perspective is a process in which the opposing parties are involved in co-creating a solution that they can live with. These processes are also empowering in the sense that they give local cultures the space to make use of their own values, which can only serve to restore a sense of confidence and promote greater self-reliance when it comes to solving problems and enabling progressive development.

Non-African governments and societies as well as international organisations will need to reflect on how they can collaborate more closely with traditional justice and reconciliation processes to promote genuine ownership of the peace process.[19] External actors must be willing to learn and not blindly (or patronisingly) transpose or impose knowledge and skills that are not immediately translatable or understandable to their host populations. We should question attempts to impose a universal conception of justice. Instead, we should draw lessons from African conceptions of justice, which emphasise communal harmony over the general tendency within Western notions of justice to prioritise individual culpability. It is always vital to learn what peacemaking strategies and responses might be appropriate in different contexts. The question that faces us today in the context of our globalised world is whether we are prepared to draw from the lessons of African models of transitional justice and reconciliation.[20]

Notes

1 Ogbu Kalu (1978) *African Cultural Development*, Enugu, Four Dimensions Publishers.
2 Claude Ake (1991) 'Rethinking African democracy', *Journal of Democracy*, 2(1): 32–44.
3 Ngugi wa Thiong'o (1986) *Moving the Centre: The Struggle for Cultural Freedoms*, London and Nairobi, James Currey and Heinemann: 61.
4 Desmond Tutu (1999) *No Future Without Forgiveness*, London, Rider.
5 Tutu (1999): 34–5.
6 Tutu (1999): 35.

7   R. Khoza (1994) 'Ubuntu: African humanism', Johannesburg, HSRC occasional paper. See also S. Maphisa (1994) 'Man in constant search of ubuntu – a dramatist's obsession', paper presented at the Ubuntu Conference (IADSA) Pietermaritzburg, University of Natal.

8   Erasmus Prinsloo (1998) 'Ubuntu culture and participatory management', in Pieter Coetzee and Abraham Roux (eds) *The African Philosophy Reader*, London, Routledge: 41–51.

9   Charles Villa-Vicencio and Verwoerd Wilhelm (2000) *Looking Back, Reaching Forward: Reflections on the Truth and Reconciliation Commission of South Africa*, Cape Town, University of Cape Town Press.

10 Nomode Masina (2000) 'Xhosa practices of ubuntu for South Africa', in William Zartman (ed) *Traditional Cures for Modern Conflicts: African Conflict 'Medicine'*, London, Lynne Rienner.

11 Accord (2002) Conciliation Resources, *Protracted Conflict Elusive Peace: Initiatives to End Violence in Northern Uganda*, London, Accord – International Review of Peace Initiatives.

12 Trudy Govier (1998) *Social Trust and Human Communities*, Montreal, McGill–Queens University Press.

13 Dennis Pain (1997) *The Bending of Spears: Producing Consensus for Peace and Development in Northern Uganda*, London, International Alert and Kacoke Madit.

14 Kacoke Madit (2000) *The Quest for Peace in Northern Uganda*, London, Kacoke Madit.

15 Jannie Malan (1997) *Conflict Resolution Wisdom from Africa*, Durban, ACCORD.

16 Tim Murithi and Dennis Pain (eds) (1999) *African Principles of Conflict Resolution and Reconciliation*, Addis Ababa, Ethiopia, Shebelle Publishing House.

17 Mohamed Abu-Nimer (2001) Conflict resolution, culture and religion: toward a training model for inter-religious peace-building', *Journal of Peace Research*, 38(6): 685–704.

18 Basil Davidson (1992) *The Black Man's Burden: Africa and the Curse of the Nation-State*, London, James Currey. Crawford Young (1994) *The Colonial State in Comparative Perspective*, New Haven, Yale University Press.

19 Some external actors have assessed how they interface in a more meaningful manner with local traditions. See for example, Department for International Development (DFID) (2000) *Access to Justice in Sub-Saharan Africa: The Role of Traditional and Informal Justice Systems*, London, DFID.

20 Susan Collin Marks (2000) 'Ubuntu spirit: example for the world', in *Watching the Wind: Conflict Resolution During South Africa's Transition to Democracy*, Washington DC, United States Institute for Peace.

Index

Women and Security Governance in Africa

Edited by 'Funmi Olonisakin and Awino Okech

2011
paperback
978-1-906387-89-1
also available in pdf, epub
and Kindle formats

When the path-breaking United Nations Resolution 1325 on women, peace and security was adopted in 2000, it was the first time that the security concerns of women in situations of armed conflict and their role in peace building were placed on the agenda of the UN Security Council.

In the field of international security, discussions on women and children are often relegated to the margins. This book addresses a broader debate on security and its governance in a variety of contexts while making the argument that the single most important measure of the effectiveness of security governance is its impact on women. But this is more than a book about women. Rather it is a book about inclusive human security for Africans, which cannot ignore the central place of women.

'In the first volume of its kind, some of the best and most engaging African intellectuals and activists have gathered to expose the fallacies of the current security paradigm to show how "security for women" must entail, at least in large part, "security by women".'

Professor Eboe Hutchful, chair of the African Security Network
•••

'We need fresh perspectives and new ways of visioning governance in Africa so that women's security becomes an intrinsic measure of development and peace. This important collection of insights from across the continent leads the way.'

Winnie Byanyima, director of UNDP Gender Team
•••

 Order your copy from www.pambazukapress.org

From Citizen to Refugee: Uganda Asians Come to Britain

Mahmood Mamdani

From Citizen to Refugee
Uganda Asians come to Britain
MAHMOOD MAMDANI
Second edition with a new introduction

2011
paperback
978-1-906387-57-0
also available in pdf, epub
and Kindle formats

In *From Citizen to Refugee*, republished with a new introduction by the author and with contemporary photographs, Mahmood Mamdani explores issues of political identity. This gripping personal account of the Asians' last days in Uganda following their expulsion in 1972 interweaves an examination of Uganda's colonial history with the subsequent evolution of post-independence politics.

Arriving in overcast London, Mamdani joins compatriots in a refugee camp. 'It was the Kensington camp, and not Amin's Uganda, which was my first experience of what it would be like to live in a totalitarian society.' Mamdani's story, as pertinent as when first published, will be familiar to refugees and those seeking asylum in Britain today.

'Urgent, intimate and personal, the tales of loss
and departure from Uganda, and racism in Enoch Powell's England,
are only offset by the liveliness of the prose.'
The Africa Report Magazine